GOD GREW
TIRED OF US

*Two Lost Boys peer inside a journalist's car at the
Kakuma refugee camp in Kenya in 2001.*

GOD GREW TIRED OF US

JOHN BUL DAU

with Michael S. Sweeney

NATIONAL GEOGRAPHIC

WASHINGTON, D.C.

First paperback printing 2008

Copyright© 2007 John Bul Dau

Illustration Credits — Front Matter, Eli Reed/Magnum Photos; 3, Eli Reed/Magnum Photos; 6, Courtesy UNHCR; 13, Randy Olson; 18, Courtesy John Dau; 27, Malcolm Linton/Getty Images; 36, Sven Torfinn/Panos Pictures; 52, Malcolm Linton/Getty Images; 74, Derek Hudson/Sygma/Corbis; 88, Wendy Stone/Corbis; 94, "Crossing the River Gilo" by Mac Anyat, courtesy UNHCR. 99, Wendy Stone/Corbis; 102, Derek Hudson/Sygma/Corbis; 119, Derek Hudson/Sygma/Corbis; 132, Joachim Ladefoged/VII; 136, Derek Hudson/Sygma/Corbis; 143, Courtesy John Dau; 148, Joachim Ladefoged/VII; 166, Eli Reed/Magnum Photos; 171, Paul Daley/Newmarket Films; 182, Courtesy John Dau; 188, Eli Reed/Magnum Photos; 197, Paul Daley/Newmarket Films; 206, Courtesy John Dau; 223, Courtesy John Dau; 235, Courtesy John Dau; 241, Paul Daley/Newmarket Films; 243, Courtesy John Dau; 257, Courtesy John Dau; 263, Courtesy John Dau; 264, Courtesy John Dau; 266, Mark Mainz/Getty Images;

ISBN: 978-1-4262-0212-4

One of the world's largest nonprofit scientific and educational organizations, the National Geographic Society was founded in 1888 "for the increase and diffusion of geographic knowledge." Fulfilling this mission, the Society educates and inspires millions every day through its magazines, books, television programs, videos, maps and atlases, research grants, the National Geographic Bee, teacher workshops, and innovative classroom materials. The Society is supported through membership dues, charitable gifts, and income from the sale of its educational products. This support is vital to National Geographic's mission to increase global understanding and promote conservation of our planet through exploration, research, and education.

For more information, please call 1-800-NGS LINE (647-5463) or write to the following address:

NATIONAL GEOGRAPHIC SOCIETY
1145 17th Street N.W.
Washington, DC 20036-4688 U.S.A.

Visit the Society's Web site at www.nationalgeographic.com/books

Printed in U.S.A.

Interior Design: Cameron Zotter

To John Garang

God made him for a great purpose: to unite and inspire the people of southern Sudan. He died too young, but his mark will never pass away. We Sudanese owe him much.

AFRICA

SUDAN

Area
Enlarged

ETHIOPIA

UGANDA

KENYA

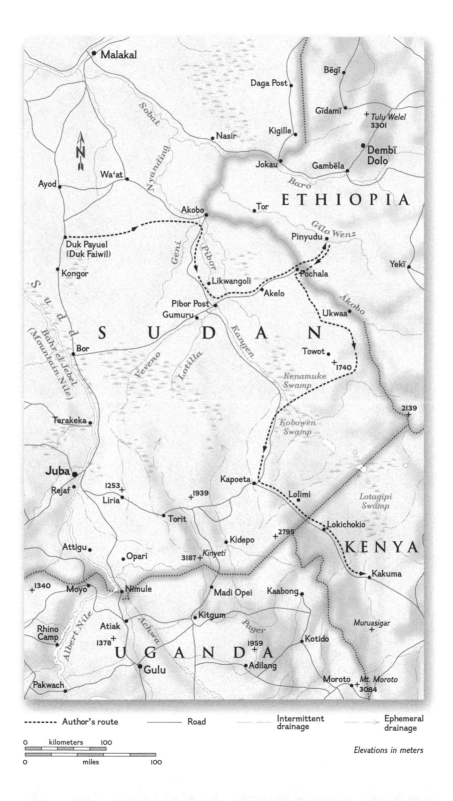

Malakal

Daga Post

Bēgī

Gīdamī

Tulu Welel
3301

Kigille

Nasir

Jokau   Gambēla

Dembī
Dolo

Sobat

Nyanding

Wa'at

Ayod

Baro   ETHIOPIA

Tor

Akobo

Gīlo Wenz

Pinyudu

Yekī

Duk Payuel
(Duk Faiwil)

Geni

Pibor

Likwangoli

Pochala

Kongor

Akelo

Ākobo

Pibor Post
Gumuru

Ukwaa

S   U   D   A   N

Bor

Kangen

Towot

1740

Sudd

Veneno

Lotilla

Kenamuke
Swamp

Bahr el Jebel
(Mountain Nile)

2139

Terakeka

Kobowen
Swamp

Juba

Rejaf

1253
Liria

1939

Kapoeta

Lolimi

Lotagipi
Swamp

Torit

Lokichokio

KENYA

Attigu

Opari

Kidepo

2795

3187 Kinyeti

Moyo

Nimule

Madi Opei

Kaabong

Kakuma

1340

Muruasigar

Rhino
Camp

Atiak

Kitgum

Pager

Kotido

1378

1959

U   G   A   N   D   A

Adilang

Moroto

Mt. Moroto
3084

Pakwach

Gulu

Albert Nile

Achwa

- - - - - - Author's route   ——— Road   ——— Intermittent
drainage   ——→ Ephemeral
drainage

0   kilometers   100

0   miles   100

Elevations in meters

INTRODUCTION

THE NIGHT THE DJELLABAS CAME TO DUK PAYUEL,* I REMEMBER that I had been feeling tense all over, as if my body were trying to tell me something. I could not sleep.

It was a dark night, with no moon to reflect off the standing water that pooled beside our huts. My parents and the other adults were sleeping outside, so the children and elderly could all be inside, away from the clouds of biting insects. My brothers and sisters and I, as well as about a dozen refugees from other villages in southern Sudan, stretched out on the ground inside a hut that had been built especially for kids. I lay in the sticky heat, tossing and turning on a dried cowhide, while others tried to sleep on mats of *aguot,* a hollow, grasslike plant from the wetlands that women of my Dinka tribe stitch together. Our crowded bodies seemed to form their own patchwork quilt, filling every square foot with arms and legs.

The name of the village as it appears on English-language maps is often shown as Duk Fawil, a variation from the Arabic.

I opened my eyes and stared toward the grass ceiling and the sticks that supported it, but I could see nothing. Inside the hut it was as dark as the bottom of a well. All was silent except for the whine of the occasional mosquito that penetrated the defenses of the double door, a two-foot-high opening filled with twin plugs of grass that were designed, with obviously limited success, to keep pests outside.

Silence. It must have been around 2 a.m.

Silence.

Then, a whistle. It started low and soft at first, then grew louder as it came closer. Other whistles joined the chorus. Next came a sound like the cracking of some giant limb in the forest. Again, the same sound, louder and in short bursts. I wondered if I were dreaming. As deafening explosions made the earth vibrate beneath me and hysterical voices penetrated the walls of the hut, I realized what was happening.

My village was being shelled.

I sprang up, fully awake. In my panic, I tried to run, but the hut's interior was so impenetrably black I slammed headfirst into something hard. The impact knocked me backward, and I fell onto the bodies of the other children. I could not see even the outline of the door. But I could hear the voices of my brothers and sisters, loud and crying as the shells began exploding, punctuated by the occasional burst of automatic gunfire.

"Is this the end of the world?" a woman screamed in panic somewhere outside the hut. There was a pause, and other voices repeated the question. I did not know the answer. Then I heard my mother calling my name. "Dhieu! Dhieu!" she screamed. Try as I might, I could not figure out where the voice came from. I strained to listen, but recumbent bodies had come alive all over

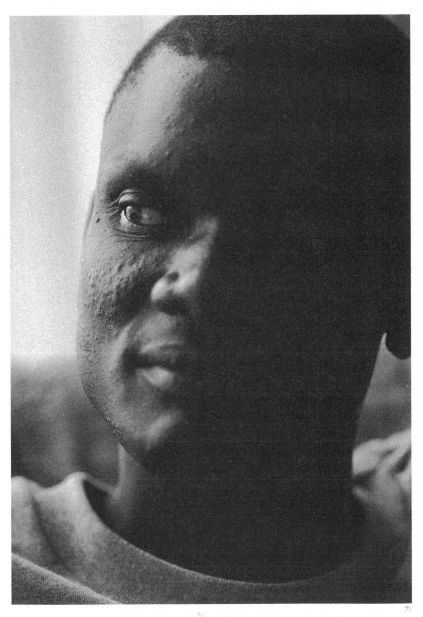

*John Bul Dau contemplates a question from filmmaker Christopher Quinn
during an interview at John's Syracuse apartment.*

the floor and children inside the hut started to scream, too. My mother shrieked the names of my brothers and sisters, who were in the hut with me, and cried, *"Mith! Mith!"* ("Children! Children!") The village cattle joined in, mooing and urinating loudly, like a rainstorm, in their fright.

My whole being focused on the single thought of finding the door. I scrambled around the darkened interior of the hut, bumping into a mass of suddenly upright bodies. A group of us, a tangle of arms and legs, flailed around the room, trying to find the way out. We ran into each other, and all of us fell, a jumble of bodies on the ground. The hut seemed not to have a door, and in the chaos and darkness I felt as if I were suffocating. It was a living nightmare.

Suddenly, I felt a hint of a breeze. It had to be from an opening in the exterior wall. I stumbled, let out a cry, and strained toward the puff of fresh air. I found myself on top of somebody, but I could see the door's faint outline. I crawled through the two layers of grass that formed the door of the hut and emerged into the outside world.

I stood and watched the strangely red dawn of a world gone mad. The undergrowth in our village is as thick as a curtain in the rainy season, the eight-foot-tall grasses blocking the view of the horizon. On this night, though, fires had burned away some of the brush. I could see neighbors' huts normally hidden to me, ablaze like fireworks. A big *luak*—cowshed—in the distance, its squat brown, conical roof awash in crimson, resembled a miniature volcano. Shells landed in showers of dirt, smoke, and thunder. Bullets zipped through the air like angry bees, but I could not see who fired them.

I started to run but did not know where to go. Suddenly, my father ran from right to left in front of me. I pivoted and followed him. He ran between the huts, and I tried to catch up with him, but, after about a hundred yards, he halted and knelt, disappearing into the grass at the edge of a footpath. I kept running. As I started to pass him in the darkness, my father reached up, grabbed my shoulder, and pulled me down beside him.

He motioned me to be quiet, and we knelt together in the grass at the edge of the path. I crumpled awkwardly. My weight pressed on my right leg, which had folded beneath me. I half-rose and tried to shift my body to get comfortable, but I had moved only a fraction when my father gestured to me to freeze.

Within seconds a line of shadowy forms, carrying automatic rifles, ran along the path toward the hut I had just left. There were perhaps nine men, dressed in dark clothes. They did not see us. They passed close enough for me to spit on them, if I had been so inclined. As they vanished beyond a curve in the path, I could hear them fire their guns. The shooting seemed to ring inside my head, and I clapped my hands to my ears. A bitter taste flooded my mouth. Perhaps the sourness of my tense stomach had overflowed. It's odd to remember such a small detail now, but the events of that night are cut into my memory as if etched by acid.

My father dropped low to the ground and seized me with one hand. With the other hand, he pulled himself deeper into the bush, dragging me behind him like a sack of millet. I started to crawl. We moved through the muck, smearing our knees and hands, until we reached the sanctuary of the forest. Inside the shelter of the trees, where the djellabas could not see us, we rested. My father did not speak, and I did not press him to do so.

The light grew. It was not daybreak, but the dance of fire on the huts and surrounding trees made it seem so. I heard more gunshots and more crying. I knew nobody in the village had a

Lost Boys gather at Pinyudu camp in February 1989 to listen to camp caretakers. John believes he is somewhere in the back.

gun, so each report of the automatic rifles could only mean more death for those I loved. I recall having two thoughts. First, I convinced myself that the women in the village had been right: It really was the end of the world. Second, I wondered what had happened to my mother and my siblings.

After two hours, the sounds of attack faded. I took stock of my situation. I had just turned 13. I was naked. I carried no food or water. My village had been destroyed. I had become separated from my mother and siblings. Armed men who spoke a foreign tongue combed the forests and grasslands, and if they found me, they most likely would kill me. The only good thing I could imagine was that I might be safe for a while.

It was then that I realized the man who sat beside me was not my father.

In the 19 years since that August night, as one of the "lost boys" of Sudan, I have witnessed my share of death and despair. I have seen the hyenas come at dusk to feed on the bodies of my friends. I have been so hungry and thirsty in the dusty plains of Africa that I consumed things I would rather forget. I have crossed a crocodile-infested river while being shelled and shot at. I have walked until I thought I could walk no more. I have wondered, more times than I can count, if my friends or I would live to see a new day. Those were the times I thought God had grown tired of us.

In some ways, my story is like those of tens of thousands of boys who lost their homes, their families, and in many cases their lives in a civil war between north and south that raged in Sudan from 1983 to 2005. In some ways, I represent the nearly 4,000 Sudanese refugees who found haven in the United States. But in other ways, my story is my own. I have a job, an apartment, a new family, and a wonderful new country to call home. I am studying public policy and world affairs at a university, and I plan to use my education to make life better in Africa and in America. I know I have been blessed and that I have been kept alive for a purpose.

They call me a Lost Boy, but let me assure you, God has found me.

SELECTED TIMELINE
OF SUDAN

OLD TESTAMENT refers to what is now Sudan as the land of Kush.

1ST CENTURY A.D. — Explorers traveling up the Nile from Egypt get no farther than the Sudd, an immense swamp. The area beyond remains legendary and unexplored by outsiders for centuries.

7TH CENTURY A.D. — Followers of Muhammad spread Islam across North Africa and push into south.

EARLY 16TH CENTURY — Muslim armies control all lands bordering the Nile from the Mediterranean port of Alexandria to the site of modern-day Khartoum. The unconquered land to the south they name Bilad al-Sudan, an Arabic epithet meaning "Land of the Blacks."

1820 — Khedive Muhammad Ali, acting on behalf of the Turkish Ottoman Empire, invades northern Sudan from Egypt, telling his commanders to seize Africans as slaves. His armies penetrate the Sudd in 1840, becoming the first outsiders known to have done so.

MID-19TH CENTURY — Slave traders from northern Sudan and Greece follow the Egyptians and Turks, creating a time Dinka tribespeople called "the spoiling of the world."

LATE 19TH CENTURY — The British persuade the Egyptian khedive to halt trafficking in slaves in Sudan, but all attempts to suppress the slave trade fail.

1880s — The Mahdi, or "Expected One," a self-proclaimed prophet, incites northern Sudanese to rise up against their foreign masters. The Mahdi's armies destroy British forces at Khartoum and behead their general, "Chinese" Gordon. Southern Sudan, resistant to the Mahdi's Islamic fervor, dissolves into tribal warfare and famine. Sudan's population declines from seven million to two million in 20 years.

1898 — The British triumph over the Mahdi's forces and take control of all Sudan, disguising their rule as a "condominium" with the Turkish Ottomans in Egypt.

WORLD WAR I — The facade of joint rule is ruined when Britain finds itself at war with the Turks.

1920s — The British encourage division between the Muslim north of Sudan and the Christian, animist south. British policies in the 1920s increasingly treat the south as autonomous: Access by the northern Sudanese into the "closed districts" of the south is curtailed, but Christian missionaries are allowed in to "educate" the native tribes and shore up the region against Islam.

1940s — British colonial rule wanes worldwide. Britain makes plans to pull out of Sudan.

1955 — Sudanese soldiers from southern tribes mutiny, calling themselves the Anya Nya, a reference to a snake living in the forest.

1956 — Sudan gains its independence. The new Sudanese government, headquartered in Khartoum, pushes an Islamic, Arab agenda that further politicizes southern tribes.

LATE 1950s — Civil war erupts when the north tries to suppress the southern rebellion by burning villages and expelling Christian missionaries.

1969 — A military junta led by Gaafar Muhammad Numeiry seizes control of Sudan's central government, vowing that Sudan will remain a single state. The southerners continue to revolt, fearing that the government plans to forcibly make all of Sudan an Arab, Muslim nation.

1972 — With the help of the United Nations High Commissioner for Refugees and the World Council of Churches, northern and southern Sudan reach a compromise known as the Addis Ababa Agreement.

1973 — The Socialist Republic of Sudan is formed, with the south—defined roughly as everything below the tenth parallel—gaining autonomy and the north declaring Islam to be the state religion.

LATE 1970s — Southern autonomy begins to erode.

1983 — The northern government initiates a policy of rotating military units between the south and north, causing a revolt of southern soldiers unwilling to leave their families in the south. President Numeiry proclaims sharia, the strict Muslim legal code, throughout Sudan.

1984 — The Sudan People's Liberation Movement, the political arm of the SPLA (Sudan People's Liberation Army), announces its intention to topple Numeiry's government. Numeiry declares a state of emergency after a Libyan plane bombs a government-operated radio station, then reputedly lands in southern Sudan. The SPLA, led by John

Garang, attacks army and government outposts in southern Sudan and the violence flares into open war.

1985 — The army seizes control of the government, deposes Numeiry, and institutes a new state of emergency. Unrest between north and south continues.

EARLY 1990s — Sudan's support of the Iraqi invasion of Kuwait, taken in the name of pan-Islamic solidarity, opens its borders to radical Islamic groups. The United States responds by cutting all financial assistance to the Khartoum government.

1992 — The forces of Sudan's ruler, Gen. Omer al Bashir, begin the largest offensive of the years-long civil war.

2001 — Serious negotiations begin between the Sudan People's Liberation Army and the Khartoum government, both exhausted by the long stalemate.

2005 — A Comprehensive Peace Agreement, stipulating a permanent cease-fire, is signed. John Garang, the former rebel leader, becomes Vice President of Sudan but almost immediately dies in a suspicious helicopter crash. Garang's successor, Salva Kiir Mayardit, vows to support the Sudanese Government of National Unity and continue the pursuit of lasting peace. Humanitarian organizations begin planning for the repatriation of hundreds of thousands of southern refugees.

1

SUDAN IS A HUGE COUNTRY, THE LARGEST IN AFRICA. IT COVERS 966,000 square miles, roughly equal to the area of Western Europe. Its first census, taken around the time it gained independence at the beginning of 1956, indicated slightly more than ten million residents divided among 572 tribes speaking 114 languages. The largest ethnic group by far is the Arab population in the Muslim north. Dozens of tribal groups compete for a voice in government. The Dinka represent the largest of the minorities, with roughly two million people today.

Independence did not end the ongoing tensions between north and south. The new government, headquartered in Khartoum, angered the southern tribes by minimizing their political voice and ignoring their Christian heritage. The Dinka and other southern tribes, such as the Nuer and Nuba, fought back. The northern government tried to suppress the rebellion by burning southern villages in the late 1950s and expelling the Christian missionaries, whom they believed supported the rebels and blocked the spread of Islam. The country found itself mired in all-out civil war.

The Muslims in the north had better weapons, but the tribes in the south fought with the conviction that comes with belief in a cause and defense of a *homeland. The southerners had no uniforms, no ranks, not enough guns to go around. Rebels calling themselves the Anya Nya improvised antitank weapons out of glass bottles filled with kerosene and stoppered with flaming rags.*

A military junta led by Gaafar Muhammad Numeiry seized control of Sudan's central government in a 1969 coup. Numeiry abolished multiparty democracy and promised that Sudan would remain a single state. However, he held out the possibility that the southern provinces could someday rule themselves within the framework of a unified government. Southern rebels took heart but continued to press for autonomy. Secret peace talks between delegations of northerners and southerners opened in May 1971, with the help of the United Nations High Commissioner for Refugees and the World Council of Churches. In February 1972, the two sides agreed to allow southern Sudan full autonomy within the context of a republic. The accord became known as the Addis Ababa Agreement, for the Ethiopian city where the two sides met. A new constitution became law after national elections, and the world welcomed the new, socialist Republic of Sudan in May 1973. The south, defined roughly as everything below the tenth parallel, received its longed-for self-governance. The north declared Islam to be the state religion, but it affirmed the right of citizens to practice Christianity.

The Addis Ababa Agreement ushered in 11 years of peace. John Dau was born in 1974, only a few months after the peace took hold.

IN THE BEGINNING, A MAN NAMED AYUEL WAS THROWN DOWN to Earth from heaven. This is what I was told as a child. As Ayuel walked across southern Sudan, he carried a bowl filled with *akop,* a kind of food. Ayuel worked some magic with the bowl. No matter how much he shared his food with others, he never ran out. People called the food "akop ayuel." When people went to look for their lost cows, Ayuel gave them a bit of his akop, and they never went hungry.

Dinka boys smear themselves with the ashes of cattle dung to treat lice.
Adults mix the ash with cattle urine to color their hair.

This made the sun angry. Why should Ayuel never lack for food, when others had to toil in the heat of the day to raise their crops and their cattle? The sun decided Ayuel had to die. But Ayuel fooled the sun. He chose to stay indoors during the day, so the sun could not kill him. Ayuel came out of his hut only after the sun went to bed for the evening.

So the sun plotted. He asked the moon to kill Ayuel at night, and the moon agreed.

One night, as Ayuel worked outside, the moon threw down a long, metallic rod that passed through Ayuel's head and fixed him to the ground. Ayuel was gravely wounded. Neighbors came and saw what the moon had done, and they cried in anguish. Then they tried to push Ayuel toward heaven, thinking they could lift his body off the top of the rod, but the rod was too high. So they began to dig, thinking they could find the bottom and slide Ayuel off the end. They dug and dug, almost to the center of the Earth, but they never reached the tip of the rod.

That is when Ayuel realized he would die there. He announced a blessing on his people, saying, "I must die now, but I will leave you with a spirit called Deng Pajarbe. People will fear you, and you will be leaders."

That is how the Nyarweng, my clan of the Dinka tribe, came to be. That is how my ancestors and my father learned of their destinies to become leaders of men. Those who find within them the spirit of Deng Pajarbe, Ayuel's gift to his people, can do great things. From the earliest age that I can remember, I knew I must find my own way to lead my people toward some greater good. I never could have imagined, of course, that I would grow up to help children survive in the African wilderness without their mothers and fathers. Or that I would help young Dinka men and women build new lives in America.

SOUTHERN SUDAN IS NOT THE KIND OF PLACE MOST WESTERNERS embrace. The temperature often reaches 120°F, and the rainy season floods the landscape with standing water, breeding clouds of ravenous mosquitoes. Duk County, which surrounds my village, is generally flat, so it holds water. Oceans of eight-foot-tall grasses, interspersed with canopied forests of acacia, patches of farmland dotted with cattle luaks and huts, and stands of tamarind and lulu trees, make it hard to see from one place to another. If I climbed to the top of a luak, I could see the land sloping gently toward the north and west. Narrow dirt footpaths disappear into the savanna, linking one village to the next. There are also no real cities in the whole of southern Sudan—at least nothing to rival Khartoum or Omdurman in the north—and no real roads, just tracks of rutted brown dirt. Anyone who ventures abroad in a car must be prepared to repair it themselves when, not if, it breaks down. Some of the paths lead into the land we called *toch,* which holds enough water even during the driest months to grow grasses to feed our cattle. Beyond toch lie the White Nile and the Sudd, its eternal swamp of crocodiles, hippos, and mosquitoes. The Sudd never drains. That fact has long been a blessing for the tribes of southern Sudan, because it always provides us with water, and my people move through it like antelope through the forest. However, outsiders see the swamp as a barrier. For centuries, from the time of the Roman legions through the arrival of Arab and British armies, the Sudd has kept nearly all invaders at bay.

Our culture centers on cows, so much so that they sustain us from day to day and figure into our initiation into adulthood, our courtship, and the very continuation of our lives from one generation to the next. There is a legend among the Dinka that God long ago offered the first Dinka man a choice between the gift of the first cow and a secret gift called "what." God told the man to choose carefully, because the secret gift was very great, but the man took one look at the cow and became transfixed. "If you insist on having the cow, then I advise you to taste her milk before you decide," God said. The man tried the milk and declared it marvelous. He chose the cow, never having seen the secret gift. God gave that gift to other people, leading them to the technological advances of Western science. The Dinka did not follow the Western pattern of development, partly because of southern Sudan's lack of metal ores and stone, but mainly because of their contentment as farmers and cattle raisers.

The Dinka lived happily, drinking their cows' milk, eating their cows' flesh, and using their cows as currency. To the Dinka, cows mean life.

It is no surprise that our isolation has helped preserve our ancient beliefs and customs. The Dinka keep mostly to themselves, raising cattle for their milk and for their value as a form of money. They raise crops of millet and maize, as well as tall, very black-skinned boys and girls. At a very early age, Dinka children take on the responsibility of tending cattle, goats, and chickens, and of keeping pests away from their farms. Early on, they are tested in their games and chores to see which of them has the qualities of leadership that guarantee the tribe's survival from age to age.

That survival has not been easy.

History here is like the River Nile. It has many branches, it flows without ceasing, and it links vastly different landscapes with long, clear streams. To understand how my people found themselves continually under attack in recent decades, it is best to start at the river's source.

My FAMILY DOES NOT KNOW THE EXACT DAY OF MY BIRTH, as there were no records kept then, but we think it was in July 1974. It was the happiest of times in southern Sudan because we thought we would have peace forever. We lived in a row of huts next to our cattle and our garden. The main hut was divided into three sections for my parents, the boys, and the girls. The boys and girls also had their own little huts. Our luak, a much larger, thatched hut, housed our cows during the wet season. Otherwise, most of the cows lived away from the huts in cattle camp.

When I was a boy, my uncles told me stories of the fighting before the Addis Ababa Agreement. Some of them fought with the Anya Nya, but my father, Deng Leek, did not do so. He served the rebellion by giving food and ammunition to the Anya Nya soldiers. I was very proud of his helping the cause of freedom in southern Sudan. I was the third of six children—three boys and three girls—born to our mother, the first of my father's four wives. My father has a total of 18 children, which is not unusual for a successful and respected Dinka man.

He liked to work hard, getting up before the sun and heading to the garden outside our hut. I usually saw him shortly after dawn, weeding. Our biggest crops were millet and maize. We also grew okra, onions, and beans in the brown dirt, and planted pumpkin vines to trail along the fences around our cattle yard. If the soil was good, we planted tobacco. My father tended the garden for hours in the morning, before the heat of midday. "When you work, you get what you want," he said. He was always building and rebuilding huts for our family and our cattle. He would cut trees in the forest and bring them back to support our shelters of mud walls and tied-grass roofs. One time when his work had bathed him in sweat, I told him, "Father, you have to stop. You have to rest a bit." He said, "The time to rest is when you can see what is in front of you," meaning, "don't stop until you've finished what you're working on."

My father was a respected man in our village, a judge and a wrestler. It is a very great thing among the Dinka to represent your clan as a wrestler, for when a wrestler matches himself against the champions from other villages and other clans, he represents much more than himself. Being the champion wrestler of any Dinka village is like winning the World Series or the Super Bowl.

Deng Leek, John's father, in Uganda in 1998. He is holding a mayuai *stick with an elephant-tusk handle, symbol of an honored leader.*

God created Deng Leek to wrestle. His chest rippled with muscles. He had big shoulders, big arms, and thick thighs and legs, in which his veins stood out against the muscle walls. I stand very straight, but my father, perhaps because of his great strength and his bulky chest, always seemed to be leaning forward and balancing on the front of his feet. Aside from his narrow, friendly face and delicate ears, he probably looked fierce to anyone opposing him. I remember looking up at him when I was a young boy and thinking how large he was. In fact, he was not tall for a Dinka, perhaps six feet one, whereas I now am six eight. I never saw him wrestle. He gave up the sport sometime before I was born, and he did not talk to me about his life as an athlete. But I did witness his wisdom as a judge.

I often went with him to see him render justice under the giant tree in the center of our village. The villagers of Duk Payuel called our tree "Kuel Adeng," the tree of the woman called Adeng. She was my great-great-grandmother and a well-respected Dinka in her own right. On the days he presided over appeals court, my father waited for the litigants and villagers to gather under the tree, then he put on his djellaba, the long robe favored by Dinka elders of authority. (Only later did the word take on new meaning as shorthand for the robe-wearing Muslim soldiers who invaded our homeland.) My father added a final touch, wrapping a colorful scarf around his head, then headed toward the great tree. Along the way, other, lesser judges fell in step with him. A policeman came too, carrying a whip made of hippopotamus skin.

I stood beside my father, who sat in the middle of the judges, and watched as the two sides argued back and forth. My father decided a lot of cases involving the exchange of land, grazing rights in disputes between two powerful families, and

the accidental killings that sometimes occur during fights at cattle camp, when rival clans clash over water and grassland. If a
man killed another man, my father ordered the payment of a
hundred head of cattle; if a woman had died, he ordered a payment of about half as much. That was the rule in our traditional,
patriarchal culture: A man's life was worth more than a woman's,
although both had great value.

My father did not have a constitution or a law book to help
him make decisions. Today, a Dinka judge goes to school to learn
to read and write and to study law, but my father had only the
laws and values of the Dinka inscribed on his heart. And his
word was absolute.

Like all heads of households, my father had to respect his family. He never spoke cruelly to us, and he never ate unless he knew
there was enough food to satisfy us children. He also never ate
any small, sweet piece of food, such as popcorn or candy, because
candy is only for children. Even today, many years after I left my
village, I have difficulty taking a cookie in the fellowship hall at
church. I look at the little food and think, "I am not a child. I will
lose respect if I eat this."

My mother, Anon Manyok Duot Lual, always seemed to be
cooking. She made a lot of food to feed her large family. My favorite was pumpkin. It is so sweet in Sudan, not like the bland pumpkins in America. I remember one time standing outside our hut
while my mother cooked it. I could smell the aroma drifting on
the air. She had scooped out the insides and boiled it. When the
pumpkin became soft, she filled it with millet powder and mixed
it with water. Then she put the lid back on top and cooked it. That
was what I smelled outside the hut, and it made my mouth water.
She also made a dish called *awalwala,* which is sort of the national

food of southern Sudan. She mixed millet powder with water and
let it set for a day. Then she ground it and made a fine, soft paste.
When it began to look like mashed potatoes, she plopped the mixture inside two halves of a gourd, added more soft millet powder,
and kept mixing to get the lumps out. If there are too many lumps
in her bowl of awalwala, she knew she would lose respect, so my
mother kept mixing and stirring it until it was perfect.

She put food on one tray for my father, one tray for the girls,
and one tray for the boys. Once a week, as a treat, she put butter
on the bottom of everybody's bowl and ladled in the hot food.
The fresh butter melted and crept around the edges of the food,
until it puddled near the top. Butter on awalwala, that was a good
day. We also drank milk every morning, afternoon, and night.
We mixed it with our food at mealtimes, and we drank it before
we went to bed.

THE DINKA CAME LATER TO CHRISTIANITY THAN PEOPLE OF THE
West, but my family, like most Dinka, honored the word of the
Lord and sang praises to his name. Some Dinka still believe in
the old gods, the gods of our ancestors who ripened the wheat
and brought the harvest. My family worshipped the god of Ayuel
and the spirit of Deng Pajarbe until I was about five years old.
When we embraced Christianity, it was so good. I learned that
the Lord doesn't need anything; worshipping him is free. The
spirit gods needed something every day.

Every year, before my family became Christians, my father
had to slaughter a cow to appease the ancestral gods. One time,
before we converted, I fell sick, and my father had to slaughter
a goat or a chicken, I can't remember which. When the sickness
hadn't left me after two weeks, he called the witch doctor. He

came to the house dressed in feathers, with the dried cover of a bull's penis around his neck; I thought it was a funny costume even then. The witch doctor blew on my hair and twisted it, and he put saliva on my head. Then he sat down and tossed the shells of a dozen snails on the floor. He read them—some were topside up, some topside down—and then made his diagnosis and announced a cure. I had fallen sick, because the spirits wanted my family to make a sacrifice, he said. My father had to slaughter a cow and share the beef (and it probably was no coincidence that the witch doctor always got his portion) to appease the spirits. That was very expensive, and I was not the only sick child in my family. When my brothers and sisters took ill, my father had to repeat the procedure, slaughtering another animal, according to the witch doctor's prescription.

When the missionaries came to Duk County, long before I was born, they said the Lord would welcome the Dinka as his people and we wouldn't need to give Him anything. Except, that is, the willingness to believe in Him and do good things in His name. I think my father came to believe the old gods were expensive and jealous, whereas the Lord does not require the constant sacrifice of animals.

In the Dinka world, the cycle of the seasons regulated work and diet. There are four seasons in southern Sudan, but they don't follow the same order at my equatorial home as they do in the temperate zones. Cool weather starts in November in southern Sudan. It never gets very cold, perhaps 55°F degrees on the coldest night. Winter was always a good season, not only because of Christmas, but because the mosquitoes went away. The grass changed from green to yellow in Duk Payuel. The wind came from the east and dried the water that collected in front of our luak after the rains. We had no calendar, but I knew when cool weather was due to arrive, because the village elders emerged from their huts in the morning, leaned on their walking sticks, and announced the changing of the season. They said they had felt it in the evening breeze.

When the tall grass turned brown, we burned it to clear the ground for hunting. We could see into the forest, where the *thiang*, a kind of large antelope, and other animals ran. Winter mornings brought fog to my village, and birds we had not seen for some time returned. Black crows with white necks visited again, as well as hawks, which are very bad birds. Hawks swooped out of the sky and stole meat from the hands of us children. They inflicted bad wounds with their sharp talons on some of us.

The mosquitoes were completely gone by January and that made people happy. No farm work could be done, so my father and the other men in the village used the time to fix roofs and rebuild huts and luaks. My father invited other men to help him cut and haul the logs for the luak. He never paid anyone for the work, but he made sure there was a batch of dark red millet wine on hand to make things go easier. The men marched off to the forest, singing as they went. Everyone competed to show how hard they could work, and they always came back from the forest dripping sweat.

I went with them to cut trees a few times, but I had a bad experience on one of the trips. I was chopping a tree when a sliver of wood flew off and struck me in the left eye, effectively destroying my vision in it. For many years, until I had surgery in America, I could see almost nothing out of that eye. Now I can see a little bit.

At the end of February, the air starts to get hot. We would know the hot season was coming, because the trees would drop their leaves in order to minimize water loss through aspiration. Cracks would start appearing in the earth, some of them large enough to stumble into.

As February ended, it was the young men's job to find the right place to keep and guard our clan's cattle. We could never be sure whether it would be the same place as the year before; the water might have gone, or the grass might not have grown thick enough. Our clan sent out five strong men, with no food, to travel for two days and search for cattle camp. Once they made their selection, the mothers and fathers decided which of the girls would get to accompany the young men of the clan to camp. When that was settled, we set off along the dirt paths, driving most of our cows before us. We always left a few behind so the boys, girls, and elders of our villages could easily get milk all year round.

Maj. Court Treatt, a British adventurer and filmmaker who made many visits to East Africa in the early 20th century, got it right when he characterized the opening of cattle camp as the most pleasant time in the life of a Dinka boy. "During the rainy season, the cattle are grazed during the day and brought into their special houses at night; but as the rainy season ceases, and the receding water leaves behind a tangled mass of nourishing grass, there comes to the Dinkas the most blissful period of their lives," he wrote. "They trek with their beloved beasts to the cattle camps on the edge of the swamps, where...they settle down to a picnic life in which every day is to them a high day and holiday."

I could never eat food at cattle camp. Anyone who did so would be ridiculed as lacking integrity or being greedy. I could only drink milk, but that was fine with me.

In March, the land grew dry. At some point, when the earth became parched, everyone from my village moved to the wetter lands near cattle camp. When clouds started to gather in April, we knew the rains were near. The rains came in May and continued for many weeks. The saturated ground sent forth a billion green shoots, and some boys returned to help their parents do farm chores.

July, the month I was born, was a time of hunger, because the crops we had planted earlier were not ready for harvest, and the food preserved from the previous year always ran low. No matter how hungry we got, however, my father would not butcher even one of the cows for food. His neighbors would have thought he was lazy for not growing enough food, and they might have poked fun at him by composing a song. Ridicule for behavior that threatens traditional ways of life provides a strong force to keep those ways intact.

Our crops started to ripen in August. Maize came in first, then millet. As soon as the millet began to ripen, birds descended on the village to try to steal it. When I was very young, I had a common job in the millet fields. My father built a platform in the fields, and I climbed to the top and sat there with a supply of clay balls. When the birds came to eat the millet, I clapped my hands, shouted, hit a dry animal skin with a stick, and threw the clay to scare them away. They were relentless. I had to pay close attention all the time and not daydream to keep the birds away.

From June until harvesttime in October, the weather was always hot and wet. The ground got saturated, and the water backed up. We built levies around our huts and luaks to keep the floors dry, but there was no way to keep dry when we walked to visit our neighbors or tend the cattle. And always, bloodthirsty mosquitoes hovered in great numbers. If we left the windows open, we couldn't sleep; when we slapped at the mosquitoes, our hands came away bloody. If we closed the windows, the air became too hot and muggy.

In the morning, if I tried to walk to a neighbor's house, snails in the mud cut my feet. I could hear other people's footsteps in the standing water—*galoop, galoop*—before I saw anyone approaching. Dew formed overnight on the tall grass between the houses and on the paths that led to our cows. My brothers and I had to get up early and walk naked along the grassy paths to tend the cows. There was so much dew on the grass that whoever led the way got soaked. My brothers and I always fought to be in the back of the line. Each time my turn came, I found a stick before I went to bed, so I could beat the grass on our walk the next morning. That knocked off most of the water before it soaked me.

No wonder everyone was so happy in November when the elders said they could feel the cool season returning.

I NEVER HAD FORMAL SCHOOLING IN DUK COUNTY. THE ONLY schools were Muslim ones for the Arabs in the north, or Christian ones in the biggest villages of the south. But I did have an informal education based on stories and riddles. Father and mother told them at home, and the children shared them as well. The youngest boys and girls took their goats and sat under a tree to swap stories. I sat with them often. We split into two groups and composed riddles for a competition. When one side failed to guess the correct answer and had to give up, the losers sent a girl from their team to the other side. This went on, back and forth, all morning one day. When the other team would ask

A Dinka herdsman stands watch at cattle camp in Bahr el-Ghazal, Sudan.
As is customary, he has armed himself with a stick.

me a final riddle that I could not answer, I would argue like a
man in my father's court. I hated to admit defeat and give up
the last girl. Now, as I look back on the game, I understand that
I learned not only how to think analytically by composing and
guessing riddles, but also how to defend what I had, to keep it
from being taken.

We also made up stories that contained moral lessons. I told
one story about an old man who decided to live alone, away from
the nearby village. He kept to himself and tended to his many
cows. The villagers did not have as much to eat as he did, but he
did not care because he was wealthy. One day a group of lions
invaded his property. They ate all of his cows and left him with
nothing. The villagers called on the old man and took him to
their village. They found him a wife, and he learned to live again

as part of the group. He never lived alone or kept his milk to himself again.

Besides tending cattle, boys were expected to gather the dung and break it into small pieces. Spreading the dung in a fine layer makes it dry evenly, after which it can be collected and burned. The smoke repels flying insects that otherwise would bite the cattle and make them angry. If I had been working hard, I liked to show my father the brown smears on my hands as evidence of my labor, to gain his approval. But I wasn't always so diligent. My father checked the dung I had broken, dragging his toe among the clods to see if I had missed any sizable bits in my haste. He corrected me when I had quit too quickly and failed to do a thorough job.

When I wasn't tending cattle or breaking up cattle dung, I played a lot as a child with toy cows made out of clay or in groups with the other children. One of my favorite games was called *alueth,* in which we pretended a lion captured Dinka boys and turned them into lions. We picked one boy to be the lion, and he stood at one end of a field near his base. The other boys stood at the other end.

The lion charged into the boys, and they tried to dodge him and get to his base, where they were "safe." If the lion caught them, he put his hand on their noses, and they became lions, too. The game continued until only one boy stood alone. He then became the lion, and the lions became boys, and it all started up again.

I also enjoyed spending time at my special tree in the village. It had a branch hanging low, parallel to the ground. Seven of us would sit on the branch and swing back and forth, watching the world go by.

It was an ideal childhood. I would not trade our homeland for any other place on Earth. It is the land of our ancestors, the land of our cattle and our vegetables, the land we pass along to our descendants. I never questioned that I would live forever in this Eden.

Events proved otherwise. The signs were there for us to see, starting in the early 1980s, when I was still a young boy.

News came to Duk County from the south. My parents told me the story just as they had heard it in the village. They said a man walking toward the town of Bor met a tortoise on the path. The tortoise spoke to him, saying, "I am sent by the Lord. I bring you news of doom. Your country, southern Sudan, will be destroyed." The man stopped and listened to the tortoise. It spoke again. "The Lord has said, 'I will punish you because you have been unfaithful. I give you three choices for your doom, and you must choose among them. One is drought, and if you choose it, I will punish you by withholding the rain. If you do not choose that, I will punish you with flood. And if you do not choose that, I will punish you with war. Now, you must choose.'"

The man ran from the talking tortoise, but the tortoise yelled after him, "You must answer me. You must choose."

So the man answered. He chose war.

When he returned to his village, he spread the word of his encounter. The people of my village debated whether the man had made a wise choice. Some said he should not have chosen as he did. If he had picked drought, they said, they could survive because the Dinka have weathered many a dry spell in southern Sudan. But drought would bring famine, and everyone, including women and children, would suffer. So some of the villagers rejected that option. They said flood would have been a better choice. If the floods came, the Dinka could go to the Sudd and catch fish for dinner. But there were those who said a flood would kill our cows, and what use would it be to become fishermen if we lost our cattle? Cattle are the backbone of our life, and we could not afford to lose them. Most of the villagers of Duk Payuel finally agreed the man had chosen wisely, but that did not settle the debate. Groups continued to argue for flood or drought. No matter which fate they chose, everyone was terrified.

More ominous news came to my village from outside. A month or two after the man met the tortoise, a crow landed on the shoulder of an old woman who was sitting and plaiting rope in the shade of her house. The crow pecked at her and said, "I was sent by the Lord to bring you news of doom. Your country very soon will be destroyed." The woman tried to shoo the bird away, but it stayed right by her, talking. The woman became very frightened. The crow gave the same message as the tortoise: "You have to choose. Drought, flood, or war." The woman didn't know what to do, so she said nothing.

In the evenings before bedtime, everyone in my village would gather outside and talk about these portents. "If there is war, can we run to toch?" someone asked. "Toch is a good place to hide." Others said no, toch could be dangerous, especially if the doom came as flood. There already is a lot of water at toch, and flooding would make it hard to live there. Still others said not to worry, that we could cut down big trees and make boats if the floods came to toch. None of this comforted me. One danger seemed as bad as the next, and being asked to choose the form of our destruction did not provide much comfort. Some people became so consumed with the impossible choice and with looking for other signs that they stopped tending their crops. My family kept on, though. Sometimes all you can do is keep going, even in the face of great danger.

At the same time, a prophet named Ngun Deng, who lived among the Nuer, a neighboring tribe, forecast a similar doom. Fighting would come to southern Sudan, he said. Many Nuer would die. In the end, the southerners would defeat the enemy, and be defeated, too. He further prophesied that the country would be invaded by "white people," by which he meant Arabs. Ngun Deng said, "Yours will be a generation of black hair." Our elders interpreted that to mean the white-haired grandparents would die without a new generation to replace them; black-haired children and young adults would be killed before they could grow old enough to get their first gray hairs.

Ngun Deng's prophesy seemed to match the forecasts of the tortoise and the crow, reinforcing the gloom that spread among my people. Then the sun turned red, as if the heavens them-selves spoke to us. My mother said red was the color of blood, and it meant that surely, blood would flow. When I asked her where the blood would come from, she said, "People will fight, and there will be lots of killing."

What could we do? Where could we run? Nowhere, said Ngun Deng. Everywhere you go, you will find problems awaiting you, he said. The elders of Duk Payuel decided that, if troubles faced us in every direction, we would stay where we were and await whatever came.

We accepted this decision and the logic behind it, because we knew our fate had been written in the Bible. Our war had been prophesied thousands of years ago. That was our doom. Biblical texts also spoke of our deliverance. That was our hope. "Woe to the land of whirring wings along the rivers of Kush," begins

Chapter 18 of the Book of Isaiah. "Go, swift messengers, to a people tall and smooth-skinned, to a people feared far and wide, an aggressive nation of strange speech whose land is divided by rivers." Because the people of Kush were so unfaithful, the Bible said the Lord would cut off their shoots with pruning knives and take away their spreading branches. But one day the Lord would hear the cry of the Sudanese and bring them to Mount Zion.

We believed what we read in the Bible, and thus we knew the prophecies of the tortoise, the crow, and Ngun Deng would come true. War would come to us, but God would be with us in our hour of torment and make us powerful again. This was the secret strength of the southern Sudanese. We would never give up, despite being outnumbered and outgunned because we knew we would triumph in the end. As Isaiah prophesied more than 2,600 years ago, the Egyptians would lose heart, and the Lord would bring their plans to nothing.

Since before the Romans tried to enter the land of Kush and failed, the Bible has told of our final deliverance. Sudan would stay strong in the Lord, and its people would persevere until their reward.

THE SOUTHERN SUDANESE SAW THEIR AUTONOMY GRADUALLY dissolve in the late 1970s and early 1980s, partly through intertribal squabbles but mainly through tensions with the north. In 1983, the government insisted on a policy of rotating military units between the south and north. Southern units of the Sudan People's Armed Forces serving in the south were ordered to serve in the north. Many of the southern soldiers balked at the idea, as it would separate them from their families and bring the feared northern soldiers almost literally to the edges of their villages. Southern soldiers stationed in the town of Bor rose in a revolt and refused to allow northerners to take their places. Strict government censorship descended on the southern provinces, but small battles broke out between northern and southern soldiers and resulted in scores of fatalities. The southern soldiers abandoned Bor and retreated. Some found their way to the villages of Duk County in Upper Nile Province. When they came to Duk Payuel, they urged the villagers to rise and fight. War had come, the soldiers said.

John Garang, a Dinka and an American-educated economist, initiated a moderate movement for reconciliation. His plan called for a form of national unity in which the many minority peoples of Sudan, who formed a majority

*SPLA soldiers carrying automatic rifles march through
the Shilluk region of southern Sudan.*

when counted together, would have the strongest voice in government. However,
as the fighting continued and north and south polarized, Garang cast his lot with
the Sudan People's Liberation Army and joined the fighting.

In the fall of 1983, President Numeiry traded his military uniform for a djellaba and Muslim turban. Numeiry proclaimed sharia, the strict Muslim legal
code, throughout Sudan and pushed through judicial changes. Amnesty International reported 58 public amputations in Khartoum in a 12-month span. No
such figures were available for sharia punishments in the south.

The Sudan People's Liberation Movement, the political arm of the SPLA,
declared its intention in March 1984 to topple Numeiry's government. The next
month, in a strange tragedy that has never been fully explained, a Tupolev-22
in the Libyan air force killed five people in a bombing raid on an Omdurman
radio station owned and operated by the government. Numeiry's government
proclaimed that the plane, although apparently supplied by the Soviet Union

to the Libyan government, had taken off from and returned to a base in southern Sudan. Numeiry declared a state of emergency. Police officers and soldiers loyal to the northern government received emergency powers to enter and search homes, open private mail, and make arrests with little evidence.

The SPLA, with Garang firmly in charge, carried out attacks on army and government outposts in southern Sudan as the nation's internal violence flared into open war. A northern offensive pushed the SPLA back to the town of Pochala, not far from the border with Ethiopia. The SPLA also set up a base in Ethiopia, where it trained its soldiers in the mid-1980s. Meanwhile, Arab military units went on daylight raids in southern Sudan, shelling villages and stealing cattle before retreating to their bases at night. As the fighting continued, a third consecutive year of drought in the south added to the misery.

On April 6, 1985, the army seized control of the government, deposed Numeiry, and instituted a new state of emergency. The unrest between north and south continued. By mid-1987, the fighting was rocking back and forth across southern Sudan, gradually moving closer to John's village.

I COULDN'T EAT.

Each night I tried to force some milk past my tongue, but the sound of bombs exploding somewhere in the distance beyond my village made my stomach hurt and my throat clamp shut, like the jaw of a crocodile. I went to bed with my stomach growling and my head roiling with thoughts of what might come. But because I couldn't eat, there was a little more food for the very old, the very young, the sick, and the needy. And they were everywhere.

It was August 1987, and food was scarce in Duk Payuel, the collection of huts in the tangled forests and savannas of southern Sudan that I had called home for all my 13 years. The rainy season was well underway, so millet, maize, and the other crops my parents had planted on our little farm had not yet ripened. It would be weeks before we could eat from the new harvest. Any food we had stored from the previous year had long been dispersed. My father, mother, two brothers, and two sisters survived day to day by drinking milk from a few cows we kept in our luak, the round thatch-roofed, mud-sided barn that all families in southern Sudan construct to keep their precious cattle safe and dry. My family's luak resembled a miniature brown mountain rising out of the sea of stagnant water that covered our farm in the middle months of every year. In happier times I loved to visit our cows and drink their milk just before bedtime.

This year, Duk Payuel had to extend its meager food supply nearly twice as far as the year before. Hundreds of refugees had swelled our village until we had to feed about 3,000 people. The newcomers had fled their homes, taking only what they could carry, and become exiles in their own country. As is the custom among the Dinka, my tall and dark-skinned people, we shared what little food we had until it was nearly gone.

The refugees told us terrible stories. They had trekked to Duk Payuel from the north and west, running on foot in front of advancing armies that had burned and shelled and destroyed everything they encountered. The djellabas, the Arab militia, killed nearly everyone who had a black face.

Like the others in Duk Payuel and throughout the surrounding Upper Nile Province, my father and mother had heard rumors even before the refugees had arrived: God had promised doom to the southern Sudanese. My parents had followed the news of civil war in Sudan with growing concern, and they had prayed. Four years earlier, at the start of the latest round of conflict, the Muslim-dominated national government had declared sharia throughout the country, imposing Muslim law—including the removal of eyes and tongues, the amputation of limbs, and other barbaric criminal penalties—on everyone, including Christians such as my family. Furthermore, our taxes in the southern provinces had disappeared into government offices in Khartoum and other northern cities, never trickling down to benefit those of us who had paid them. The Dinka and other southerners had protested, but they had only brought on crushing retaliations from the better armed, better financed, and vastly larger armies of the government in the north. My family and the rest of the Dinka just wanted to be left alone. The djellabas had no intention of granting our wish. They torched and they killed.

SOME OF THE SPLA SOLDIERS CAME TO DUK PAYUEL AND nearby villages to recruit. They told us of their sanctuary in Ethiopia. They said we could get guns and training and then return to help force the Arabs out of southern Sudan. Plenty of Dinka, especially among the refugees who flooded our town, answered the SPLA call.

The Arab soldiers from the north started attacking our villages. They killed civilians as well as soldiers because they accused villagers of harboring mutinous soldiers. In some cases, they were right. But my family, like most in Duk Payuel, tried to stay out of the fighting. We were farmers. We raised cattle. What did we know of politics and war?

This did not stop the northern soldiers when they came to Duk County. They killed everyone with black skin, whether they were SPLA soldiers in khaki or simple farmers in civilian clothes.

The refugees in our village said the djellabas had killed young boys and abducted and raped young girls. Some of the abducted females were sold into slavery, they said.

Duk County kept swelling with refugees. My father's collection of huts by the luak and millet field sheltered as many as six refugee families at a time. So many people came in July and August of 1987 that the adults gave up sleeping indoors. They stretched out on the dirt, under the stars, and let the mosquitoes drain their blood so that there would be space for the children to sleep together on the floors of the village huts. Night after night, I tried to sleep, with no success, in a hut crammed with 20 other children.

As the fighting got closer, we could hear the sound of guns, bombs, and shells. The elders of my village ordered the men to set up a patrol. Groups of five to ten villagers started making rounds at night, looking for signs of advancing Arab soldiers, but as the boredom of nightly reconnaissance hikes wore thin, they trickled back to their homes. They didn't want to be separated from their families if an attack should come or to return from patrol and find that their families had fled. Theirs was an ill-advised decision, unworthy of a Dinka—to sacrifice the good of the village for the good of one's immediate family.

One night, my mother and father stood between the huts of our farm as the sound of bombs exploded in the distance. The attacks came from Antonov warplanes and djellaba artillery units. We did not know whether to stay and hope the bombings would miss us or take our chances and flee. I heard wild rumors in the village. Some villagers, numb with fear, said the djellaba had a bomb that followed its victims wherever they went. "If you try to run away, it goes from place to place until it finally tracks you down and kills you," they said. Others said, with some grain of truth, that the djellabas wanted nothing more than to kill Dinka boys.

My father suggested the villagers round up the boys of Duk Payuel and take them to the Sudd, far from the violence. That sparked an entirely new debate: Would it be better for the boys to be safe in the wetlands but separated from their families, or under the protection of the clans but in harm's way? And what if the djellabas came between the boys and their families, cutting off all communication?

Some argued we should flee to the east, away from the Nile and the Sudd. The ground was drier there, and travel would be easy. Unfortunately, the elders realized, what's good for the goat is also good for the lion—government troops could easily follow any exodus into the dry lands.

A group of refugees in our village took matters into their own hands. One night they fled to toch, the wetlands of cattle camp, which they thought would provide a safe haven. There they were attacked by djellabas, Arab militia. A few survived and straggled back to Duk Payuel. They said the djellabas killed most of the children and men and abducted the women and adolescent girls. Ngun Deng had been right. This would be a black-haired time.

That was when I found I couldn't eat. I lay on my cowhide at night and listened to the explosions competing with the sound of my stomach complaining about its emptiness. The heat was unbearable. That may not sound like much compared with the danger of living in the path of an advancing army, but the mosquitoes, ovenlike temperatures, and pools of water on the ground that prevented us from making a comfortable bed outdoors meant we never had a moment's respite.

I tried to put my trust in my father. He was the wrestler who defeated all foes. He would protect our family and keep us together, I thought.

But I was wrong. I was living in a bad dream. The social order that had knit the Dinka together since God created the world began to unravel. Groups no longer gathered under the giant tree where my father dispensed justice. The rituals of courtship—the dances, the meeting of family members, the talk, talk, talk so common to my people—came to a halt. Cattle camp became a memory. The only collective action of any significance was the pooling of any extra scraps of food to share with the refugees. I am ashamed to say it, but in the time of our greatest crisis, most of the people of Duk Payuel turned away from their social traditions and focused on saving their own families.

One night, my body was tense, as if it were trying to tell me something. I could not sleep. I could not eat. I lay on the ground, listening intently to the world outside. All of the children were in my hut, but I do not know if any of them slept.

It was the middle of the night. Pitch black and silent except for the occasional whine of tiny insect wings. Suddenly, there came the whistling of a shell. I thought perhaps I was dreaming, but then I heard voices outside, crying out.

I jumped up with a start. I scrambled in the blinding darkness to find the door to the hut, bumping into other children as panicked as I was. Finally, I saw a wedge of light, found the door, and ran outside as incoming shells set my village ablaze. I saw the man I thought was my father and raced after him into the tall grass just as a squad of djellabas headed toward the huts I had just left. All that night, as we waited in the grass for death or daybreak, I thought the man who pulled me to safety was my father. When the sun began to rise, I learned I was wrong.

ABRAHAM DENG NIOP WAS MY NEIGHBOR. I DON'T KNOW HOW I could have mistaken him for my father, even in the dark. True, he had seven parallel scars on his forehead, like my father, that marked him as a Dinka man. But he walked bent over, keeping his eyes on the ground, and he didn't have my father's powerful upper body. He was much smaller—obviously so, even though a shirt and trousers covered him. Abraham had a brown tooth that I could easily see any time he spoke. He had pierced his ears, and his skin was a lighter brown than that of my father. He never said much, and only then after thinking very carefully. When he visited my father and the two spoke together, I saw Abraham's eyes focus on something I could not see, as he reasoned out what he wanted to say. When he came to a conclusion, it was as if something clicked, and his face opened up. Abraham and my father liked to talk, as all farmers or ranchers do, about what to cultivate, what they might have to pay in taxes, and how certain plots of land never seemed to produce as much food as they should. I remember one time in particular when they discussed the best way to deal with a wildcat that had been sneaking into our gardens and stealing our chickens.

Abraham had a wife, two daughters, and a son. The boy, Majak, was my best friend. We played alueth and cattle camp games, but mostly we wrestled. One of Abraham's daughters was also near my age, and we played with clay cows. Sometimes, our families went to toch together in dry season. Abraham was a hunter and brought us game. When he killed a thiang, he gave my family some of the meat. My father returned the favor, buying Abraham's wife some clothes when he purchased clothes for my mother.

I knew him and his family well. But he was not my father, and I worried for my family, as Abraham and I waited for the end of the djellabas' attack. Abraham said next to nothing, as the minutes dragged slowly by.

After about two hours the guns fell silent, and we heard no more sounds from the village. Abraham told me we ought to try to move. We started to head toward Duk Payuel, but we heard Arabs close by. We turned east, away from the village, and started to run along the paths. We might have been tempted to try to go cross-country, but my legs were too short for me to pick my way quickly through the underbrush, and I knew I could not move silently through the forest. So Abraham and I ran on the open path. My fearful heart pounded in my ears.

Every time we heard noises coming toward us, we ducked into the forest or the tall grass and knelt. Arab soldiers kept passing. When they disappeared, we started running again. East seemed a good direction; we heard no guns as we ran toward the rising sun. I did not run well. I kept stepping on snails and clams, which had burrowed everywhere in the muddy ground. My feet turned bloody. I stumbled as I tried to plant my toes and heels without opening the cuts. Abraham grabbed me and pulled. Like most Dinka boys, I slept naked except in winter, so I had no clothes on when I left my village that August night.

We did not hear any Arab troops for a few hours, and we started to think we would be safe. Around 8 a.m., we happened upon some other refugees. A Dinka woman and her two daughters said they wanted to go east with us. Like me, they obviously had fled in the middle of the night. The mother wore a sheet wrapped around her body, and the girls wore only underpants. Seeing them reminded me of my own parents, and I asked

Abraham about them. "They are coming, they are coming," he said. He convinced me that we would rendezvous with my family somewhere to the east. That made me feel better about running away from my village.

The woman's name was Adut. I have forgotten the names of her two daughters. Abraham and I told them they could join us as we headed east. We walked and ran without stopping to eat or rest. We kept at it until midnight, about 24 hours after the start of the attack on Duk Payuel. Finally, exhausted, we clambered off the path into the dark forest. As the women and I settled down to try to sleep, Abraham announced he would not join us. "I want to go back," he said.

"Oh, I want to go back, too!" I cried.

Abraham insisted that Adut would take care of me, and I would be all right. I refused. I didn't know her, I told him, and I wanted to see if I could find my parents. I was starting to doubt the story he had told me of his plans for a rendezvous.

Abraham had considered the matter and made up his mind. He did not want any debate.

"You will stay," he commanded.

I cried, "No! I don't want to." But he didn't listen. He started to leave us and headed west, back the way we had come. I started to follow him.

"The woman is OK," Abraham said, as he looked back at me. At that, as if some unspoken communication had taken place, Adut sat me on the ground. She whispered to try to comfort me, and she began to pull pieces of grass out of my hair. Abraham started to leave again, and I struggled to escape the woman's embrace so I could go too. Abraham raised his face from the ground and stared silently at us. There was a moment when nothing happened, and I knew he was thinking again. Then, Abraham broke the spell.

"OK," he said. "I will stay."

He stepped back toward our little group and spoke to the girls and me.

"Go, find me some firewood in the forest so we can cook," he said. We carried no food or kitchenware, so I had no idea how he planned to prepare dinner. Out of respect, however, I told him I would go look. The two girls and I galloped off into the trees to gather wood. Soon we were out of sight of the two adults.

When we came back, Abraham was gone. Adut said he had set out to find something for us to eat, but I knew better. He had gone back to Duk Payuel. I thought he must be as worried about his family as I was about mine. I also knew I had no hope of catching him on my bloody feet. Reluctantly, I settled in to rest for a while. My stomach growled, and I felt numb.

Around 8 p.m., Abraham returned. I was so relieved and happy, but I could not read his face. He said he had met with my family, and my father wanted me to know I should keep moving east with Abraham. They would catch up later, he said. I didn't realize then that this was a lie. He had not seen my family.

We slept in the forest that night, and the following morning the two girls woke up still tired. The younger one felt so weak she could not get up. Her mother did not have the strength to carry her, so Abraham lifted the girl and put her on his shoulder. I felt weak too, but I stood and staggered a bit until I felt better. Abraham said he knew where we could get something to eat. We walked and walked until we had to rest awhile in the long grass. Abraham disappeared and returned with an *amochro*, a root the size and shape of a flattened softball. Amochro has a crisp, white flesh and tastes a bit like an apple. He gave it to the girls and me, leaving nothing for the adults. There was only one root, and Dinka custom said the adults could not eat until the children had satisfied themselves. The root held a lot of water, and it took the edge off my hunger and thirst.

As we ate, the sun ascended higher in the sky. The air grew warm and humid in the high grass where we sat. Abraham moved us to the shade of an *ngap*. In English, you call it a fig tree. It kept the sun off us, but it would not have ripe figs on its branches for six more months. I remembered the story of Jesus cursing the barren fig tree when he was hungry.

Abraham left us for a short while to go looking for more food. He came back carrying a pot with a broken edge and— praise God—a pumpkin. Both came from an abandoned house, he said. He gave them to Adut to cook. Then he cut into a tree known for its sticky sap. He collected the sap and a bunch of twigs and sticks. Arranging everything on the ground, Abraham started rolling a small stick back and forth between his palms. The friction made the sap-covered sticks catch fire. Adut filled the pot from a nearby pool of standing water and set it on the fire to boil. Soon we had sweet pumpkin to eat, and we were happy. We drank deeply from the pool. It was full of small sticks, insects, and frogs' eggs, but we were so thirsty we did not care.

We deliberately did not eat all of the pumpkin, because we did not know where or when we would have our next meal. So we carried the leftovers with us and kept going.

We fell into a daily routine. Abraham told us he had thought about it, and he decided we would be safest if we walked during the day along the paths in the grasses that towered over our heads, while keeping alert for the sounds of approaching soldiers. As darkness fell, he insisted on moving deep into the forest to avoid detection. He chose our place to bed down very carefully. The best place was a ring of tall grass amid the trees with no standing water amid the roots. When we found such a place, we tramped the grass flat, like dogs turning in a circle before they lie down. Abraham said that, while it might be tempting to sleep directly under the trees, those sites likely would invite encounters with predators and snakes.

As darkness fell and my mind grew quiet, I thought about my family, and I prayed to God. "Where are you?" I asked God. "In my village, they said you are everywhere. If you can hear me, please let me find something to eat. And please let me find my mother and father." I thought about how comfortable I had been with my family, and how bad my life had become. I hated my life and asked why I had been born. I thought of drowning myself in a river as an alternative to the days I knew lay ahead. Those thoughts followed me as I slapped at the mosquitoes and waited for sleep to come.

Every morning, I woke stiff and sore. My bleeding feet still hurt, and I also felt the pain of tired muscles. Even though I had walked all the time as a child, tending cattle and doing chores, nothing could have prepared me for walking from dawn to dusk, day after day. My legs ached from the constant strain, and my stomach rumbled from lack of food. My bare feet bore a hundred scratches, and mosquito bites made my skin look like the surface of a pond during a spring shower. Abraham always rose first and pressed the rest of us to get under way. A couple of times during our first week on the path he hit me and cried "Get up!" before I managed to stand. When the sun started to climb, we started walking—me, with a decided limp until my legs grew limber with exercise and heat. East we headed, always east.

The pumpkin lasted less than three days. Afterward, we went two days without finding any food. We broke our fast when Abraham and Adut sneaked into the garden of an occupied house and stole some millet. They ran back to us, and nobody saw them. We did not bother to pound the millet as we did in our village, to remove the seed covers and pulverize the grain. Adut merely put it in the pot, covered it with water, and set it to boil. I was so hungry I did not mind chewing the husks.

A WEEK INTO OUR FLIGHT FROM DUK PAYUEL, I STARTED TO grow a bit calmer. I still had not been reunited with my family or gotten enough to eat, but at least I had not heard bombs or guns for several days. If only that feeling could have lasted.

The air grew strangely still. Sounds carried far. I could hear each slap of our feet on the path, loud like an approaching storm. I started to feel afraid for no apparent reason; I felt something vibrating in my head in a premonition of something bad—the way I had felt before the attack on my village. I started to look and listen more intently at the turns in the path ahead of us. The channel through the high grass twisted left and right and passed clumps of trees. Abraham led the way, followed by Adut and her two daughters. I brought up the rear. The air grew thicker, as it does just before the storm breaks and the rains come. Only, it did not rain. The path bent to the left to skirt a low mound, and finished circling the mound in a long arc back to the right. Abraham disappeared around the curve as the women and I came to the end of the straight part. I looked to the top of the rise on our right and saw a strange man dressed in a khaki shirt and shorts.

Another man's voice shouted something in Arabic up ahead, where Abraham had just disappeared into the grass. Abraham understood Arabic and later told me the man had ordered us to stop and identify ourselves.

Just as the women and I stopped at a small clearing, within sight of Abraham, I heard the distinct clack of someone sliding the bolt of an assault rifle.

"This is the end of my life," I thought. I wanted to run, but then I thought the gunman probably would just shoot me in the back. In a split second, I weighed my options of running away or staying and taking my chances. I stayed.

Nineteen djellabas carrying guns and ammunition spread out in a line perpendicular to the path, blocking our way forward. "You! Move this way!" one of them ordered Abraham. He stepped to one side of the path, where the man pointed. "You!" another said to Adut, "you move to the other side." The girls and I stood in the middle of the path.

Abraham was wearing a good shirt, nicer than what most of the soldiers wore. A group of djellabas ordered Abraham to take it off and give it to them. Abraham touched his shirt for a few seconds, pondering what to do. One of the djellabas, the shortest one, pushed Abraham to the ground with the butt of his automatic assault rifle. His clothes bristled with 20-round magazines.

The soldiers beat Abraham with sticks and rifles until he surrendered his shirt. On the other side of the path, another group of djellabas beat Adut. The girls and I stood helpless, watching in silence.

A soldier with a dark mark at the edge of his eye walked up to me. He grabbed fistfuls of my three-inch-long hair and twisted. I cried out in pain, but he kept pulling and twisting. I decided I might get him to quit if I stopped crying, so I forced myself to make no noise even though the pain was excruciating. I looked at the ground and tried to send my mind far away. The man kept twisting until a clump of hair came out by the roots. He threw it in my face. That seemed to satisfy him, and he stopped.

One of the djellabas said something that must have meant "Let's go," because they stopped beating Abraham and Adut. They left us, heading west where we had come from. Adut had not been beaten too badly, and she could walk. Miraculously, the girls had not been touched. But Abraham had been pummeled until his shoulders bled. He rested for a short while then insisted on getting under way again.

We left the path and struck out through the grass and forest toward the south till we found a new path heading east. We took it in hopes of avoiding any more soldiers.

At midafternoon, our hopes were dashed. Another group—a mixture of black Sudanese and Arabs, led by a man who spoke Shilluk, the language of another southern tribe—surprised us and made us halt. We sweated for a few minutes, while the tallest Arab looked us over. Finally, he made a motion with his hand, telling the rest of the soldiers to let us go. They disappeared behind us to the west. After a few minutes we heard gunshots from their direction. We had no idea who or what they shot.

By then it was eight days since we had left Duk Payuel. We had arrived almost at the border between the Dinka and the Nuer people. We came to a small village called Waat. Abraham and Adut sneaked into one of the village farms and stole more pumpkins and a handful of millet stems. The stems were as sweet as sugarcane, and we chewed them for their juice; it helped keep

Injured soldiers of the SPLA rest at a hospital in southern Sudan in 1997.

hunger away. Abraham felt it was a good time to let us rest, so we stayed there for a day. From there, Abraham explained, we would walk into Ethiopia. The SPLA had sanctuary there. We could join the rebel militia in the Bongo area, if we so desired, or simply live there for a while in peace and wait for the civil war to sort itself out. He kept telling me that my family would head east, too, and must be somewhere nearby, but he did not say anything about his own wife and children.

On our second day of rest, Abraham announced we had to move. I told him I wanted to sleep one more day, but he refused. He sensed more government troops would come. He was right, of course, but he could not have known how soon. Shortly after we set out toward the east, we fell into an ambush along the path, sprung by a militia loyal to the government in Khartoum. There were about 20 men, heavily armed and dressed in khaki.

Most were Arabs, but some of the men came from black southern tribes who must have cut a deal with the northern government
in return for short-term loyalty. They carried water canteens,
ammunition clips in clusters of four, rocket-propelled grenades,
huge knives, and a dismantled mortar base and launching tube.
Somewhere in their packs they must have had shells for the
tube. They immediately focused their attention on Abraham.
Their eyes widened when they saw the bloody wound on his
shoulder, which looked like the bruises and cuts caused by the
kick of a rifle. They spoke to him in Arabic, so for me watching
the interrogation was like pantomime. I imagined they wanted
to know if he was with the SPLA or could tell them how to find
the rebels.

The soldiers threw Abraham to the ground. They stomped
on his head with their boots. I screamed in horror. A small man
turned a fierce look on me. He strode to where I stood and hit
me, again and again. Then he grabbed my ears and started to
pull them away from my head. Finally, he settled on beating me
with a stick. Others joined in, kicking me and punching me. I
didn't know what they said, but I gathered they wanted me to
stop screaming. But I couldn't stop, and I was too terrified to
speak. All I could manage was a shriek that made the soldiers
beat me more fiercely. Others grabbed more sticks and began
beating Adut and her daughters.

The little man who had started the beating pointed his gun
at my stomach. I understood. Somehow, I sucked in a gulp of air
and held it. I told myself not to look into his eyes.

I stopped crying.

My tormentor put the gun on his shoulder and picked up his
stick. With just the stick this time, he beat me until I collapsed

and stopped moving. I could still hear, and I knew another group had continued to beat Abraham.

I think I passed out. When I regained my senses, the soldiers had gone. My mouth felt huge from the beating, and I am sure I looked swollen and purple. Blood flowed from my head and shoulders. White and yellow stars danced across my vision, as I tried to focus my eyes. I crawled to where Abraham lay senseless. Amazingly, he was not dead. His head looked as if it had been pummeled with rocks, his right ear had been torn, and his torso, arms, and legs were bloody and bruised. I sat beside him until he woke. We tried not to move as we regained our strength.

Adut and her daughters were gone. The soldiers had taken them. For what purpose, we could only guess. All of our guesses were unpleasant. We looked briefly for their bodies near the trail and in some huts abandoned after a recent djellaba raid, but we did not see them.

Abraham stood in the gathering darkness and said we should get inside for the night. We limped to a hut and collapsed. Next morning we were still too sore to move. We lay in a stupor in that hut all day, recovering from our wounds. Then we started walking again.

Those next days remain a blur. Nothing but painful walking, searching for food, and sleeping. We crossed the boundary separating Dinka from Nuer. A group of men bearing the Nuer ceremonial scar patterns on their foreheads met us on the path. I expected another beating, but thankfully they meant us no harm. They looked at Abraham and must have assumed, because of his age, that he had a wife and daughters; they probably assumed I was his son. I stood beside Abraham as he answered a question.

"They were killed," he said. He raised his hand to point to the west. His jaw was set, and a tear trickled down his cheek. I was thunderstruck. He had kept the deaths of his wife and children to himself for two weeks, so I would not feel despair. Now it washed over me. My friend Majak, my wrestling buddy who played with clay cows, died in the attack on Duk Payuel. So did the rest of Abraham's family.

"Let them go," said the Nuer who seemed to be in charge. "Let them go."

Abraham looked at me with the streak of water on his cheek. "Let's keep moving," he said.

He found a tall tree and climbed to the top to look around. When he came down, nothing had changed. East, he said. East.

During the day we trudged like robots. "We will keep going," Abraham said. "Until we are killed." I believed him.

THE WALK TOWARD ETHIOPIA BECAME A SORT OF GAME WHERE the object was to go as far as we could before we died. I awoke sore and tired every morning, but at least there was plenty of water to drink. Gradually, I got my strength back after the terrible beating the militia had given me. With only two of us, we moved faster through the forest and the underbrush. Gathering enough to eat became simpler, too, now that we had only two mouths to feed. Abraham took me when he went looking for food and began to teach me the signs that led to edible fruits, flowers, and grasses. "There will come a time when I will not be here for you," he said, "so you must be able to find your own food. When I am not here, keep going east. Keep moving until someone kills you."

He took me to a pool of water near the trail. It covered two or three acres, huge for southern Sudan. Our food had run out, but he said he would show me how to find something to eat in a pond. The pool had a kind of grass called *apai* growing on the surface. Abraham waded into the water, uprooted a handful of apai, and brought it to me on the shore. He cut off the bottom part of the stem and cleaned it. "Chew this," he said. "It has some nutritional value. And sometimes you can even swallow the residue."

It tasted sweet. As I chewed, he gave me another lesson.

"Everywhere you see water, the water attracts animals. It attracts people. It attracts our enemies," he said. Then he told me a Dinka story. "God brought four things to the land of the Dinka," Abraham said. "One was water. Two was a cow. Three was a goat. And four was millet. And God brought together a man, a lion, a hyena, and a bird. He told them, 'Choose what you want to be yours from among these four things. But choose wisely, because you can choose only one.' Now, the man was all set to choose the cow. But a fox came to the man on the night before the choosing and asked him what he would pick the next day. The man said, 'I am going to take the cow.'

"The fox replied, 'No, that is not a wise decision. You should choose water.'

"And the man asked, 'What can I do with water?'

"The fox said, 'If you choose water, everything will belong to you in time.' And he explained why this was so.

"The man was convinced. So on the morning of the day of choosing, God gave man the first choice. The man said, 'I am going to take water.' And God gave him water.

"Then the lion chose, and he picked the cow. The hyena picked the goat, and the bird picked the millet. That ended the distribution.

"The fox had told the man the truth. The fox had said the lion would eat cows all of its days, but it also would need water. If the man fenced his water, he could make the lion pay for a drink. So, the first time the lion came to the man to ask for water, the man said, 'No, you have to buy it. You must give me a cow.' The lion weighed his options, to give a cow or to stay thirsty. While the lion thought about it, the fox went to him and said, 'Give the man a cow. There will be no problem. When the man leaves his cows grazing outside, you can grab one and run away with it.' So the lion gave the man a cow. Then the hyena came to beg for water, and the man said the same thing, 'You have to buy it.' The fox told the hyena, 'Give the man a goat. Later, when the man has left his goats unattended, you will take it back.' So the hyena gave the man a goat. The bird came to the man to ask for water, and the man said, 'You have to buy it.' Just as he had with the lion and hyena, the fox explained the situation to the bird, and the bird gave the man some millet. Thus the man controlled all things, while the animals watched him constantly to steal back the things they had chosen.

"Now, why do I tell you this story?" Abraham asked me. "The answer is, water attracts all life. Men, lions, hyenas, and birds. Water is the source of life, as well as a source of life's problems.

"So, this is a big thing. Every time we chew apai by the water, we must go to the far side and get into the water amid the grass. If people come, you must lie down in the water and keep only your nose and lips above the surface. That way, people cannot see you. Sometimes you can raise your head a little bit and listen. But you must never move or make a sound, until you are sure you are safe. Never get up, even if you think they see you. Never get up unless someone tells you to get up."

It was only a day or two later when we came to a big river covered with apai. Abraham and I did exactly as he had said. We crossed the river, picked our apai, and submerged our bodies in the water as we chewed.

Within a minute or two, I heard voices speaking in Arabic. There were gunshots and laughter. I was so scared. My heart beat so loudly I could hear it in my ears. I lay on my back and reached down for the river bottom, grabbing a handful of mud and roots. I pulled gently to lower my shoulders and head under the water. The air in my lungs kept trying to pull me to the surface, but I fought to stay down with just enough of my lips and nose above the water for me to breathe. Abraham did the same.

I could see a bit through the muddy water and the reeds. A squad of Arabs came to the water's edge only a few yards from where Abraham and I hid. They took off their shoulder packs and set them on the ground. Some of them fired their guns— in the joy of finding good water, I guessed. *"Allah akbar!"* they shouted. That was one Arabic phrase I knew: "God is great." A few sat and pulled out tobacco for a smoke. Some prayed, kneeling to face the east. One man urinated into the water not far from us. Others stripped off their clothes and dived into the water. They were so close I could feel their waves rock me back and forth.

A man who must have been their leader arrived at the river's edge. He was obviously older than the other soldiers, as he had white hair tucked under an officer's cap. He blew a whistle, and everyone stopped what they were doing and ran to stand in front of him. The men began to move out; apparently he had given an order to march. One by one, agonizingly slowly, they filed past us and disappeared.

The whole episode took about an hour. It felt like four to me as I struggled to regulate my breathing and keep my head from bobbing above the surface. When I was sure they had gone, I emerged from the water. Abraham came out too. I shook with pent-up fear. We dashed into the forest and felt temporarily safe.

This was the land of the Nuer, and Abraham and I stayed alert for any encounter. We did not know whether the Nuer would be friendly or not if they found us.

We kept moving. In a couple of days, near sunset, we heard the sounds of an approaching group, a lot of feet slapping on the dirt. Abraham and I hid. I counted 17 in the group, all male, including two adults. It was a strange meeting. We thought they might be our enemies. Abraham and I listened to their voices. They spoke Dinka! We stepped out from behind our tree and shouted, "Hey, how are you?"

They ran into the forest. They must have thought we were the enemy. Abraham shouted after them, "Stop! Stop! We are your people." After a while, they drifted back, and we all introduced ourselves. They were also refugees heading toward Ethiopia. Most of the boys were naked, like me. I felt happy to have companions my own age. Maybe I could make new friends.

We decided to walk together for companionship and safety as we moved deeper into Nuer territory. We met many Nuer, and I decided that some were good and some bad. None of them bothered us. Some gave us food, and some did not. It was the middle of September, and the harvest was coming in, so there should have been plenty of food to offer strangers. However, war and famine had reduced both Nuer stockpiles and Nuer generosity. Even when a good soul gave us some food, it was never enough for 19 people. We stayed hungry all the time.

TOWARD THE END OF SEPTEMBER WE CROSSED ANOTHER TRIBAL boundary, separating the Nuer from the Murle tribe. We had almost reached the Murle town of Pibor. The Dinka knew the Murle as a violent tribe, whose customs included kidnapping children. Before the civil war came to Duk County, the Murle had raided our villages, stolen our cattle, and kidnapped young Dinka boys and girls. According to Murle tradition, the more people you kill the more respect you earn, and the more children you abduct and raise as your own, the more numbers you have for cattle raids.

We were in a weird and foreign land, and we swung in a wide arc around Pibor, to avoid being seen by the Murle there. We redoubled our lookouts, as we moved east through Murle country. Three of the boys and I climbed trees every day to do reconnaissance. My legs had grown strong on the journey, and I could climb any tree I saw. I was also very skinny—naturally so to begin with and especially so because of slow starvation. Abraham told me to climb as high as I could and scan the horizon for anything that moved.

One day another boy and I climbed the same tree. The boy's feet were wet with sweat, and he lost his hold. He fell to the ground and broke his right arm. I clambered down and ran to him. He said he could not move. Perhaps the wind had been knocked out of him, or perhaps it was something more serious than just a broken arm. I tried to lift him, but he was too heavy for me to carry. I sat him down and encouraged him to try to walk. He moaned that he could not. I tried to pick him up again, and I managed to stagger about four steps before I had to put him down. It began to get dark. I told him I would summon help. I half-carried, half-dragged him a short distance to a curtain of grass and laid him inside, where he could not be seen. I marked the spot by tying the tops of three clumps of grass together and ran to get help. Abraham and the other two adults returned with me. They examined the boy and said we would have to wait until he felt strong enough to walk.

We stayed under that tree for five days. Abraham and the other adults announced we would start sleeping during the day and go wandering for food at night, in order to minimize our chances of encountering the Murle. I stubbed my toes and nicked my ankles and shins as I stumbled about the forest at night, but I found nothing to eat. Neither did the other boys—not even an amochro fruit. We were fortunate that no hyenas found us in the forest. They smell blood across great distances, and we were bloody. I think the djellabas' guns must have scared all of the predators away.

We grew desperately hungry as we waited for the broken boy to heal. The flies that swarmed under the tree and made our lives miserable did not share our problem. But we did find water. Abraham taught me that, when I bedded down for the night and the world grew quiet, I should listen for the croaking of frogs and mark the direction. Frogs only croak near water, he said.

The broken boy began to feel better. I pulled up some of the tall grass and twisted it into a crude rope, with which I tied the boy's arm to his body. The arm was clearly dislocated, with the elbow sticking out at an impossible angle. The boy could not control the movement of his hand. I tried to tie everything so it would move as little as possible as he walked, but he grimaced in pain as he stood and took a few steps. It was the best we could do. We told him he had to walk. If he didn't, he would die.

He walked.

We went farther into Murle country. Abraham told us it was a very dangerous place. If the Murle caught us, he said, they would kill the adults. Children would be forced to eat snake. We believed that eating snake meat made people forget their families.

We closed in on the town of Pibor, which had been occupied by northern soldiers. We swung in an arc to move around the town without entering, and in a day we came to the far side. Apai and *abaar* provided our only food. Abaar is like a wild form of millet. It has tiny fruit and a big stem, which we chewed for juice.

God and I had many a conversation. I did most of the talking. I got mad at God for all of the injustices in my life. "In the church in my village, they say God is always with you," I told him. "If I am here, on the verge of dying, where are you? And why are you letting the Muslims defeat us? Is their God stronger than you? Please, God, I am naked and the cold at night is very bad. And I need something to eat.

"And God, if I must die, at least let me see my mother and father first. After that, you can kill me."

I did not cry any more. There was no point in tears. One of the other boys whimpered from time to time, though. Desperation takes some getting used to.

We became very thirsty. It was the end of October. The land was drying, and winter was not far away. Abraham said the Kangen River, east of Pibor, would give us water. But when we got to the riverbank, we learned that the Kangen is seasonal. It flows in the wet season then dries up. The angry sun had paved the riverbed with cracked and pitted plates of dried mud. We poked about for water under the dirt but found none.

We had been walking in silence for days. With little hope to keep us going, and with every day like the one before it, we found little to talk about. I felt as if my mouth had stopped working. Then, Abraham noticed hawks and vultures circling overhead not far in front of us. They must be eating something or preparing to do so, I thought. Abraham had the same thought. "Where the bird is, there is water also," he said. "Let's go."

In our village church in Duk Payuel, we had sung a song about carrion birds. "Where you see vultures, there is a dead animal. When the vultures circle, there is a dead animal," we sang. Jesus said the same thing in the Book of Matthew: "Wherever the corpse is, there the vultures will gather." I sang that Dinka church song to myself, as we walked forward.

The two adults we had met in Nuer country led the way, followed by Abraham and the boys. I hung near the back, helping the boy with the broken arm. We boys encouraged one another, saying how good it would be to find water. We had begun to find our voices again.

Without warning, two Murle in a tree shot the two adults in front. I did not see this; I only heard the shots and learned the details later from the survivors. The two Murle had killed a gazelle and were grilling it on the far bank of the Kangen. The smell of roasting meat had attracted the birds. While the meat cooked, the Murle stood guard in the tree. They had seen us approaching and opened fire.

The boys exploded into the bush on the right side of the path. I ran, frightened, and the boy with the broken arm hobbled with me for a while, surprisingly fast. Abraham ran left of the path. Automatic rifle fire pinged around us—*tadumtadumta-dumdumdumdum.*

We did not know what had happened to the other two adults, but we assumed later that they had been killed. They never rejoined us, and Abraham said he saw one of the men fall after hearing the crack of a gunshot.

Abraham had coached us on what to do in a situation like this. "When you meet someone with a gun, you must run," he told us one night. "But don't keep running. Jump into the forest when you are out of sight. Then stop, sit, and listen to see if anyone is following you. Pretend you are not there—don't make any moves at all, because the whisper of the grass can give you away. Then, if you think the enemy knows which direction you went, go the other direction."

This lesson returned to me as I hid in the long abaar. The tips of the grass blades swayed, but I assured myself it was only a gust of wind. When the stirring stopped, the air grew still. I could feel the slime of thick sweat from my terrified dash emerging all over my body. I wiped my forehead with my fist. I stayed still for perhaps a half hour, but heard nothing. Only then did I move. I doubled back through the brush toward the east, to circle around the site of the Murle camp. Some of the other boys already were there. Two hours later, Abraham showed up. We crimped our fists, put the bent knuckles of our thumbs to our mouths, and blew to make the call of the *akunguet* bird, as Abraham had showed us, to bring in the last of the boys. The Dinka believed that when the bird cried at night, filling villages with its trilling, train-whistle moan, something bad was about to happen. It was a small irony that Abraham had chosen that birdcall for our recognition signal in enemy territory. He said the enemy might know how to imitate the akunguet as well as we did, so he taught us to blow three short blasts followed by a trill created by fanning the fingers. *Foo foo foo—whirrrr.* That was our code.

I heard that signal on and off for the next six hours, as the survivors came back together. We figured we had scattered across an area of about two square miles. Finally, everyone had reassembled, except for the two adults shot by the Murle.

While we had been running and hiding, I had forgotten my thirst. Now my dry throat reminded me of why we had hurried toward the circling birds in the first place. Abraham told us the way ahead would only get more difficult. We would have to travel exclusively by night, he said, because the sun would only increase our thirst. He told us to lie down in the shade of a lone tree and to be prepared to start walking after dusk. Everyone did as he said. Once again we had forgotten how to talk. Crawling insects called *achuks* and flying insects called *rungs* made us miserable. The only sound we made all day was the slapping of our palms against our skin, as another bite pierced our flesh.

I thought about the time of day and how in Duk Payuel I would have been drinking my milk at that exact hour. I pictured my mother moving to the kitchen and cooking pumpkin. When I finally fell asleep, I dreamed I was eating awalwala—the thick, creamy Dinka dish of cooked millet—with butter on the bottom of the plate. When I woke up at sunset and found my belly still empty, I was very disappointed. We had gone a day and a half without any food, not even apai or abaar to chew.

Night fell, and the breezes kicked up. A bright moon rose. Abraham said it was a good time to leave. "Where are the other two men?" one of the boys asked. Abraham said, "I don't know. Maybe they will be waiting for us up ahead. We need to move, so maybe they will find us." It wasn't a lie exactly; he could not be sure they were dead, but he must have had suspicions.

We stood up. Everyone limped from stiffness and the insect bites. Starting out was always the hardest part of the day for me; the last ten minutes before I knew we would set out were like a reprieve for a condemned man. I loved doing nothing while waiting to begin. Abraham broke the reverie. He yelled at me and some of the other boys to get up and start walking. I hated him at that moment.

We walked for hours, until Abraham told us to stop and sleep. We flattened the grass beside our path and drifted off.

When I woke up, my body screamed for water. We had gone two days with no food or drink. The sun rose at 6 a.m., and we decided to move forward to try to find water before it got really hot. One of the boys complained about our constant walking. "If I die, my bones will walk back home," he said with a sniff. I knew he shared my dislike for getting started, so I replied, "If you die, your bones will never move!"

Just as thirst started to make us stagger, Abraham said he smelled water. I did not believe him. He had told lies to me many times— sometimes for my own good, to keep me moving forward in hopes of finding my parents, but lies nonetheless. But he was right this time. The path opened onto a mud hole. Snakes lay coiled at its edges, and flies buzzed above the moist, black earth. We did not care. It looked like paradise. Everyone dived into the mud. "Eat the mud," Abraham said. "It will keep your throat moist." I clawed some from the ground and put it in my mouth. It tasted sweet, with a bitter hint of rotted apai. I ate more and more, as did the other boys, while Abraham warned us of the danger of eating too much. We ignored him. Finally, he pulled us out of the mud.

We kept moving. The mud had helped take the edge off our hunger and thirst, but by midafternoon all of our torments had come back. The line of boys stretched long and thin, with gaps between the groups. As we marched in the broiling sun, some of the boys must have given up and sat down to die. Abraham and I were at the front of the line, and we did not realize how many we had lost.

Eventually, the boys at the front with us sat and refused to move. I was one of them. "I can't move, Abraham. I will die here," I said. Abraham said he smelled water up ahead, but I knew he had to be lying. I looked at my body. It had become gray, almost white, as I grew dehydrated. I pushed my swollen tongue outside my mouth, like a panting dog. I tried to cry, but my body could not summon enough water to make tears.

Abraham grabbed me beneath my arms and lifted me. He dragged me forward about five yards. When he saw I refused to work my legs, he dropped me to the ground beside a small thorn tree. Abraham turned his attention to the handful of other boys, dragging and finally dropping them too. I did not see my friend with the broken arm. When he disappeared I do not know, but I never saw him after I curled up under the thorn tree.

Abraham came back from trying to help the stragglers. He called my name. I tried to hide from him by crawling farther off the path, but the thorn tree snagged my skin and made it too painful to move. Abraham appeared at my tree and told me to get up. I did nothing. He grabbed my legs and pulled, but I held fast with my arms to the trunk of the tree. He dropped my legs. "I need water," I croaked.

Abraham still carried his dented cooking pot and a small cup he had picked up somewhere along the way. He thought for a minute, and then shot a stream of urine into the cup and handed it to me. I drank. It tasted very, very bitter, and it didn't seem to make me feel any better. Abraham sat beside me, and I cried.

Abraham didn't know what to do. The sun began to set, and our band that once had numbered nineteen had fallen to only four—Abraham, me, and two other boys. "If we go farther, maybe we can find water," Abraham said.

I did not feel confident, but I prayed once again. "God, what wrong have I done that you have given me all these trials?" I quietly sang some gospel songs, thinking it would make me feel better. "Don't let your heart get upset," I sang. "You are in the hand of God." That didn't make me feel better either.

The air grew colder after dark. I found the coolness refreshing, and I summoned the strength to stand. I decided if I was going to die, I would die walking. So the four of us started walking. We walked until about 1 a.m. and then settled for sleep.

TODAY WILL BE THE DAY I DIE, I TOLD MYSELF AS THE SUN WOKE me at dawn. My fourth day with nothing to drink except mud and urine. It was a fine day to die.

Then God did a good thing. He led us to water.

Abraham had walked so far ahead I could not see him. But I heard the three-note call of the akunguet. Abraham appeared ahead, holding his cupped hands in front of him. Water dribbled between his fingers, so by the time he reached us, all he could show were his shiny, wet hands. "Look, water! There is water ahead," he said. I tried to stand, but my legs seemed numb and tangled, and I fell. Again I tried to stand and fell. I stood by sheer will power and walked with the other boys into the vast Kangen Swamp.

The swamp never disappears, even in the dry season, and it attracts animals all year round. We crawled into the *buchbuch*, the dirty water mixed with mud and apai at the edge, and drank and drank. Abraham told us to go farther into the swamp, where the water was cleaner, and he pushed us to make sure we got the message. I crawled forward and sat, letting the water close over me to my neck. I dipped my head and drank. "I am alive!" I thought. "I will never die of thirst again."

We drank far less than we wanted to, as Abraham warned that too much water after so long a thirst could kill us. I contented myself with chewing apai and letting the swamp water fill my thirsty pores. Grasshoppers clung to the apai, and we knocked them off and killed them. Turtles about as big as a man's hand crawled along the edge of the swamp, and we caught them and killed them, too. Abraham made a fire out of grass and sticks. We plucked the wings from the grasshoppers and roasted the bodies on sticks. Tasty. Then we set the turtles to roast in their shells. When they were done, we peeled off their belly plates and scooped out the yellow meat from their legs, neck, and organs. Delicious; like heaven. It was our first protein since leaving Duk Payuel, almost three months earlier. Two of the turtles were females, and their bodies held caches of leathery roasted eggs. I put one in my mouth. It was about the size of a grape, and it tasted salty. When I put it between my teeth and closed my jaw, it popped like a balloon. I swallowed the yolk and white matter and spit out the empty shell.

We felt safe there, next to the Kangen Swamp, because nobody lived nearby. We saw no houses and no people of any kind. For two days we dined on grasshoppers. On the third day, we slid into the deeper water and started walking toward the distant, eastern shore. I worried about crocodiles in the water but did not see any. The water came up to my shins at first, and then up to my waist. Nighttime came, but there was nowhere to lie down, so we had to keep moving. Moonlight scattered across the ripples created by our sloshing steps. We entered Kangen Swamp at daybreak, and we left it the following dawn—24 hours of nonstop walking. Before we left the eastern edge, Abraham put some swamp water in his pot to carry with us.

We came to Pochala, a Sudanese town just west of the Ethiopian border. Enemy troops occupied it, so we did as we had at Pibor—we swung around it in a wide arc. Our route took us into the lands of another tribe, the Anyuak. Half of the Anyuak ancestral lands lie in Ethiopia, half in Sudan. The first Anyuak we met gave us a little food. The next group we came upon had just killed a bull elephant and were butchering and skinning it in a village near Pochala. They gave a chunk of belly meat to Abraham. He boiled it for at least three hours, but he never could get it tender. He pulled the gray meat from the pot only to discover he had nothing to cut it into portions for the four of us. We passed it from hand to hand. The meat had the size and shape of an American football, round with pointed ends. Each of us in turn bit into one of the pointed ends and twisted the meat with both hands to try to tear off a bite-size portion, but elephant meat is tougher than an automobile tire. I got an abaar stem and peeled it to reveal the white, sharp blade within to use as a knife. It was no more use in cutting the meat than a feather would have been. Abraham finally bit off a small portion and gave it to me. He did the same for the other boys, and that way we got a bite of elephant in our mouths. I chewed and chewed, but it never seemed to get any smaller. I drank some of the broth from the pot instead, and it was much better.

Abraham got too tired of fighting the elephant meat with his teeth and stopped trying to bite off small bits. He had succeeded only in removing the parts that stuck out from the center, turning the football into a round softball. We plunked the globe of gristly meat into the pot for carrying and started walking again. That day we met more Anyuak, Abraham addressed them in Arabic, which they spoke. I also learned a few Anyuak words.

In the morning, we had to travel through an Anyuak village in order to avoid the enemy soldiers in Pochala. The village had a king named Agata, and, according to Anyuak tradition, strangers passing through must meet the king. Escorts took us to his home, and Abraham talked with him, telling him we had nothing to eat and pointing out the obvious fact that we boys were naked. The king gave us a gray, wool blanket. That night, all three of us boys slept under that single blanket outside the Anyuak huts. We almost came to blows trying to decide who got the middle. The boy in the middle never got cold, because the outside boys turned left and right in about equal measure. When I got to be in the center, I never pulled on the blanket. I left that to the outside boys. We divided up the middle-blanket time for seven nights, after which Agata gave us two more blankets. Abraham still didn't have his own blanket, but the three of us boys had one each.

Abraham told Agata we wanted to go into Ethiopia. The king said many other refugees had passed through, and he had rendered them the same service, giving them food, shelter, directions, and advice. The best place was Pinyudu refugee camp on the other side of the border, he said. He gave us his blessing for travel, so the Anyuak would know not to attack us, and he provided us with a little bit of corn for the journey. When the Anyuak weren't looking, we threw the elephant ball away.

We walked from village to village and came to the Gilo River. When we crossed it, we knew we had finally made it to Ethiopia. It was the end of 1987.

The first Anyuak we came to on the east bank confirmed that we had crossed the border and introduced themselves as Ethiopians. We soon arrived in Pinyudu and found that several thousand Sudanese boys had gotten there ahead of us. Some had come via Pochala, as we had, and others through the towns of Nasir and Akobo.

Pinyudu wasn't much to look at. No houses. No fences. No evidence of a permanent settlement. Nothing but people sitting under trees. Yet we were safe and free. I thought to myself, this was a place we could stay.

The camp was relatively small then. Abraham stayed with us for about two months before he went to live with the adults. We three boys joined residential groups administered by the Ethiopian Anyuak. As we settled in, dark-skinned Sudanese trickled into camp every day, sometimes a hundred in a single day. Dinka constituted the largest group, but I also met Nuer and other tribes. The boys fended for themselves at first, but as more adults came to camp they became supervising caretakers and teachers, freeing the oldest boys to help tend to the hundreds of young ones. During the short time I lived with Abraham and the other two boys, he finally told us what he had seen at the Murle camp. All the while we walked, he had told us the other two adults might join us; but in Pinyudu, when we felt safe for the first time since August, he finally told us that he saw one of the men shot to death. I let my mind wander to the boy with the broken arm, and I wondered if he were still alive. Did he find Kangen Swamp?

The adult caretakers put me in charge of 1,200 boys. I was only 13 years old. Other boys were older than me; I don't know why the adults picked me to supervise. I had many duties. When a boy got sick, I had to make sure somebody remembered to cook for him. I forced the worst of the sick boys to go to the camp clinic, built by the Ethiopian government. Later, when world relief organizations brought food, I made sure my section of camp received its fair share.

CHOLERA STRUCK THE CAMP THAT FIRST WINTER. WE HAD NO latrines and no water to wash ourselves; everyone was very dirty. Flies hovered over every living thing. When we wanted drinking water, we got it from the stream next to camp. It was the same water in which we took our showers and relieved ourselves. We were boys, we did not know any better.

The disease announced itself with excessive diarrhea. I saw boys squat at a moment's notice in the middle of camp. Their eyes sunk into their skulls and their teeth clamped together so they could not talk. Out of 50 boys in a group that slept under a tree, about 10 suffered on any given day and some died.

I did not catch the disease. As one of the lucky, healthy ones, I ministered to the sick. The sufferers wanted to drink and drink, but I decided they could have only a small glass of water. The cows of Duk Payuel once suffered from a disease that caused bad diarrhea, and my father treated them by preventing them from drinking as much as they wanted. I thought the same would be

A Lost Boy wraps himself in a blanket at Palotaka,
an internal refugee camp in Sudan's Equatoria region.

good for sick people. They begged, but I gave them only a small drink. I don't know if there is a medical explanation for what happened. I merely gave treatment and observed the results. If I kept them from drinking more than a glass or so, they lived. If they found a way to sneak a lot of water, they died quickly.

The sick gathered under the trees during the daylight hours and called for their mothers and fathers. When they died, I organized the gangs to carry the bodies outside camp for burial. We buried at least one boy from my group every day, and often as many as three. I had no shovels, axes, or spades, so I told the burial detachment to find sharp sticks. We marched out to the land beyond the camp perimeter and with the sticks and our hands dug troughs eight to ten inches deep—as deep as we could go with our crude tools. We placed the bodies in the shallow graves and covered them with a few inches of soil. At night, while we slept in camp, hyenas and lions visited the graveyard to dig up the bodies. The hyenas woke me with their crazy, mocking laughter. When I visited the next morning, an arm or leg stuck out of the ground from rigor mortis. Gradually, after the care-takers taught us how to dig latrines downstream from camp, the cholera began to disappear.

Boys also caught whooping cough, chicken pox, and measles, all of which I had suffered and developed an immunity to while growing up in Duk Payuel. The sudden proximity of so many boys in such unhealthful conditions made diseases spread quick-ly. We did not know about germs. All we knew was that when one boy took sick, many others followed.

The magnitude and immediacy of death drove some of the boys insane. They refused to touch the dead bodies. They smeared their heads with excrement and then ran up to me to try to force me to smell them. I remember one boy crying out the name of his cow from his village. I tried to model good behavior for such boys, but it was hard. I took my turn at burial detail, and I led the gravediggers in singing hymns as we placed the bodies in the ground.

I had two close friends at Pinyudu—Manyok and Ajak, both Dinka. Ajak was goofy but a good man. He and I played alueth, *alier* (which is like hockey), and football (which Americans call soccer). We had no ball at first, so we stuffed some donated socks into one big sock, tied it shut, and used that for a ball. Later, the United Nations provided a soccer ball for every thousand or so boys. That was a nice gesture, but I seldom got to play with the ball. It was a treasure not widely shared.

Manyok and I made a bed of sticks to go in one of the huts my group built. We made poles out of four small trees to make the supports and fashioned a mattress out of grasses. We put a rail down the middle to separate his half and my half. One day he took sick. I did not know what it was, or how bad it was. He struggled with his sickness for about a week. I awoke one morning and saw him lying on his side of the bed. I tried to wake him, so we could go fetch some more saplings for huts, but he did not wake up. I shook him, and nothing happened. "Manyok, what are you doing? What's wrong?" I was scared. I listened for his breathing but heard nothing. I ran to find a caretaker. He followed me to the hut and examined Manyok. "This guy is dead," he said. Just like that. No easing his way into the news, which is the Dinka fashion whenever someone dies.

I took the body to a camp doctor, who told me Manyok had died of typhoid fever. I had slept in that same bed, but thankfully I did not catch the disease.

It was my duty as leader of my group to appoint a burial detail. I put my own name on it, and we carried Manyok to the graveyard. By that time, we had a hoe, so we buried him properly. I led our group in singing a hymn in Dinka for Manyok.

In addition to the contagious diseases, everyone in camp suffered from *tuktuk*. It is an insect that burrows under the skin of the feet, like a flea. I got bit and didn't know it for a day or two. I saw tuktuk (Westerners call it chigoe flea and the disease it causes tungiasis) in a crack in the skin of my foot. It had laid eggs, and its body had grown fat and white like a tick. I got a thorn and opened the skin to try to remove the insect and its eggs. The hard part was removing the head, because it had burrowed its jaws into a blood vessel and held on tightly. This was one of many bites to come. More often than not, I split the tuktuk body open when I tried to remove it, and that meant tuktuk eggs spread throughout the foot. My feet hurt so much I had trouble walking. I wasn't the only one; the whole camp walked on the clean bits of their feet as if they were stiff or drunk. Some boys' feet got so bad they could not walk at all, and I assigned a few boys to help them check their feet. The worst cases pushed themselves along the ground with their hands. Naturally, their hands got tuktuk infestations. The pest didn't go away until we started getting kerosene from the UN in 1990. The caretakers said we could kill the tuktuk, if we washed our feet regularly in kerosene. I tried it, but it made my wounds sting and my feet swell. Nothing seemed to help as much as checking my feet five or six times a day and immediately removing a tuktuk if I found a new one. Shoes would have helped too, but nobody had any. Once everybody practiced good hygiene and used the kerosene in extreme cases, the tuktuk epidemic ended.

Our food shortages eased when the United Nations started bringing us cooking oil and powdered milk in sacks. I put water in the empty oil containers and added a little powder. I gave the milk to the children who suffered from mental illness, and it helped a few of them to feel better. It was a comforting food, reminding them of home. I also put milk in an empty oil can and left it out in the sun all day. The heat turned it into something like buttermilk or yogurt, which we Dinka loved.

I saw white people for the first time at Pinyudu. Their shirts said "UN." We thought the UN was something for white folks. They brought us bags of dry corn and ground maize flour along with more oil and milk. The Ethiopians gave my group an oil drum, and we cut it in half to make kettles to boil water. We ate boiled corn with oil and milk. We cut the corn flour sacks into sheets and used them as dishes.

In mid-1988, the United Nations gave us axes and sickles, but for our first rainy season in Pinyudu we had to make huts without sharp tools. I led my group into the forest outside camp. I demonstrated what to do, so they could copy me. I climbed to the high branches I wanted to use for roof supports, grabbed them, and jumped. As I fell to the ground, my weight bent the branches until they snapped. Everyone did the same. That is how we got small logs for our home.

My group started out with about 200 members. We cleared a space beneath a tree by pulling up the grass with our hands. I tried grabbing it near the ground and twisting it with my hands, but I mostly succeeded in making my hands bloody. It took a long time to clear a decent space without a sickle or knife. We set the grass aside to dry.

I had the boys collect bark from the forest and soak it overnight in water to make it tender. In the morning, I could ma-
nipulate it into crude ropes. I directed the boys to put two poles
together, and I tied them with the bark rope. Once we had
enough supporting branches forming a grid of crossbeams overhead, we covered the roof with the grass we collected from clearing the ground. My first hut was only ten feet in diameter. We
didn't use it for sleeping. Rather, we kept our food rations and
other belongings dry under its roof. I slept outside during the
dry season. When it rained, well, I didn't sleep much. Mostly
I sat beneath a tree and waited for the rain to stop. That could
take hours.

Some of the boys at Pinyudu talked to the white workers
from the United Nations. They thanked them for the food but
said they missed the butter their mothers used to make. So the
UN brought us lots and lots of butter. I put it on our cornmeal
and wondered, how did the UN come to own so many cows
to give us milk and butter? I asked my friends. They said, "It's
not milk. The UN cuts open a special tree, and the inside of
the tree fills with white liquid, which they dry with a special
chemical. That is what they give you." As for the butter, they
said it was really the fat of the thiang antelope. It tasted like
butter to me, and I liked it. Some people can never allow others to have a bit of happiness, if they themselves are miserable. When the UN brought us canned chickens a few months
later, the naysayers insisted that nobody could own so many
chickens. The bird inside the can had to be *gon*—a nasty bird
that eats insects and human feces and travels in large flocks
throughout southern Sudan. A lot of boys refused to eat the
chickens after that.

The United Nations also gave us blankets and secondhand clothes. It was a very important day when a boy got a blanket. The thick material consisted of a patchwork of red and blue, and it had a great smell. I still had my gray wool blanket from King Agata, so I was not as needy as most boys as winter arrived. When I got my UN blanket, near the end of the distribution, I buried my face in it and inhaled. I can still remember that fresh, organic aroma. It smelled clean, like sunshine. I put it over my head and ran around camp, smelling it and saying, "This is mine." I also got a shirt. The pocket was stitched with a strange, three-letter word. I tried to say it, with the help of some friends. "Oosaw," we said. I could not figure out how to pronounce those letters, U-S-A, but I figured it must be a rich country to give away so many clothes.

The UN blankets had two sides and an air layer in the middle. Some of the boys sliced through the stitching along the edges and separated the two halves. They sold one section to the Anyuak market outside camp in return for much coveted monkey meat. Abraham went to the market and bought a needle. Somehow he got some thread, and he cut and stitched a UN blanket to make some clothes. He made me a fancy red-and-blue pair of shorts to go with my Oosaw shirt.

I never went to the Anyuak market alone. For one thing, I prized my blanket too much to cut it up and barter it. For another thing, it was too dangerous. Boys who visited the Anyuak to barter their blankets or to steal mangoes or maize started disappearing, and we did not know why. The Ethiopian government arrested one of the Anyuak, and he confessed: The tribe had killed the boys to use as bait to attract leopards, which the Anyuak highly prized for their valuable skins.

To us boys, a blanket was a very valuable thing. As leader of so many boys, I often adjudicated small conflicts, usually involving theft. Blankets had become a chief medium of exchange, so they made a tempting target for thieves.

Some of the camp residents believed in magic. One time, a boy had his blanket stolen. He came to me and accused another boy of the theft. There was no evidence, but the plaintiff wanted justice served. What could I do without evidence? This was not the kind of case that lent itself easily to the wisdom my father dispensed on the bench. I tried to dismiss the case, but the boy whose blanket had been stolen would not let it go. He hired a 12-year-old boy who claimed to be clairvoyant. I can't remember the clairvoyant's name. Everyone just called him Ateermadang for the song he sang about himself. In the Dinka language, *ateer* means dispute and *madang* means stop. When the boy went into his routine to enter the world of magic, his spirit took the form of a girl named Dispute. He sang, *"Hen yok ateer ke ci miol ee ma-guong!"* And the crowd around him joined in, singing, *"Ke ci miol maganydak."* After repeating that as many as five times, they sang a plea to solve their disputes, which began with the line, *"Ateer-madang, nyan ateermadang."* The lyrics translate roughly as:

Ateermadang: "I found a girl of Dispute, drunk with the itch disease!"

Audience: "She is also drunk with madness!"

In unison: "Please, girl of Dispute, stop! Stop! Spare the life. And we will solve our dispute in our own way."

The plaintiff approached Ateermadang and asked to hire him to investigate the blanket theft. "I will help you," Ateermadang said, "but not until you cook me something special. I would like some akop with dry meat on it." It makes me laugh now, to see how easily Ateermadang got what he wanted, which was a free meal. At the time, however, I believed that under the right circumstances, a magic boy could speak with the spirit world.

Ateermadang came to the hut of the plaintiff and walked inside with his arms folded, elbows forward, like a praying mantis. He asked everyone to sing his "ateermadang, nyan ateermadang" song so he could go deeper into his trance. The boys surrounded him and sang. As they grew louder Ateermadang started leaping and speaking in tongues. The singing stopped, and Ateermadang froze. He appeared to have crossed some invisible boundary.

Ateermadang made everyone leave the hut, and he closed the door. Nobody could see him inside, but I heard him mumbling. He seemed to be talking to God. I could not make out the words.

Finally, Ateermadang emerged from the hut and asked a few questions.

"Who did you see yesterday near the hut?" he asked the boy who had lost his blanket.

"Him," said the accuser, pointing at the defendant.

Ateermadang made a great show of communing with the spirits and intoned toward the defendant, "You took this man's blanket!"

"No! No! I did not!" yelled the defendant. "I was not there; I did not take anything."

I did not know what to do, so I fell back on the time-tested method by which boys settle disputes.

"Ateermadang said you stole the blanket. If you do not confess, we will beat you," I said. I told a group of boys to beat the defendant, yet even as he suffered the blows, he never admitted the theft. Such is justice when you're 14 years old. We never found the stolen blanket, either.

As it turned out, the camp later learned Ateermadang had lied about his special powers. He confessed the whole thing. The boy admitted he was just pretending to be clairvoyant to get others to cook him good food, with lots of protein. I felt bad for everyone who had trusted in his powers. Innocent boys had been wrongly accused, just so Ateermadang could eat.

It took awhile before Ateermadang accepted that he had wronged other people and felt shame. He said he did not need to play act any more. No doubt his decision became easier to bear once the UN started regularly supplying us with food.

Things began to get much better. I played hide-and-seek and a version of alueth in the stream. Sometimes my friends and I formed a circle in the water and tried to splash each other, like boys all over the world, or to jump around and whip each other with our legs. We fished with sharpened poles during the dry season, spearing small fish that had become trapped in pools as the river receded. Once in a great while we caught and killed a crocodile. It wasn't hard, because Dinka boys knew the secret. We surprised the crocodile while it was in a thick stand of apai and could not twist and turn. One boy held its tail, and three or four of us flipped it onto its back. That's when everyone stabbed the crocodile in its vulnerable belly. By that time we had a few knives fashioned from UN containers. Once the croc was clearly dead, we cut off the tail and cooked it. Crocodile tail is a delicious, light, flaky meat. It looks like salmon.

Even I—yes, I, skinny John—began wrestling, as our group and other groups in camp put on contests. It was just like home. I picked out my opponent in the public circle. "You want me?" he asked. "Yes, I want to wrestle you, tomorrow." When the day came, everyone watched, jumping and cheering. I was not nearly

as good as my father, but I had fun. After two years into living at
Pinyudu, it was possible for me to admit that I was enjoying life
again. I still thought about my parents, but not as much.

Pinyudu grew more and more like a big Dinka village. True,
the camp had nearly all boys and only a few hundred girls, and
there were few adults. But we had gravitated toward the traditions and cultures of our families. We built huts of sticks and
mud, just as our parents had. Every year we patched the roofs or
replaced the worst of the huts before the rainy season. We had
our daily chores of cooking and cleaning, which I rotated among
the boys in my group. We played and swam and even started to
dance and sing again, just as we had at cattle camp.

Our village even had its first strange visitors from far away. An
American congressman on a fact-finding visit came to Pinyudu.
I don't remember his name, but I do remember how we prepared. Our caretakers taught us to chant the first words I ever
learned in English: "Welcome, welcome UNHCR (United Nations High Commissioner for Refugees). Welcome, welcome,
American congressman."

The words meant nothing to me at the time, but I felt some
hope that the outside world had begun to take notice of us homeless boys from southern Sudan.

3

Untold thousands of Sudanese boys walked hundreds of miles through the wilderness to seek refuge in Ethiopia in 1987 and 1988. Relief workers reported seeing 17,000 "walking skeletons" arrive at the Ethiopian camps. An American diplomat cabled the State Department that all of the refugees "had the dull concentration camp stare of the starving." Their evident suffering resembled World War II photographs of the victims of Nazi concentration camps, the diplomat wrote, and "were as bad or worse" than anything seen in Ethiopia during the 1984-86 famine. Interviewers concluded that hunger, thirst, disease, animal attacks, and human violence claimed many lives before the refugees could reach the Ethiopian border.

They came in search of food, education, and freedom from suffering. Some came to find the SPLA training camps, so they could learn to fight the djellabas. The SPLA called the boys they recruited "child soldiers" and ran a training camp in Ethiopia. They took some of the oldest, strongest boys and left the rest to get an education. This generation would need to be educated to help Sudan once the war was won.

Four southwestern Ethiopian relief camps supported 265,000 Sudanese refugees in mid-1988. Most were boys and young men. Relief workers who

Thousands of Lost Boys trudge along a path in southern Sudan after leaving Ethiopia.

surveyed camp residents found variations on the same story: They had fled Muslim troops and government-backed enemy tribesmen who attacked their villages, killing men and boys and taking women and girls as slaves. Mothers and daughters were not as ready to move quickly when the attacks came, a Sudanese leader of the refugees said. They fell behind and were more likely to be caught. Only a few hundred girls and a handful of women made it to Ethiopia. In all, about two million of the six million Sudanese living in the southern provinces had fled their homes because of famine or civil war by mid-1988; many settled in other parts of Sudan.

Newcomers "are nothing but skin and bones when they arrive," an aid worker who visited the refugee camps in Ethiopia, including Pinyudu, told the New York Times. *"They tell us that 20 percent of the people who left with them died along the way." Other estimates placed the number of deaths in transit from all causes—hunger, thirst, disease, and violence—as high as three in five. One boy told an interviewer he followed a trail of human bones to find his way to Ethiopia. Sadly, his odyssey and those of the other Lost Boys and Girls did not end in Ethiopia.*

"CALM DOWN, CALM DOWN," OUR CAMP CARETAKERS KEPT shouting at us as we stood on the banks of the rain-swollen Gilo River. But we could not stay calm. We were trapped between the crocodile-infested river shallows and hundreds of Ethiopian soldiers, who were trying to kill us or drive us into the water.

Only a few moments before, I had been eating some boiled maize on the riverbank. It had been a calm and overcast afternoon in May 1991. I had unslung my pack and placed it on the ground to make an easy chair for my back while I ate lunch. Around me, hundreds of other boys relaxed and moved lazily, not doing much of anything, and certainly not doing it in a hurry.

Then I heard the *fttt* of rocket-propelled grenades being launched and the *whump* of nearby explosions. Boys burst into a dead run like carrion crows startled by a stone. Some passed me and headed toward the river, surging below a ten-foot embankment.

I leaped up, scattering cornmeal, and looked for the source of the sounds. On the horizon, a line of Ethiopian soldiers advanced toward us. They wore dusty military uniforms of tan and pale green. Some strode forward in their black boots, firing rifles and RPGs; others must have stayed in the rear because I heard the whine of incoming mortar shells zooming over the soldiers' heads in long parabolas. A few armored vehicles rumbled across the plains, firing shells plumed by telltale puffs of black smoke. Bullets zipped through the air. They were close enough for me to hear their birdlike *kee kee* as they passed.

"We are attacked!" someone yelled. Others took up the same shout. Many boys started to cry. Some had the frozen look of panic in their eyes.

I snatched at my traveling pack, which I had sewn in Pinyudu refugee camp from plastic sheets and rectangles of cloth sliced from bags that said "USA." One handle snapped as I tried to lift it to my shoulder. I threw the useless bag down and ran toward the river.

Not being a good swimmer, I frantically looked for a place where the edge dipped gently to meet the river. While I searched, tall, coal black Sudanese boys made leaps of faith around me, jumping at full speed without looking to see where they would land. I froze. Why was I looking for an easy way to enter the water, when soldiers were trying to shoot me from a few hundred yards away?

Here's faith, I thought. I leaped, too.

I hit the mud at the reedy edge of the river. The impact smashed the air out of my lungs, but I had no time to recover. I struggled into the muddy water and began to kick toward the far side. A big man, from the Nuba tribe by the looks of him, appeared in the water beside me. He could not swim and grasped at anything to keep from drowning. Seeing me, he wrapped his arms around my head in his panic and pushed down. I fought to force him off, but he was too heavy and strong. We slipped beneath the surface. I tried to scream and got only a mouthful of water. In the silence of the river's depths, I became aware of many other legs and arms churning the water around me into foam.

The Nubian kicked his legs and got his head above the water for a moment. In pushing up, he relaxed his hold on my head. I broke free and popped up beside him, taking an enormous gulp of air. The Nubian grabbed my head again.

"Sadi ana! Sadi ana!" he yelled. It was one of the handful of Arabic phrases I had learned in Pinyudu. The Nubian whose panic had nearly drowned me was pleading, "Help me, help me!"

"I can't help you," I panted in Arabic, just before I went under the water again. At home in Duk Payuel, I learned how to swim on my back, much better than on my front. When I surfaced, I flipped face up and started to backstroke. I stared up at the sky and paddle wheeled across the water.

Time slows when your life is in danger. Every second takes a minute to pass, and even the smallest event gets chiseled into memory. It took a moment for me to realize the Nubian had let go. Good for me, bad for him. I began moving toward the opposite bank with a steady stroke. I turned my head left and right to look for the Nubian, but I could not see him in the chaos of waves and flailing limbs. All over the surface of the river, similar dramas of survival were being played out as swimmers struggled toward the far shore and nonswimmers grasped for anybody or anything that floated. Shrapnel tore into bodies and sent pieces of arms and legs flying through the air. Some people sank to the bottom and did not resurface. Others grabbed onto floating corpses and body parts.

Bullets pinged into the water and screeched overhead. They made a dull splat when they hit flesh or the mud of the western bank. Open wounds turned the water red. Crocodiles will smell our blood, I thought, but fortunately I did not see any in the water near me.

Another boy grabbed my torso; I was not sure of his tribe. "If you hold me like that I can't push water! I can't carry you!" I screamed. He relaxed his grip. I wrapped one hand around his upper arm and began paddling with my free arm. After a few strokes, I switched hands and kept going. We made slow, steady progress that way, with me changing my grip from hand to hand as I kicked and reached for the far, tree-lined shore. It was only a few hundred yards, but it seemed an eternity.

At last I felt the mud beneath me. We had made it across. The ten-minute crossing of the channel seemed as if it had taken an hour. My companion gave me a final push to plant his feet and scrambled up the bank. I followed, crawling on all fours. As I reached the top of the bank, I turned and looked at the eastern shore. Smoke and dust rose in clouds from the far bank. I heard the *crump* of mortar tubes somewhere to the east and the rattle of automatic rifles.

Shells exploded on the ground in front of me. I would have to run through the bursts to escape, I thought. But at least the river would stop the advance. Only a madman would pursue his enemy through swift, crocodile-filled waters. I thanked God that armored vehicles could not float.

I turned and hustled in a deep crouch, half-running and half-crawling across the grass and into a field showered by dirt clods kicked up by bursting shells. Bullets fired from the far shore sped by me, cutting down boys who rose up too high. I looked for my companion on the swim across, but he had disappeared. I never saw him or the Nubian again. I kept going until the shells stopped exploding around me. Then I walked until I was sure I was safe.

Hours later, after the survivors reassembled, we shared stories of the crossing. A few of the lucky ones had held onto a rope the caretakers had managed to string across the river and hand-walked to safety. Others found small boats along the riverbank and tried to make the crossing in them, but at least one of them overturned in midstream. Four young men who had sat in the boat went into the water; a crocodile took one, and the other three drowned. One boy who made it to the other side incongruously had a live goat thrust into his open arms by another survivor. Blood burst as the boy held the goat. He checked to see if he had been hit. No, the bullet had hit the goat, killing it instead of him.

Perhaps 20,000 Sudanese boys went into the Gilo River that day. Nobody knows how many died in the crossing. Maybe 2,000, maybe 3,000, maybe more. Some drowned. Some caught a bullet or shell fragment. Some found their way into a crocodile's belly. I know the crocs had a feast, because others who made it to the western shore told me they had seen their friends in the beasts' cold jaws. One man showed me the stump of his

*Refugees flee across the Gilo River ahead of Ethiopian troops
in a painting done by a 17-year-old Lost Boy at Kakuma.*

hand and told me a crocodile bit it off while he swam. Later, in
Kenya, the boys started calling him Mkono Umja—"One Hand
Man" in Kiswahili.

A week before the attack at the Gilo, nobody could have fore-
seen such chaos and death. We had grown accustomed to life
in Pinyudu and had expected to live there a long time. We had
our homes, our meals, our games, and even some of the sweeter
things in life, such as our traditional songs and dances. I certainly
did not think the war we had left in Sudan would find us.

But if I had listened more closely to our caretakers, I might
have suspected something was up. In April 1991, they told us of
troubles facing the Ethiopian government, which had sheltered
us and allowed the UN to bring us food. Ethiopia had its own

civil war—rebels, friendly with the northern Sudanese, were fighting against the socialist government of President Mengistu Haile Mariam. The caretakers said that if the rebels took power, they would not let us stay. "If they come," the caretakers said, "we will have to run away to a different place." That did not sound too bad. I could go to another camp if I had to.

The boys in my group discussed the likelihood of our leaving Pinyudu. That spring, the rains came to dusty western Ethiopia as never before. We stood in a circle under a tree near our hut and talked as the rains pelted the camp.

The Ethiopian People's Revolutionary Democratic Front captured Addis Ababa on May 21 and sent Mengistu packing. He fled to Zimbabwe, leaving the government in the hands of our enemies. In Pinyudu, at the edge of Ethiopia, we heard the news almost immediately. The new government gave us a week to leave. That left us with no opportunity to harvest the corn and vegetables we had planted near our huts.

"Now," the camp manager announced at an assembly, "we have no choice. There is another war, and there is no place for us here."

I wondered where we would go. Back to our villages, I hoped. I wanted to look for my family. But then I considered more carefully. Nothing had changed in Upper Nile Province. The northern djellabas still controlled most of the villages, and there would be no life for me anywhere near such people, as long as my country was at war with itself.

"Pochala would be a good place," someone said. It was not far from the Ethiopian border and still in the hands of the SPLA. I was not too excited about returning to a Sudanese town certain to draw the attention of the djellabas, but I could see no good alternative. We had to choose the lion in Ethiopia or the hyena in Sudan.

Pochala, I thought. I would have to go there, even though it meant returning to the hand-to-mouth life I had lived with Abraham on the walk to Ethiopia. As I thought about my future, I discovered a nagging voice in the back of my mind that said something bad would happen soon. It was the same feeling I had felt in Duk Payuel in the days before the djellabas came.

OUR EVACUATION FROM PINYUDU HAD BEGUN AS AN ORDERLY affair. The caretakers announced that the best way to stay organized was to have one group leave each day, starting immediately. The first group of 1,200 set out that very day, walking and carrying food and supplies toward the western border. A second group took off shortly after noon the next day. At that rate, clearing camp would take a couple of weeks.

I was in the third group. Every boy had a bag like the one sewn from American cloth sacks and bits of plastic tarpaulin. I told my housemates to put their tools and extra clothes in the bottom of their bags and put a little food on top. I made sure everyone carried a bit of corn or vegetable oil.

"There may be no food later," I said. "Carry what you can." Around 3 p.m. on the third day of evacuation, my group started moving toward the Gilo River at the western edge of Ethiopia. We followed in the footsteps of the first two groups. The brown land, dotted with hardy grasses and pools of mud, passed monotonously underfoot. Bushes, flowers, and trees encouraged by the rains had sent forth armies of fresh shoots, covering the plains with a pale green blanket. Mosquitoes buzzed around me as I walked. Every evening we made camp under the sky, opened our bags, and cooked corn meal mush for dinner. Our cooking fires sent drifts of white smoke into the night sky, and blossoms of orange flames dotted the dark landscape with a comforting glow. If not for my nagging suspicions, I might have been able to relax and treat the journey like an adventure. I tried to sleep, but the weather was cool, and the clouds that gathered tickled me with drops from a steady drizzle.

It took four days before my group reached the Gilo. The first two groups already had arrived. Many of the boys could not swim, so the caretakers debated the best way to get to the other side. Someone suggested trying to hire the native Anyuak to ferry us across in their little boats. The caretakers investigated and found that idea had two problems. First, it was a seller's market. The Anyuak had a monopoly on boats, and they set their price too high to accommodate everyone. Second, the boats were so few and the numbers so large—and swelling by 1,200 or so every day—that it would have taken many days to get everyone across.

The caretakers settled on a plan to string a rope from shore to shore a few feet above the water and secure it to trees at each end. They scouted the best location for anchors on both banks of the river. Meanwhile, more and more boys packed the eastern side of the Gilo.

Each night brought cool temperatures. Each morning dawned warm and pleasant. Each day, I wondered, would this be the day I would cross? Would I be safe?

I did not know that as the refugees from Pinyudu assembled on the grassy bank of the Gilo, military units dispatched by the new Ethiopian government were approaching the river from another direction. The shooting started on my fifth day. I was just beginning to relax and eat as the sun struggled to fight through a scattering of clouds. I did not hear or see any warning. Only after I had crossed to the western side did I learn that boys in another group had met an SPLA soldier on the east bank before the attack started. He reported fighting between Sudanese militia and Ethiopian soldiers at Pinyudu, after the refugees had left. It was common knowledge that the SPLA had soldiers in and around our camp to recruit for the southern Sudanese militias, and that they trained on Ethiopian soil. The SPLA soldier had said he expected the Ethiopians to pursue all of the Sudanese to the Gilo, and he was right. If only that message had gotten to everyone sooner, perhaps more lives would have been saved. As it was, it seemed a miracle that only a few thousand of us died in crossing the river.

Like most survivors of that day, I still have bad dreams about the Gilo River. And I wonder still, what does war do to people to make them shoot children? Do those Ethiopian soldiers ever get nightmares?

AFTER MY ESCAPE ACROSS THE GILO, I STAGGERED FORWARD FOR many hours. Nobody in my group had any food; we had left it on the eastern shore as we dived into the river. About 18,000 boys from Pinyudu trudged toward Pochala. Boys from other refugee camps in Ethiopia joined us. The line stretched so long that two days passed between the first boy and last boy crossing the same spot in the muddy road.

The Anyuak of Sudan welcomed us. I found some fruit growing in the Anyuak forests, and they gave us some of their own food to eat. It barely took the edge off my hunger. My stomach growled and my legs ached, but I kept walking, willing my feet to pull free of the sticky mud and take one step closer to Pochala.

Lost Boys on their way toward the Kenyan border
sleep in the desert of southern Sudan.

We arrived to find Pochala a friendly but broken town. The SPLA had captured it from the djellabas, but the fight for control had reduced much of the town to ruin. Caretaker adults—perhaps 200 of them had survived the Gilo—showed us where we could find temporary shelter. I and a few hundred other boys spent our first nights in an abandoned military barracks.

Soldiers came to talk to us, telling us about the war in Sudan. Some of my friends met soldiers from their villages, but I never met anyone from Duk Payuel. The soldiers gave us a little of their food. It never lasted long. The SPLA could not support tens of thousands of children on their own.

We had no idea then that we would have to stay in Pochala for nine months with no guaranteed supply of food. The wet season rains pelted us and covered the ground with mud. Pochala became an island surrounded by swamp, impossible to cross in a car or truck. No food came over the submerged roads. I started feeling hungry all the time.

During my second month in Pochala, I heard the sound of an airplane overhead. For a split second, I hoped it might be a United Nations plane making a food drop. Then the sound resolved itself into the characteristic *ooooovvv* of Antonov engines. It was a warplane from the Khartoum government. The plane flew over the town and dropped a string of bombs. They kicked up fountains of dirt as they hit near the camps, and a few boys were injured. As soon as the plane left, I started digging, because I knew the Antonov would return. Everyone else must have had the same idea, for soon the streets of Pochala were crisscrossed with trenches.

I built a hut from branches and mud where I could store any food I found, and a trench not far from the door to the hut that I could dive into. It wasn't many days before the Antonov returned, and my trench served its purpose. The plane came back a few days each week, and my body instinctively jerked toward the trench as soon as the faintest engine noise drifted over the trees.

Food became extremely scarce even as the swamps began to dry. The SPLA soldiers said they had no more food to give us, and we were on our own. Most wild fruits hadn't ripened yet. I knew of a few that should have ripened and combed the forests for amochro, which Abraham had showed me how to find, as well as *waak,* a shrub that bears a white, sweet fruit with a funny aftertaste. I also resigned myself to eating the fruit of the *gumel.* It's a huge tree, with a sweet-and-sour fruit about the size of a baseball. Everyone knew eating the gumel fruit brought on the symptoms of malaria, but that was better than starving. I weighed my options and ate. The fruit made me sick, yet it kept me alive.

We also took clothes to the Anyuak and bartered them for food. In my circle of a few dozen boys, we asked one who had a T-shirt to give it up so we could get some corn. Another boy washed it and took it to the Anyuak outside the village, and we got enough corn to keep us alive for a few more days.

The exchanges always had risks. The Anyuak nearest Pochala quickly realized how desperate we were, and they offered less and less for our articles of clothing. Things got so bad that one local trader offered only a cup of corn for a shirt. We refused. The Anyuak sneered at us. "Go and eat your clothes," they said.

We traveled farther from town, and indeed the price rose higher. But there was danger in wandering too far. I heard about some boys, not from my group, who wandered so far in search of a good price that they were captured by hostile Anyuak and killed.

I found myself using words like "killed" and "died" in conversations without giving them much thought. How much I had changed, I thought. In the Dinka tradition, children were shielded from death. In fact, the news of a loved one's passing was kept from children as long as possible. An elderly neighbor was supposed to break such news, very carefully, first to the adults of a family after having prepared them with small talk and references to the mortality of men and women. Then the adults gently told the children. Everyone cried, even the men, and the women sometimes threw themselves on the ground in their wailing and mourning. In Duk Payuel, my relatives took off all of their jewelry, wore only black clothes, and let their hair go unattended after a death. It was all an elaborate process meant to demonstrate the esteem in which the dead person was held.

Sudanese children cook beans at a camp near the Kenyan border.
The UN supplied refugees with food during their journey.

In our refugee camps, however, the necessity of burying so many children telescoped the ceremonies of mourning into a few moments of silent grief. I helped bury the people I knew, I said a few words of prayer, and I moved on. I had no black clothes to wear, and my hair already was very dirty and likely to get much dirtier. I felt as if I had grown up too fast. Death had become all too familiar.

I asked the caretakers why the UN, which had fed us in Pinyudu, couldn't bring us food in Pochala. They replied that the town had no roads for overland supply and no airfield where planes could land. Not long afterward, the caretakers put us to work clearing space for a landing strip. I helped dig up roots and cut down trees with axes supplied by the SPLA. Slowly, the strip took shape on the outskirts of town.

The first time a giant cargo plane flew over the town, I ran away. I thought it was another bomber, and a big one at that. The plane dropped bags onto the open fields. Only after it had flown off did I and some of the other boys go to look at the bags and discover they were full of food and secondhand clothes. Soon we came to distinguish the deep throbbing of the relief planes' engines from the droning of the Antonovs and ran to pick up the shipments as they streamed toward the ground. Some planes from the International Red Cross and the UN landed, and others dropped maize, oil, beans, and medical supplies from midair. One drop killed two boys when bundles of food and medicine fell on them. After that, all planes landed for deliveries for a while.

The food came just in time. Pochala's refugee population had swollen to perhaps 80,000 with an influx of southerners made homeless in the new round of fighting. Many boys I knew had sold all of their clothes to the Anyuak and were naked again. When clothes arrived in the airplanes, I worked with some of the older boys in my group to distribute them wisely. I decided that if a boy was completely naked, he had first choice on an article of clothing. Boys who already had shirts or pants chose much later. Most boys picked through the clothes and selected an adult shirt. The shirt tail hung around their knees, covering them like a dress. Underneath they wore nothing. That seemed a good choice for naked boys who only got to pick one article of clothing—it kept them warm but could be hiked in a hurry when they felt an attack of diarrhea coming on.

I didn't get any new clothes for a long time. I still wore the colorful blanket-shorts that Abraham had made me, and I was naked from the waist up for several months. The shorts had suffered many tears over the months I had worn them, but I had learned how to sew and kept them patched. The SPLA kept me supplied with needles. Finally, I got a long T-shirt and wore it with my shorts.

As the weather grew cooler and drier, the Antonov sorties grew more frequent. We wondered if the northern government deliberately targeted boys, as we were the vast majority of the town's occupants. Bombing runs hit Pochala every day, in the morning and afternoon. I started to anticipate the explosions. I played soccer with my friends, using a ball made of socks, and we suspended the games around 3 p.m. to be near our trenches when the bombers passed over. Still, casualties started to rise, not only from direct hits during the air raids but also from the Anyuak. They didn't like their forests being bombed, and they shot a few boys and SPLA soldiers in Pochala to scare the rest of us enough to move on. The Anyuak called us *ajuíl,* the name of a small antelope that lives in the forest. It always seems to be on the move, wandering without a home. The Anyuak couldn't understand why we wandered without settling, preferably elsewhere.

Raids also hit the town of Torit, where a bomb exploding in the market killed more than 30 people. And once, 200 soldiers who crossed into Sudan from Ethiopia attacked Pochala briefly before withdrawing. Some boys left Pochala with Red Cross workers, who promised to reunite them with their families, but most refugees stayed. They had no families to be found.

IT'S STRANGE TO SAY IT ABOUT SUCH A VIOLENT TIME, BUT I WAS happy. I had a daily routine of cooking, games, and building huts and trenches to keep my mind occupied. Corn and beans made a good dinner, and the UN planes also supplied us with fishhooks. I went to the Pochala River and caught plenty of fish.

I discovered the constants and the variables in the algebra of survival. If I had plenty of food but risked violent death, I felt better than if I had starved in peaceful times. My first rule, every day, was to find enough food to make it to the next day. Then I could afford the luxury of worrying about the enemy.

Often I thought about my parents. Perhaps being once again in my home country brought back their memory. I saw a woman one time in the town who looked and dressed like my mother, and I began to think about my village. When the bombs fell, I remembered the night the djellabas came. And every time I ran into Abraham—he had survived crossing the Gilo without harm, and I met him in Pochala—he reminded me of friends and family in Duk Payuel. Abraham had become one of the caretakers, serving as a surrogate father to a thousand boys. He made sure we cooked our food properly, had our illnesses treated, and maintained our trenches and latrines.

I knew the civil war was drawing closer to Pochala, because the Antonov sorties were increasing and refugees coming into town told tales from other villages. Reliable news was scarce, though. Nobody had a television, and radios were extremely rare. The only radio signal that reached into southern Sudan came from the BBC. I didn't know anyone who spoke English, so the news broadcasts that occasionally mentioned the Sudanese civil war might as well have been in Latin or some other dead language. News traveled almost exclusively by word of mouth. It took many years for me to learn of the events in my country that plagued the boys of southern Sudan.

The Sudanese government, under military rule and led by Gen. Omer al Bashir, continually pushed to transform the nation into an Islamic state. Bashir's forces began the largest offensive of the civil war in March 1992, aiming to break the SPLA's lines of supply and communication in the south. Relief operations based in Kenya and Uganda proved ineffective, as roads leading to refugee camps in southern Sudan fell under the northern government's control. The United Nations cut back its airlifts as the assaults escalated. Human Rights Watch/Africa reported many abuses, including "arbitrary killing and looting of civilians." Northern troops burned everything within 12 miles of the newly captured towns of Rumbek and Yirol in an attempt to deny food and support to the SPLA. Those actions alone added 100,000 more people to the list of refugees made homeless by the civil war. Meanwhile, internal strife between two rival factions of the SPLA led to additional fighting in southern Sudan, killing thousands of civilians caught in the middle.

The year's worst fighting occurred in July, when the SPLA faction led by Col. John Garang captured the town of Juba in a massive counterassault aimed at rolling back the government's southern sweep. Summary executions and torture, including the administration of electric shocks and the crushing of testicles, became common.

ACCOUNTS OF WAR GREW INTO WILD RUMORS. I HAD NO experience of the world outside Sudan and Ethiopia. If someone told me a story about the United Nations or a foreign country or the djellabas, I tended to accept it. Every night, one of the caretakers walked through Pochala shouting the news of the day as he went from one cluster of huts to another. "You've got to take care of yourselves tomorrow, because the Antonovs are coming again"—that was one of the messages he shouted a lot. Sometimes the Antonovs came the next day; sometimes they didn't.

I wondered, like the other boys, about the UN. The people of the UN had to be Christians, I thought, to be helping Christians in Sudan. Other Dinka boys said the UN—they pronounced it

"WEE-enn"—had to be stupid to give away so much food and clothing. Or they said the relief planes only gave us the food that the UN deemed fit to feed its cows.

In January 1992, the bombardments increased again, and the caretakers told us to prepare to move out. They said the northern armies had drawn near Pochala, and soon the town would fall into their hands. I wanted to go west, initially to the Kangen Swamp and then on to Duk County. Wiser heads reasoned that if the djellabas could take an SPLA center such as Pochala, they could certainly seize places that were less well defended. In the end, the caretakers consulted with the SPLA and decided to vote. The soldiers urged them to flee from the fighting but not to the land of tribes hostile to the Dinka, like the Murle. The caretakers went off by themselves to decide. Finally, around seven one night, they reached an agreement. They sent out the news, dispatching the town crier.

"We go to Jebel Raat," he shouted. The words mean "mountain lightning," hardly the most comforting name for refugees fleeing war. That meant we would walk south, toward Kenya. South, farther from our homes, but also farther from the djellabas.

From Raat, a town controlled by the SPLA, we would keep going to stay ahead of the soldiers. A line of villages stretched south from Raat like beads on a long string: Pakok. Buma. Kapoeta, the largest town in eastern Equatoria. Then Nairus. Finally, at the end of the line, Lokichokio, a town just over the Kenyan border. If we made it to Kenya, we would be safe once again. It sounded easy. In reality, the journey from Pochala to safety across the border measured 500 miles. Unlike my journey from Duk Payuel to Ethiopia, I would travel this time in a pack of thousands of boys, all following well-marked paths through the savannas, forests, and deserts of southern Sudan. Djellabas in airplanes could not miss us if they tried. Nor could the native tribes whose homelands we would have to cross.

"You will leave soon," the crier said. "Get some food together to start the journey. Along the way, the UN will give you food and water, and you will be okay."

On the appointed day, I stood with my group, ready to begin walking. We had sewn new carrying bags from pieces of tent canvas and emergency medical bags the UN had dropped on us, and we filled them with maize, beans, and plastic bottles of vegetable oil. Everyone carried enough food to last several days. Like the other boys in my group, I had sewn shoes out of plastic bags and rectangles cut from tent coverings. They looked strong, but they fell apart after only two days' march.

We set off on a morning at the end of the dry season. We sang to keep our spirits up, for we did not know what lay ahead.

I sang in the Dinka language:

Lord, bless our journey,
Give us joy and peace.
Let the love of your word be our victory,
And take our fatigue away.
As we go through this wilderness,
We thank you and worship
Because your words we have listened to.
Help us believe in you in our heart and life,
Now and forever and ever.

We sang other songs, too, to be brave and to break the tension with humor. One boy sang his own song, "I am malaria," which meant, "I am strong; I can hurt anybody." Another boy sang to tell the world he was a lion. Some walkers sang about the men going forward and the women being safe; perhaps 500 women and girls, refugees from their villages, marched with us.

When I saw a boy by the side of the road, apparently resting, I chided him for not marching with us. "What are you doing? Are you a woman?" That was an insult to a Dinka man. The boy replied, "No, I am waiting for somebody." He could not admit he was resting if he wanted to keep his self-respect.

Most boys walked with heads held high, boastful and strong, because that's how we felt. The heat of early March enveloped us like lava, but we did not feel it. We strode southward with pride, because we moved on our own volition, not at the barrel of any djellaba gun. Caretakers walked with us, on both sides of a two-track Anyuak path, to make sure we did not disappear into the grass or fall behind.

The air felt dry, and the parched ground gave us good footing. The Anyuak had set small fires in the forests around where we walked, to clear the brush. Like the Dinka in Duk County, they wanted to open up the ground beneath the canopy so they could hunt for big game. The grass and brush was so dense that if the Anyuak hadn't cleared it, they could have stood within ten feet of an elephant and not known it. Ash from the fires drifted down on my head as I walked, like gray leaves falling from a tall tree. Smoke and fog mixed in the morning to enclose the path within misty walls. At night, I could see the Anyuaks' fires burning in the distance.

Caretakers had briefed our group before we began walking to be alert for large predators, but I did not see any. Two boys who straggled at the end of the line did fall to Anyuak arrows, though. The news spread through the line, from mouth to mouth, and we picked up our pace.

After about two weeks, the head of the line reached Raat, but it took three more days for the last of the marchers to enter the village. I stayed in the town for three days. We had eaten most of the food we had brought with us. My group moved out when it was our turn, but others kept coming. I doubt the village could have held us all at the same time.

And so we came to the next village, Pakok. There we found Ugandan rebel soldiers who had crossed the border to find sanctuary in Sudan. What a crazy world—each country in revolt, pushing its rebels to seek sanctuary in a neighboring country that was in turn dealing with its own problems.

We also found yams, maize, and groundnuts in Pakok. Whatever we had to barter with, we traded for food. We stayed there for some time, because food was so abundant.

We finally left for Buma at the end of March, confident that the UN would bring us water and food on the long journey. Our caretakers had told us so. I did not know that Red Cross relief workers had delivered food and water to previous lines of boys making their way toward the Kenyan border, or that the Khartoum government had evicted the Red Cross for a few months, accusing them of assisting the SPLA.

I TRUSTED IN THE LORD AND BELIEVED SOMEONE, SOMEWHERE would help us. We felt so strongly that we would find assistance in the wilderness that my group used most of our water supply more quickly than we should have. Some we drank, and some we used for boiling beans and cornmeal.

I remember a blindingly clear day, with so much sunlight that it hurt to look at the sky. It was the middle of the hot season in southern Sudan. The call of a crow seemed to carry forever in the still air. A few cirrus clouds, impossibly high, barely moved as the sun crawled from east to west. I marched in the heat and drank my water until it nearly ran out. I wiped the sweat from my forehead with my fist. That night, my group pooled our beans and cooked dinner. We used the last of our water; I assumed we would get more from the UN the next day.

Come the morning, the sun rose angry and hot as we stood and started walking again. Around noon, some of the smallest boys began crying because of heat and thirst. My feet started to burn on the dirt path. I noticed some of the boys around me leaving the path and walking through the grass, where the ground had a bit of shade. I stopped and bent my knees to examine the bottom of my left foot. The skin had turned red, and my toes had swollen with fat blisters. I popped one of the blisters, and hot water ran across my foot. It hurt like a bee sting. I checked the right foot, but it was not as bad. I tried limping for a while by putting my weight on my heels, to keep the dirt out of my open blisters, but that proved very awkward. So I took off my T-shirt and tied it around the toes of my left foot. It didn't help much, and I couldn't get traction on the dirt. Finally, I tore the sleeves off my shirt and tied one sleeve around each foot. I saw other boys doing the same. It helped for a while. Then my feet started to hurt again. I checked my right foot, and blisters had formed on those toes, too.

I could barely walk. I looked for Abraham to help me, but he was nowhere to be found. I hobbled as best I could; I did not want to fall to the end of the line and get captured or killed by the Anyuak. Dripping with sweat, pain, and exertion, I kept moving forward, hour after hour.

At last I stopped. All of my blisters had burst along the way, and I felt woozy. I tried to forget about the heat and my dry throat, but I could not. All around me, other boys cried for water but got none. Too tired to care, I fell asleep right beside the road. For three hours, people tramped by a few feet from my head, but I did not stir. When I woke up, feeling a little better for the rest, I fell into line and started walking again.

Things became really bad. The sun hammered us from above. Boys tried to urinate, but nothing came out. They walked from person to person, holding out their cups and begging for someone to pee a little bit so they could drink it. A few boys could still urinate, and they obliged some of the beggars. I begged, too.

I didn't find anyone who could help. I envied the boys who had a cup of urine to drink.

I staggered forward, not sure how far I could go. Then, I saw a miracle. A UN water truck came toward me, following the two-track path. Boys stepped into the grass to make way. "Here comes salvation," I thought. But the truck did not stop. It passed me and headed for the end of the line. For once, being last, where the Anyuak and wild animals could pick off stragglers, had its rewards. A few boys tried to jump in front of the truck to make it stop, but the caretakers pulled them away. Suddenly, the marchers realized that the fastest way to get water was to double back. Hundreds started retracing their steps, heading for the end of the line, afraid more of dying of thirst than of Anyuak and lions.

I caught up with the water truck and got my drink. It tasted wonderful.

From that day onward, the UN returned every day as we walked toward Buma. The relief workers knew our route and met us in the afternoon. Always they came in one water truck and one Land Cruiser bearing the blue UN flag. No more did we crowd toward the end of the line. We kept walking forward, stopping to dunk our heads in the mobile water tank when we came upon it. The caretakers timed us. I stuck my head underwater and took a big gulp. After a few seconds, I felt a hand on the back of my neck, pulling my head free. That was the caretakers' signal to move along and make way for another boy to dunk and drink.

The UN trucks also delivered bags of food, which the trucks deposited by the side of the path. We got spoiled by the steady drops. We always carried food from the night before, but as soon as we saw the new food we cast off the old. In about a week, following our daily routine, we arrived in Buma.

The SPLA controlled the town, but the Murle controlled the surrounding forest. On our way into Buma, the Murle captured one of my cousins, Aleer Kongoor Leek, who had strayed off the path. They didn't kill him. Instead, they tried to make him into a Murle child. The more children a Murle family has, the more powerful it becomes and the more cattle it can claim in its recurring cattle raids. My cousin broke free several months later and rejoined his group. He told us three Murle men had fought to take possession of him. They took him to Murle land and gave him to an old woman. Her son had been killed in one of the wars, and she had no surviving children. She tried to make him eat snake without telling him, because anyone who eats snake forgets his family and is ready to join a new tribe. But Aleer found the snake bones in his food and refused to eat. For six months, he was forbidden to go outside and play with the Murle boys, so the adults could watch him closely inside their huts. After a while, Aleer said, the Murle men began his training. They took him to the forest and told him to hide. Then they went looking for him. Whenever they found him, they beat him, he said. Aleer got better and better at hiding in the forest, which is characteristic of the Murle. He learned to anticipate where the Murle men would move by watching their eyes. He learned to run long distances with one leg tied behind him, in order to prepare for the possibility of being wounded but not killed. He carried Murle boys great distances, to prepare to help comrades injured in war, and he became quite strong. The Murle began to trust him. Since he never ate the snake meat, however, he remained a Dinka in his heart. One day, when he went far into the forest, he ran away and made his way back to camp.

I stayed in Buma for about a week. During that time, news reached us that the djellabas had captured Pakok. The UN truck drivers said we would be safe for now, but we itched to get moving again, in case the Arabs were not far behind us.

We set out again, bound for Kapoeta. The natives we met along the way were Taposa. Their women wore an animal skin on their back and another on their front, and no other clothes. The men stayed naked. The Taposa disliked the long line of boys, whom they saw as invading their land, and I think they sought to curry favor with the djellabas by harassing us. While I rested under a tree near the path, I saw three Taposa moving in the brush. They started shooting, killing one boy and wounding another. A couple of boys picked up their wounded friend and carried him until the following day, when the UN car arrived and they put him in it.

The northern government's Antonovs found us and began bombing us again, but I think the Taposa frightened me more. They wore scars on their arms or their chests, one scar for every man they had killed. It was rumored they killed for fun. One day on the road between Buma and Kapoeta, we passed through a tiny Taposa village. Everyone was dancing. They had just returned from a war with the Murle. Three of the dancers held out the heads of Murle men they had killed. They jumped and shouted and shook the heads. It was very scary, but they did not harm me that day as I passed through.

Finally we approached Kapoeta. The djellabas had bombed the town not long before my group, which was third in line, came near the northern outskirts. Everyone was frightened. One of the caretakers had a radio and understood English. He tuned the dial to the BBC's "Focus on Africa" and listened to a news report. It said the northern soldiers were closing on the SPLA base of Kapoeta from the east. We figured the soldiers probably would arrive in three days. The broadcast also gave the world one of the first glimpses of our plight. "Twelve thousand boys"—the reporter probably had undercounted the total—"are on their way on foot through southern Sudan to escape the war."

THE REGION AROUND KAPOETA WAS A NEW AND FORBIDDING landscape. The dirt changed from black and fertile to red and dusty. The wind blew constantly through the moonscape of the Tingilic Desert, making a whistling sound though the *achap* trees that I saw for the first time. Achap grow only about four or five feet tall, and typical of a desert shrub it has thousands of thorns, nasty and curved like fishhooks, instead of broad leaves that can release precious water into the air. Groves of achap crowded both sides of the powdery trails outside Kapoeta. If achap thorns caught a walker's shirt or pants, he could never get them free without tearing the clothes. I saw boys get snared by achap, struggle for a while, and then give up and take off the clothing. The Taposa had learned to adapt, however. They crawled through the achap groves and sought refuge in their shade by first covering their arms and legs with animal hides. They hid among the thorns as we passed. Then, they collected the food we had left behind, and sometimes attacked the last ones in line.

The day of the first Taposa attack, a boy in my group became very ill. We had eaten beans for dinner the night before, and they had not been cooked properly. I had only a handful, but this boy had eaten too much. The gas in the beans made his stomach swell like a beach ball. He inflated to such a large size that he could barely move his arms and legs, which stuck out from his torso like tree limbs. I gave him a homemade remedy for intestinal gas, making him drink soapy water and then having him suck on a scrap of soap. I thought the treatment would clean out his insides, but the soap had no effect. He lay flat by the side of the achap groves, moaning and complaining that he was in too much pain to move.

I didn't know what to do. I was thinking about other treatments when—*boom!*—a hidden group of Taposa fired a volley of gunshots into the line of boys on the trail. Boys ahead and behind me began running. I panicked; I had to get my group out of there, and quick. I hit the boy's distended belly with a stick, trying to force the air out of him. He merely cried in pain.

"This is the end of my life! I'm going to die," he whimpered.

"Stop!" I screamed at him. "Get up. We have to go."

The boy tried to sit up, but he couldn't get his balance with his round belly. He wobbled and lay back on the road.

I was a leader of my group, and his safety was my responsibility. I could not just leave him. I rounded up a couple of boys who had not run away, and we tried to roll the round boy along the ground, rotating his enormous belly like a ball. No good—it was too slow and too awkward, and no doubt uncomfortable for the boy. We tried to make him defecate to shrink the swelling, but he cried, "I can't do it!"

I got out a blanket and fetched two wooden poles. I set the poles parallel on the ground and tied the blanket between them to make a stretcher. We rolled the round boy onto the stretcher, and another boy and I hoisted it onto our shoulders. A third boy carried our food rations. The stretcher swayed left and right as we walked. Each jerky movement put the round boy in agony and taxed our strength.

"Stop swaying!" he yelled. "It hurts!"

But we couldn't stop. We had to get him away from the Taposa. We carried him for perhaps a half mile before we had to put him down and rest. When we started again, falling in line with the never ending stream of boys, I took a turn carrying our food and another boy shouldered my end of the stretcher.

We came to grove of achap trees. A few Taposa warriors stood among the achap, not afraid to be seen. We approached apprehensively. The Taposa watched us and the rest of the boys in line. Just as my group was about to pull even to the Taposa, they aimed their guns and fired into the air above the line of boys just ahead of us.

I let go of my food bag, and the boys carrying the stretcher dropped the round boy from shoulder height. Everyone except the round boy ran away, dodging achap thorns as we looked for a place to hide in the bush.

I didn't expect the round boy to be alive when we quietly returned a few minutes later, but there he was, still on top of the blanket. The Taposa apparently didn't want to kill him or anyone else; they only wanted our food. All of the bags we had dropped in our haste had disappeared, along with the Taposa.

As we gave thanks for our good fortune, we saw a UN car approaching. The driver didn't stop, passing us without a glance at the round boy on the ground. The round boy said he would try to walk, but he still could not even sit up. He threw himself flat and said he would die if the UN car did not return to pick him up.

Fortunately, the car did return from the back of the line. As it drew even with us, I waved and pointed to the round boy on the ground. The car stopped, and two men got out. One of them, a Kenyan, took a look at the boy. He went back inside the front of the car and emerged with a white tablet, which he put in the boy's mouth. Then he and his companion lifted the boy into the car and drove off.

I found the round boy at Kapoeta. He felt better, and the swelling in his belly had subsided. We called him Man Who Ate Beans, but it became something of a misnomer. He refused to eat beans, ever again.

Other refugees had come to Kapoeta before us and stayed long enough to begin formal schooling. SPLA soldiers acted as their teachers, drilling them in their ABC's in the open desert air. One soldier told a visiting journalist he considered the young boys who made it to Kapoeta to be among the most fortunate in southern Sudan. "I call them the lucky boys," he said. "They are

Lost Boys wash themselves in a half drum at Kakuma in 1992,
when the camp was little more than fields and achuil trees.

lucky because we give them education. To us, a classroom is a tree
that brings shade."

I stayed only three days in Kapoeta. I arrived in May, just
ahead of the northern offensive. Caretakers told us to move on,
and we headed south toward the next town, Nairus. In the middle of the night, the SPLA soldiers awakened the relief workers in Kapoeta, including representatives of the UN Children's
Fund (UNICEF), and urged them to evacuate toward the
Kenyan border. On May 28, a few days later, Kapoeta fell to the
northern soldiers, cutting the main road into southern Sudan.
Airplanes flew overhead and occasionally bombed us as we hurried toward Kenya.

The Taposa met us as we came to Nairus. They offered to sell
us milk from their cows, goats, and sheep. I traded some of the

UN food for a glass of milk. It was the first real milk I had had since leaving Duk Payuel four years earlier. I'm not counting the powdered milk I drank in Pinyudu. I saw a Taposa woman milking a cow and asked her to give me a drink. It was so, so good.

Not all Taposa greeted us so warmly. They liked our UN food, and a couple of times they kidnapped a boy and held him for a ransom of beans and vegetable oil.

The caretakers hadn't originally planned to move us over the border into Kenya. We had hoped merely to go far enough in Sudan to escape the fighting. But the djellabas seemed bent on chasing us wherever we went, from Pochala to Buma to Kapoeta to Nairus.

Each town fell to the attacking soldiers, yet no matter how many towns and cities they conquered, they could not defeat the SPLA in the countryside. Garang's forces gave battle when they thought they could win and avoided it when the odds were against them, all the while biding their time.

I hoped to stay for a while in Nairus, and I did—for about two months. Then the northern soldiers approached the town and stepped up their air raids once again. I dug another trench, like the other boys, and dived into it every time I heard the Antonov engines overhead.

The planes came every night. One evening, we heard an especially long and loud bombardment in Nairus. A rumor spread through the streets: "The djellabas may come tonight."

"Time to go," I thought.

The caretakers agreed. Some of the bombs had landed in the city and killed a few boys. The town had several thousand permanent residents, and the arrival of so many refugees had doubled its size without doubling its housing. Sleeping boys crowded the streets at night, making temporary shelters of tree limbs and blankets. They were easy targets for well-placed bombs and shells. One morning, everyone set out on foot for Lokichokio, just inside Kenya. The town served as UN headquarters for all of East Africa, so we felt we would be safe there. The United Nations would feed us and keep us safe from the war.

The walk to Lokichokio took only about a day. We crossed the international border without recognizing having passed any magic line. Our spirits felt lighter for our new freedom, yet sadder too for leaving our homeland. We carried no water, expecting once again for the UN to provide for us. When we finally got to Lokichokio, we did find some water that the UN had left us in a drum. A UN representative greeted us as we entered the town. He was so rude—he dipped his hat in our tank of water to rinse it. Perhaps he did not know it was our drinking water.

Around this time, the SPLA renewed its push to recruit soldiers from among the refugees. Abraham decided to volunteer. He got a new khaki uniform, black boots, and an AK-47 assault rifle. Morale soared among the recruits as they danced and jumped and sang songs that inspired courage. Every morning around four, Abraham and the other new soldiers fell out for training when the SPLA whistled. Everyone ran and sang until daybreak.

Lots of people, especially caretakers, volunteered. The SPLA chose the ones who looked strong and healthy. Some of the shortest young men wanted to join so badly they stood on folded sacks to make themselves look taller as the recruiters walked along to choose the most promising prospects in the lines of volunteers. I tried to join, too. "Now is the time to fight," the caretakers had told us, and I believed them. I wanted to go with Abraham. I liked the look of the uniforms and I thought I might kill some of the enemy before they killed me.

But the recruiters dashed my hopes. They knocked me out of line, rejecting me without giving a reason. I suspect I looked too skinny and weak, and they feared I would die even before I got to the combat zone. With great sadness, I watched Abraham march off to war without me.

Abraham Deng Niop: *When we got close to the Kenyan border, I left the Lost Boys and joined the SPLA. That was 1992. From that time until 2001, I fought with the SPLA, in many places and in many battles. All that time, while John remained in Kakuma, I did not hear about him. Then, in 2002, I learned he had traveled to live in the United States. Some of the Lost Boys who had gone to America had talked to people in Kenya. I went to Kenya in 2002, and I talked to people I knew, and I asked them about John. They gave me John's phone number, and we got connected again. That's how things worked—people know other people and their families, and they ask around until they find the ones they are looking for.*

John and I talk on the phone a lot. We talk about what John is doing in America, at the university, about what I did in the SPLA. About family issues. About life.

John urged me to go back to school. I live in Kampala now. The schools are much more expensive in Kenya than in Uganda, so I am studying in Kampala to get the equivalent of a high school degree in computer engineering. John has supported me by sending me money for my tuition. I hope to finish my degree and go back to Sudan, to Duk Payuel, to settle into life there again.

I stayed in Lokichokio for two months. Then the UN decided to relocate all of the boys to a new refugee camp that the United Nations High Commissioner for Refugees was organizing at the tiny town of Kakuma, 74 miles from the border. At the time, Kakuma consisted of two buildings in the middle of the desert, with almost no green thing growing nearby. With a little help, I made it in one day. The United Nations sent open-topped trucks to transport the boys to Kakuma. About 50 rode at once, standing shoulder to shoulder on the truck bed like farm animals. I stood by the edge, so I kept my balance by holding onto the side of the truck. Those in the middle were less fortunate. The Kenyan driver zoomed along, and the truck swayed back and forth as he made turns or hit bumps in the road. The rocking knocked most of the riders in the center off their feet. Boys in the front of the truck bed hammered with their fists on the roof of the cab to tell the driver to stop or slow down. Most of the time he ignored the noise.

As the boys tried to keep from falling, they grabbed onto nearby arms, necks, and clothing. Boys lost their shirt buttons to hands snatching at any available clothing. Fights broke out among boys who tore each others' shirts. One boy clutched at another's shorts as the truck jerked, and the unfortunate boy found himself naked, his pants around his ankles with no space for him to bend over and pull them up. He recovered his shorts—and his dignity—only after the truck stopped and everyone piled out. By that time, red dust kicked up by the tires coated everyone on the bed. All I could see were eyeballs looking out from suddenly unfamiliar faces. It might have been funny if some of the boys hadn't suffered injuries in the jostling.

That was my first ride in a car or truck. For the first time, I moved faster than the thiang or the lion, and I glimpsed a vision of the modern world: fast, blurred, and chaotic. My eyes burned and shed tears from the wind in my face. The speed also made me dizzy as I tried to keep my balance and comprehend the world zipping by.

I made the trip with a bundle of sticks that had been my hut in Lokichokio. Others did the same. I tied a green, ropelike piece of clothing to the bundle to show it was mine.

WHEN WE ARRIVED IN KAKUMA, THE CAMP ON THE ARID PLATEAU of northwestern Kenya seemed the end of the Earth. Every night, the wind blew in off the desert and deposited red dust over everything and everyone. I woke up my first morning in camp and didn't recognize myself or anyone else. We all looked like a different race: red black men. Cars that drove into camp in the middle of the day kept their headlights on to try to cut through the clouds of grit and the whirling dust devils that danced across the campground. When I tried to walk across camp, my legs sank to the knee in fine red particles.

Red hills surrounded the camp, and dry riverbeds lined the low spots on the dusty plain. The temperature nearly always hovered around 100°F. The camp had no electricity, no latrines, no running water, none of the things to make life easier for the thousands of refugees who began scattering across the site.

The Kenyan government and the United Nations High Commissioner for Refugees began expanding and improving the site for the camp in 1992, as soon as the first boys from southern Sudan arrived from Lokichokio. Kenyan immigration law required incoming refugees to live in such camps, and it forbade us to work for wages in Kenya. Thus, I and the other boys became dependent on donations to keep us alive. By settling into Kakuma I had made a leap of faith just as surely as I had when I jumped into the surging Gilo River.

The day we arrived, only a few gray skeletons of trees grew at the camp, so it was good that we had brought hut-building materials from Sudan. We boys began assembling huts of mud and sticks, with grass-and-leaf roofs, much like our homes in southern Sudan. Three to five boys shared a hut, and we grouped our huts by tribe into a few dozen. That helped foster a village feeling in camp. I threw together my first hut from the materials I had brought with me. The floor was bare dirt. It may not have looked like much, but for a boy who had spent most of a year on the move and constantly alert for air raids, it seemed a castle. Even better, there were no mosquitoes in the desert air.

Soon after I arrived, God blessed the camp. The rains came, and the rains stayed.

The dust settled and formed cakes of mud. The desert achuil trees soaked up the moisture and started to sprout tiny green leaves. They spread their branches and touched the limbs of other trees, like boys holding hands. The Turkana, the native tribe, were amazed. "These Dinka come with rain," they said. It sounds odd to say so, but the Turkana, a desert people, did not like it when it rained a lot. They had no permanent shelters to keep them dry. Their homes consisted of large sheets of paper tied atop lashed poles made of achuil wood, so the rains made them miserable and wet. They lived all the time with famine and drought, and so felt understandably jealous of the food the UN had given us.

In the first few weeks at Kakuma, I tried to make friends with the Turkana. I traded some of my food for their firewood and milk. But they still never had enough to eat. When I ate dinner, I could feel their eyes watching me. Those times, I gave them a little of my food. They seemed old even when they were only in their 30s and 40s.

UN workers dug down to the water table and opened a permanent well. It was the cleanest water I had ever tasted. They put chlorine into the well to kill any lingering bacteria. Of course, I did not know about bacteria at the time. Everything I had drunk at Duk Payuel, Pinyudu, or on the road had been standing, stagnant water.

I felt blessed. Shortly after arriving in Kakuma, I began attending "synagogue" every evening around sundown. An Episcopal priest, John Machar Thon, named our camp's nightly Christian worship services after the rituals of the Israelites, who fled with Moses out of Egypt and gave thanks in the wilderness to the Lord.

Like the Israelites, he told us, the Sudanese had fled again and again from persecution and yearned for their homeland. He said it would be fitting if we worshipped as the Jews did when they wandered in the desert, and if we tried to live as they lived. Thus, the refugees in Kakuma formed "synagogue" groups to worship, sing, and pray at night to bring us closer together, as well as closer to God.

I belonged to a group of about 75 boys, who gathered for two hours every evening. We sang in Dinka. Sometimes we knelt and prayed, sometimes we felt the spirit moving us to prophesize, and sometimes we just held each other. We jumped and clapped hands. And we danced. Ours was a demonstrative, emotional synagogue. It was the sweetest thing when I felt the spirit of the Lord moving through me. It was like drinking cold water on a hot day. I knew the Lord had kept me alive in the desert and in the forest, and I was sure he must have a plan for me to do something good with my life.

Settling into Kakuma, so far from home and so destitute of possessions and power, I could only begin to imagine what that good thing might be. All I could do was prepare myself for whatever God would send my way.

To do that, I knew I had to embrace my new mother and father: the classroom and the book.

Amazingly, only five boys died on the march through southern Sudan to the Kenya border, according to the International Red Cross. Four died from gunfire, and a crocodile ate the fifth. That did not mean the boys escaped unscathed. Most interviewed by relief workers in Kenya suffered emotional and psychological wounds. A psychologist who examined the boys described them as "one of the most traumatized groups of children I have ever met." They suffered flashbacks and without warning heard screams and sounds of suffering. Surveys of the boys in Kenyan camps found that 74 percent had survived shellings or air raids, 85 percent had seen someone starve to death, 92 percent had been shot at, and 97 percent had seen someone die in violence.

The Lutheran World Federation, which administered the Kakuma refugee camp for the UN, tried to make it a welcoming place for boys. By September 1992, the camp had 19,000 residents, three-quarters of them children as young as six and seven. Organizers decided to create a volleyball court and soccer field shortly after camp opened in order to let the children experience the joy of play. Boys eagerly awaited completion of a basketball court that year. They said they

Refugees, some perched in an achuil tree to get a better view,
watch a soccer game at Kakuma.

wanted to be like Manute Bol, the seven-foot-seven Dinka who starred with the
NBA's Philadelphia 76ers. They first had heard about him through a song sung
in Bahr el-Ghazal, his homeland; it said he had gone to America. They were
thrilled when he visited Kakuma in the mid-1990s.

The boys settled into their new camps in Kenya like professional refugees.
They built huts, planted and watered crops, and worked out systems for deliver-
ing water and food to every boy. The UN's Operation Lifeline Sudan, which
coordinated relief efforts for southern Sudan, supplied the refugees with tents,
water, and other necessities. An open-air factory at the camp produced mud
bricks for a community center and other buildings.

Boys interviewed at Kakuma by a Western journalist expressed hope and
faith that their lives would improve. "I want to be a priest," said a 13-year-old.
"If not a priest, a doctor. If not a doctor, I will be a teacher." Another said, "We
want to be kings when we grow up." A third boy volunteered, "I want to be a

relief worker—to give food." A Catholic priest at camp, aware of their history and their aspirations, said, "They will have a future only if there is peace."

I STARTED FIRST GRADE WHEN I WAS 18 YEARS OLD.

I sat in the red dust of Kakuma refugee camp in northern Kenya, anticipating my very first formal school lesson from a real teacher. The midmorning sun roasted me and about 60 other children as we nervously sat and waited. Everyone in first grade, from the boys of seven and eight to young adults like me, crowded into the oval of shade beneath an achuil tree that served as our classroom. As the sun rose higher, we scooted first toward the north and then to the east to keep cool as the shade rotated with the passing of the hours.

Kakuma's teachers were a mix of Sudanese adult caretakers and educators from the Kenyan school system. They didn't have fancy school supplies. My teachers made their own blackboard and markers. They built a three-legged easel out of long sticks and a handful of nails. Atop the crossbeam they placed a blackboard fashioned from the bottoms of a half-dozen square tins that originally held vegetable oil, topped with a layer of corrugated cardboard. In place of chalk they marked on the cardboard with lumps of charcoal rescued from the camp's fire pits. When they were done, they wiped the smudges clean with a cloth.

My first teacher was a Sudanese man, Atak. He walked through the seated children and strode to the tree like a man in charge. He had to be, leading so many children from so many ages, all bursting with desire to learn. No wonder, then, that his very first lesson focused on discipline.

"Good morning, pupils. I am your teacher, Atak," he said in Dinka. "When I say 'Good morning, pupils,' you say, 'Good morning, teacher' to me. Let's try it."

"Good morning, pupils!"

"Good morning, teacher!"

"This is our first lesson. It is about respect," Atak said.

There was no lesson a Dinka appreciated more than a lesson of respect. Atak taught us to rise up when he walked into the circle of shade under the achuil and to stay standing until he told us to sit. We learned to say "Thank you" for everything he taught us. Atak practiced leaving the tree and returning, and we practiced standing and saying "Good morning" until it became automatic.

After Atak was satisfied with our manners, he took roll by asking us to stand and state our names. When my turn came, I said, "My name is John Bul Dau." He wrote the words in his register, next to the other names, and I sat down. At the end, he told us he would read his roster, and he wanted each of us to respond when we heard our names by saying a brand new word. It was in another language, he said, and it became the first English word whose meaning I understood.

I heard Atak say the word. I practiced shaping it with my mouth, and got ready to use it when my turn came.

"John Bul Dau," Atak called out.

"Yes," I said.

It was a good word. Yes, I am here. Yes, I want to learn to read and write and do mathematics and discover the world and its rivers and cities and peoples and cars and planes and...everything, everything. If I studied, I thought, I could become a caretaker or a teacher or a pilot or a mechanic. I could learn to make things, maybe make airplanes to fly into the sky and face the djellabas in their Antonovs. I could do good things for myself and for my people. Yes, yes, yes.

We sat for five hours under the shifting shade with no break for lunch. At the end of the first day, the teacher gave us an assignment. Atak drew three black lines on the cardboard. The first two strokes leaned toward each other, their bases far apart and their tops touching like branches at the apex of a luak. The third stroke joined them at the waist. I had seen this shape before, on the pocket of my shirt in Pinyudu.

"This is an 'A,'" Atak said. "I want you to draw this shape in the dust with your finger."

I leaned forward and put the tip of my forefinger to the ground. I traced the magic shape as best I could. All around me, five dozen boys did exactly the same. We made no sound. Atak left the tree and wandered along the rows, praising the ones who had done it correctly. "OK," he said when he saw what I had drawn.

He walked a little farther and came to a boy whose letter looked like a hut about to collapse in a rainstorm. Atak bent over, took the boy's hand, and told him to hold his finger straight. He put the tip of the boy's finger in the dirt and slowly drew a perfect "A."

Atak left us that afternoon with our first homework. He gave me and every other boy a piece of paper with that same letter on it and told us to go home and practice drawing it. I ran home to my hut with several other boys. We spent the evening after dinner playing school. One of the boys played the teacher, and everyone else played the students. "Teacher" had us draw our letters over and over, praising those who did well and rapping the hands of those who struggled.

Thus began our nightly ritual of reading and writing. Every night, a new boy played teacher and the rest practiced drawing letters on the ground. Those whose letters looked most like the part

A Lost Boy writes his lessons in the red dirt of Palotaka, Sudan.
John Dau did the same thing when he was learning his ABC's at Kakuma.

of the alphabet assigned for that day won the game. I felt proud about my crude penmanship even if I didn't use a pen. Reading and writing would become my ticket to success, I thought. Those who used their minds got ahead in the world.

I started reading everything I could. There wasn't much at first since there weren't enough schoolbooks to go around. I read the sides of oil cartons and words on packages from the United Nations. I started by picking out the individual letters even before Atak began to show us how they joined hands to make words. I remember seeing the "R" for the first time on a UN food bag and thinking how funny the letter looked. And I found the letter "K" and thought how easy it would be to remember. It was the first letter in "Kalashnikov," and its shape mirrored the outline of the gun's barrel, grip, and magazine. It made me happy to learn the letters and get good marks on my first quizzes under the achuil tree.

It was a big day when I began to read out of books for the first time. Some had pictures in them, and I read about people from faraway places. The pictures showed animals I had never seen and happy children running to school in a real building. The boys and girls in the picture wore socks and shoes. Atak showed me the picture and said, "You could be somebody like those people in the picture, but only when you go to school and learn."

Atak began teaching us words. He showed a picture, said the word in English, and wrote it on the board. Man, boy, woman, girl, fire, water, fish—a lot of basic words a Dinka would need to know. It was so much to remember. I stayed up at night practicing the new words by saying them aloud with the other boys. If the moon gave me enough light, we stayed awake as long as we could, giving and taking elementary dictation. "Window," the teacher-boy said, and we all wrote it down. When I didn't get it right, the teacher got a small stick and smacked me. It was okay. I smacked him back when it was my turn to be the teacher. Sometimes we got into fights when the "discipline" got out of hand, but we always made peace and went back to our lessons.

A new teacher came to help Atak and teach us mathematics. For his first lesson, he told us to go home and return the next day with a handful of small sticks. Our first lesson would be pluses, he said. Then we would learn minuses.

He held up five sticks in one hand, one for each finger. Then, in the other hand, he held up five more. "Five plus five is ten," he said, and he wrote a "1" and "0" on the board. I copied it in the dirt. One. Zero.

It was fun. But nothing could compare to the day I got the first book of my very own. I remember the smell: clean and new like grass. The book contained exercises for young students, divided into three parts: English, mathematics, and science. Kakuma schools had so many students that we sliced the books to separate the three sections. That tripled the number who could learn from a book at any one time. The teachers put names on the top of the sections. I practiced copying my name from the book over and over in English.

"CLASS ONE," AS THE TEACHERS CALLED MY ENTRY-LEVEL GRADE, met under the achuil for two semesters, every day except when the rains canceled our lessons. The UN improved the camp's education program by erecting a huge building to house Class Two. I advanced enough to take lessons in the new building and marveled at the real classrooms. The rooms had a slate blackboard from Kenya, complete with real chalk. The floor was poured concrete, bare at first but soon covered with benches. It had no electricity, of course, as the camp had no power lines to connect to Kenya's grid. Nevertheless, I studied indoors, rain or shine, every day, racing with the sun to complete my lessons before it grew too dark to continue.

When I was in the equivalent of third grade, I got a schoolbook, a reader, called *New Friend.* We had to do the readings in class. We had so few real teachers that some Sudanese took on the role without adequate preparation. As my class read a chapter of *New Friend,* we came to a story about two Kenyan children, Tom and Atieno, who woke up one morning to find a hole in their garden where a casaba plant had been. They decided someone had come during the night and dug up the plant, and they agreed to stay awake the following night to see if he returned. They kept their watch by the light of the moon until clouds covered the sky and they fell asleep. The teacher told us we had to know "cloud" as an English vocabulary word. One of the pupils asked what the word meant. I watched the teacher's face, and it was clear to me he thought very hard about his answer. "Cloud is a big bird that is believed to live in South America," he said. "It is so big, when it flies it covers the moon at night." We said, "Okay." I didn't learn the truth until I entered sixth grade. After that, when I saw that teacher I laughed and laughed.

My list of classes increased. Arts and crafts joined the curriculum, and primary science classes expanded to include home science, with lessons in cooking and hygiene. I learned how bacteria spread and caused disease. The Kenyan teachers demonstrated how to clean and cook vegetables and fruit, and one day they showed us pictures of kitchen sinks, water taps, and microwave ovens. I had no idea what they were. Utensils? Coffee pots? What could they be? I nodded my head and pretended to understand. More pictures: telephones, lightbulbs, clothes freshly folded from the dryer. More smiles, more nods, more notes to prepare for tests about things that might as well have been from another planet. I was much more comfortable two years later, in Form One—ninth grade—when I studied the properties of matter. They were more abstract than the lessons about kitchen appliances, but I understood them much better.

As I progressed through the Kenyan school system, I learned about agriculture and GHC. That stood for geography, history, and civics, all in one course. The lessons focused on all things Kenyan—the Bantu, Semitic, and other peoples; industry and trade; history and government; elected officials; and Kenya's natural resources, plants, and animals. I remember learning about the flamingo breeding grounds and salt flats of Lake Magadi, and how ecotourism brought Western money into Nairobi's treasury.

I learned practically nothing of Sudan. To this day, I know more about the history of Kenya than about my own country's long and sad experience.

I had to master the basics of a Kenyan education, including knowledge of Kiswahili, the predominant language, in order to sit for and pass the Kenya Certificate of Primary Education exam. If I passed, I could proceed toward a certificate in secondary education. It was much harder to get.

I read until my eyes hurt and my head felt numb. When I got home to my hut at the end of a day's lessons in GHC, science, English, and Kiswahili, I did what students do all over the world. I threw down my book and went to play soccer. After dinner and nightly praise worship, I practiced my lessons and went to sleep. At dawn I washed and headed off to school again, to master every subject.

My education included life beyond the schoolyard. I met some of the Turkana tribesmen outside the camp and made a few friends. Some of them weren't so bad. They saw that I and some of the other boys didn't get enough to eat, so they agreed to sell us beef and other meat. They said the strange meat had come from a cow, but rumors in camp indicated the meat was something else. One time, some of the boys and I watched the Turkana skin and butcher a donkey, and we asked them what they were doing. They told us they were getting ready to eat the donkey. That gave us quite a shock, because all of a sudden we knew where the mystery meat had come from. After that, every time my group bought meat from the Turkana, we insisted on getting a piece with enough evidence to show where it had come from. If we bought a goat, we wanted an entire leg—with the cloven hoof attached. Once we worked out the rules of the exchange, we were grateful that those Turkana kept us fed.

There were other Turkana, however, who crept into camp at night and stole food. Bold raiders, armed with guns and wearing sharp, spiked bracelets on their upper arms, entered boys' huts after dark and took away as much food as they could carry. Turkana robbed three of the huts where I slept during the worst rainstorms with my roommates, who included my cousin Aleer and the Man Who Ate Beans. The Turkana raiders came to the door after dark and demanded whatever we had. Gunmen killed one of my friends, Deng, simply because he had no food to give them. Needless to say, I didn't wander outside at night, not even to walk between buildings. If the Turkana found me alone, they might shoot me too.

It's funny. Many outsiders looked at the refugees in Kakuma and took pity on us for how little we had. Others, including some of the Turkana, looked at us with jealousy for how much we had. The United Nations provided us with palm branches to thatch our huts and firewood to cook our dinner, as well as food rations.

UN food trucks arrived roughly every 16 days. Sometimes they came later, held up by bad weather on the roads or problems with donations not arriving on time. Each boy received six kilograms, or about 13 pounds, of food, typically dry maize kernels or wheat flour and a half cup of lentils. I easily held the ration, the size of three baseballs, in two hands. Every resident of Kakuma had to make the food last until the next delivery. I gathered the 12 boys from our group of huts and had everyone pool their maize. We put our collected rations in a Kenyan mill and paid a little money to have it ground into flour. Some of the boys had a little money, and we used it to buy sugar and salt to flavor our dinner.

As the caretaker-appointed leader of my group, I asked everyone what time of day they wanted to eat. It could only be once a day, I said, as we had to make the food stretch more than two weeks. We talked about it and settled on 10 a.m. After that, I decided which boy would cook on a particular day. I measured out one day's worth of cornmeal, and the cook of the day dropped it into a kettle of boiling water. When it became a liquidy yellow porridge, he added a little sugar and salt. Then we called the rest of the boys to eat. Each boy dipped his cup in the porridge and drank it. That was it for 24 hours. No meat, no milk—just enough food to keep us going for another day. Each morning dawned with our stomachs growling. We started classes around 8 a.m. and took a break for meals a couple of hours later. Then, back to our lessons until midafternoon.

Even with such careful rationing, the food never lasted long enough in the seasons when we could not grow and harvest our own vegetables, or when the trucks came late. We always ran out of corn after 12 to 14 days and had to fast until the next food truck arrived. We weren't the only ones. All over camp, the food ran out at about the same time. We called the time after eating our last rations the "black days." The phrase referred not to our sour mood but to the lack of light. Nobody kindled cooking fires at night, leaving the camp pitch-black.

I drank a lot of water to take the edge off my hunger and encouraged others to do the same. We also played games and shared stories about life in Pinyudu and on the road to Kakuma

*John Dau, second from right, drinks porridge with
his best friends after school in 1999.*

to distract each other. When we couldn't avoid talking about
our hunger, I told the boys in my circle, "Hunger does not know
nguik." That meant, our hunger might seem intolerable, but it
wouldn't kill us. Nguik is the spot on the cow where the butcher
thrusts his spear point for the kill. If hunger did not know where
to find that spot, it could not take our lives.

The UN trucks brought corn, oil, and bags of lentils to three
distribution centers at Kakuma. Once, in 1994, they brought
dates, the sweetest fruit of the desert. They unloaded the food in
huge buildings inside a fence.

We refugees queued up to get our rations. The camp caretakers issued everyone a food card, which looked something like a

driver's license. Each boy had to be responsible for getting his own food, but sometimes boys would loan me their cards, so I could pick up their rations along with my own and save them a trip to the distribution center. Each card had the numbers 1 through 12 printed along its edge. As I received my ration, a caretaker cut off the number corresponding to that particular distribution and pressed my finger in invisible ink. At the end of 192 days—16 days times 12 distributions—I got a new card. Some boys tried to cheat the system and go through the line twice with stolen cards, but their fingers glowed blue or purple when the invisible ink was exposed to ultraviolet light. The caretakers confiscated their stolen cards, and the Kenyans put them in jail.

Those were some of the rare times I saw the Kenyan police administering true justice. Most of the time, police officers abused the law to their own advantages. Camp policemen were Turkana. They sympathized with their fellow tribesmen, who raided our camp at night, and turned a deaf ear to our complaints. They got little pay and seldom had enough to eat themselves, so they shook down any Sudanese they caught during their patrols outside the camp. The Kenyan government declared that refugees could not leave the country, no doubt to promote civil relations with the Sudanese government, and tried to keep us from wandering outside Kakuma and making trouble with the natives.

I tried seven times to leave the camp and make my way back to Lokichokio. "Loki is good," my friends said. "You can get sponsors there, and you can get someone to take you into their home in Kenya." I had been living in Kakuma for a couple of years by that time. I wanted to get out of camp and into a real town, either in southern Sudan or with a sponsoring family in Kenya. The djellabas never took Nairus, in southern Sudan, and I would have loved to go there. Or maybe, I thought, I could join the SPLA or go looking for my family. All of those options seemed better than staying year after year in Kakuma. Twice, I actually made it into Lokichokio. I loitered there for a couple of days, trying to get news of the war and find a way to get over the border, but I never had any luck. The police caught me and took me back to Kakuma.

Kenyan police officers never seemed to help me and the other boys; they just wanted to rob us and get away with it. We were penniless and powerless people from another country. What good was our word against that of a native Kenyan?

My worst encounter with the police occurred in 1998, after I became secretary for an Episcopal church begun by a missionary in Kakuma. Everyone loved the missionary, Marc Nikkel, because he was so good to the Sudanese. Some of the youngest boys called every white man they saw "Mak," thinking his name had something to do with the color of his skin. Older boys called him Thon Akon, which means "bull elephant." He was a big man. While he was in America battling cancer, which claimed his life in 2000, refugees surrounded his residence at Kakuma to pray and lay hands on his bed, asking God to let him return from hospital to sleep once again in Kakuma. One of the good things he did was to raise money to build libraries at the camp. As church secretary, I was selected to take some of the money to Nairobi to buy books to fill the shelves. I received a government-issued, 30-day pass that allowed me to leave Kakuma so I could buy books and bring them back. I hired a taxicab to take me to Nairobi. Not far from Kakuma, the Turkana police halted the cab at a roadblock and arrested me. They told me my pass was no good, even though it clearly stated I was legally outside the camp on that day and could return at any time before the pass expired. I argued, but they seemed deaf to reason. "It would help if you would give us some money," they told me. I replied that I didn't have any money other than what I had to pay the taxi. They searched me and found 500 shillings I had been given to buy books for the library. They pulled my hair, punched me, and took the money. Then they threatened me with their guns. They said if I tried to make trouble for them, they would make even bigger trouble for me.

A friend of mine from camp had a similar experience. He had raised a rooster outside his hut, and when it grew big enough, he decided to take it to the town of Kakuma to sell it. One of the Turkana police spotted him carrying the bird and asked him what he was doing. "I'm going to Kakuma town to sell my rooster," he said.

"How much do you want for it?" the policeman asked.

"One hundred shillings," my friend said.

"I'll give you 50 for it right now," the officer said.

"No, thank you," said my friend, and he kept walking toward town.

The officer apparently met with some of the other police, and they plotted how to get the rooster from him. The boy hadn't walked very far before another police officer appeared and asked him what he was doing.

"I am going to sell this rooster," said my friend.

"You cannot do that!" said the officer. "It is a violation of our law!"

He grabbed the boy and took him to the town's police station. My friend told me later what happened when he got to the booking desk. A sergeant behind the desk asked the arresting officer about the charge, and the officer said the boy had been attempting to sell the national symbol of Kenya. The Kenyan presidential flag features a rooster, which also is the logo of the nation's main political party.

"Do you not know it is a crime in Kenya to sell a rooster?" the sergeant said. It was an obvious lie, and my friend refused to believe it. He protested, but the police threatened to jail him and make him pay a fine. The talk grew hotter and louder until another officer stepped into the room and played his part. He said he was the supervisor in the police station, and he expressed astonishment that anyone would try to sell a rooster. He threatened my friend but said he would issue a pardon on behalf of the Kenyan government upon surrender of the evidence. My friend left the rooster and returned home without a single shilling for his troubles.

No wonder the Dinka in camp tended to stick together. Kenyans picked on us, yet there was nothing we could do about it.

My group made sure to keep its Dinka ways. Like every other group, we maintained the nightly tradition of synagogue. We felt moved to show our love for God, following the suggestion of Episcopal priest John Machar Thon, and worshipped from six to eight every night. I worshiped with my group, number 36, which shared synagogue with group number 35. Together the two groups had as many as 600 to 800 worshippers in the congregation. We set up our worship space between our collections of huts and surrounded the space with a fence made from the branches of the achuil and a tree we called *kakuma,* just like the camp. At first we

Lost Boys perform a traditional dance on a Sunday in Kakuma.
Dancing kept spirits up and fostered a sense of community.

left the space empty, but we later added clay benches to make it more comfortable. We never added a roof. Looking up at a billion stars during the singing of hymns made us feel closer to God.

I supervised the synagogue where I worshipped. That meant I had to keep the list of preachers and remind those who signed up to show up on their designated days. I also conducted meetings and made sure we had tambourines and drums. If someone new wanted to preach, he auditioned for me. Preachers who made the cut usually isolated themselves and fasted before speaking in synagogue.

On Sundays I went to one of the big churches the missionaries built in Kakuma. Some of the boys reestablished the dances of cattle camp. We danced every Sunday night, and the boys sang songs they wrote to impress the few girls we knew. I sang a song I had written in Duk Payuel about a big bell:

Hi, people! Look at the guys who falsely claim they have a big bell
But fail to watch me as I play the superbig bell my father bought for me.
He is known as the Master of the Bell.
Once when he sold a bell, it brought us 12 cows
From which I still drink the milk.

SOME OF THE BOYS AND GIRLS IN CAMP GOT MARRIED. THEY couldn't have cattle exchanges as they would have in Sudan, but they carried out the negotiations on the promise of some-day making them good. Each side got a friend to record the negotiations, to make sure the proper exchanges took place, as promised, sometime in a happier future. Meanwhile, in the ab-sence of cattle, bridegrooms and their friends and families gave small gifts to the families of the brides. A few had managed to grow small plots of okra and sorghum using water from the community tap, and they sold their crops and gave the profits as part of the dowry. The system seemed to work. The new couples lived in the Dinka fashion, with the boy and girl going off to live near the boy's group of huts. A few of the wives got pregnant and gave birth. Everyone living nearby helped take care of the new families. Boys gave up part of their food ra-tions and gave them to the new couples, so they could have a feast for all of the in-laws. Girls brought their neighbors to live alongside them for a few weeks and help them during the biggest transition of their lives. We formed something like a Dinka village in the midst of poverty and hunger on the high plains of Kenya.

I thought about my own future. I saw no reason to get married right away. "Finish school, get a job, and then get a family," I told myself. I would wait until after I passed my

comprehensive high school exit exam before seriously thinking about getting married.

My first big challenge came in the form of the KCPE, the Kenya Certificate of Primary Education. In Kenya, primary school
is classes one through eight. I worked very hard through class
seven, then sat for a test to get into class eight. At the end of that
class, I would have to take the KCPE test and pass it if I wanted
to go on to high school.

The tests to progress to high school eliminated quite a few ap-
plicants. Teachers gave all of the preparatory lessons in English,
except for the class in Kiswahili, so I not only had to master new
subjects, but I also had to do so in a foreign language. The KCPE
covered mathematics, GHC, agriculture, the sciences, English,
Kiswahili, music, and arts and crafts. I learned faster than most,
and the teachers permitted me to skip classes five and six and go
directly to seven.

I knew I had to score a minimum of 350 out of 700 on what
they called the mock test at the end of class seven to be promot-
ed and continue my education. I watched my friends take the
test while I studied, and many of them cried when they got their
results. Not for joy either—a score below 350 meant the end of
the line for a refugee student, with no appeal.

The pressure felt tremendous. I had to pass the exam or all of
my studies would have been in vain.

Two missionary libraries finally had been built and stocked with
books, and I spent many hours reading there. My biggest problem
was getting inside. Most boys wanted to study just as hard as I
did, and long lines formed outside the library doors every day. The
librarians would not allow anyone to remove a book from the
building, so I had to wait in line for as long as two hours for people

on the inside to finish reading and make room for those outside to take their places. The caretakers and teachers set up a system to try to ease the crowding. They designated certain days for certain schools to use the libraries. I made a note of which days had been set aside for my school and jumped out of bed before dawn to get a spot near the head of the line. Even with the caretakers' system, hundreds of students had to queue up. From the inside, as I sat with my books, I could hear the rumbling of feet outside as the queue inched toward the door. I spent a lot of time hand-copying the library's books, so I could read them at my hut. There were no photocopy machines, and even if there had been, I would not have had the money to run them. So I sat and copied out 80-to-100-page books of agriculture, geography, history, and civics. I made my own miniature library, in my own handwriting.

I studied it all. In America, students ask the teachers, "Will this be on the test?" and they try to find out what part of the text-book they don't have to read. *Ha!* What a piece of cake that is. That is not school. That is not the way to get anywhere in life. In Africa, the teachers told me, "It's all on the test. You must study everything, cover to cover." To this day, when I study a book, I study it all. And I love the freedom of the American library. I can check out any book I want and take it home.

For an entire year I spent most of my free hours at the library or studying my hand-copied texts at home. I barely slept the night before the class seven test. My heart beat like a hammer, as I sweated out the multiple-choice answers. When the grades came back, I learned I had earned a mark of 365. I had passed, but barely.

I moved on to class eight. I studied at school as I always had, but afterward I learned and relearned the lessons in study groups

I had formed with my friends. We found an empty classroom and met there in the late afternoon. Each time we gathered, we picked a boy to act as teacher. He wrote the lessons on the blackboard and quizzed the other boys.

The first time my turn came, I gave a lesson in history, which was my favorite subject. I had a few pennies from doing jobs for the caretakers, and I bought some chalk to write the names and dates on the board. I started with the history of the Turkana district of Kenya then expanded to the history of the province, nation, and all of East Africa. I talked about the triangle trade, which sent American food and cotton to Europe, European manufactured goods to Africa, and black African slaves to the New World. I lectured on the Germans in Tanzania, the French in Chad, the Portuguese in Mozambique, and the British in Nigeria and Ghana. I explained how the British employed "indirect rule" through power-sharing arrangements with native peoples, while the French ruled through "assimilation," running things from the top down and requiring native peoples to act like Frenchmen. I talked very little about the history of Sudan because the lessons aimed to prepare boys to pass a Kenyan test. Still, I told what I had learned about the British experience in Sudan, including the killing of General Gordon at Khartoum at the hands of the Mahdi. I had read that on my own, outside the required textbooks. I shared what I had learned through my own inquiries about the history of the Nilotic tribes—the Dinka, Nuer, Shilluk, and other black people who live near the River Nile—as well as the histories of the other ethnic groups of Sudan.

I also taught CRE, Christian Religious Education. Kenyan schoolchildren were expected to know something of the history contained in the Bible. I taught the story of King David and his sons, particularly the treachery of Absalom, who tried to overthrow his father's throne and seize power himself. As with my history lesson, I gave a practice exam at the end of my talk. I marked the finished papers and explained why the students had made mistakes. Nobody had to smack hands anymore for bad marks; everyone had plenty of motivation to do well without facing the additional threat of corporal punishment.

As the day of the KCPE approached, I thought about how the exam would put me on equal footing with every other boy in Kenya. My identity had been reduced to a serial number on the top of the exam packet. Those who scored the test would not know whether I was Dinka, Turkana, Bantu, or anything else. My grade depended entirely on how well I knew the material. I, who had nothing, would compete with boys and girls who had grown up with the benefits of a well-financed education.

I went to the take the exam thinking I had something to prove, and I proved it. I scored 408, well above the minimum of 350. With that score, I could enter high school in Kakuma. If someone had sponsored me, I could have left the camp to attend high school elsewhere in Kenya. But that would have cost 17,000 shillings, roughly $250 per semester or $750 per year, a fortune for anyone at Kakuma.

I progressed through Kakuma secondary school, from 9th grade to 12th grade. Then once again I had to prepare for the big test that awaited me at the end, the Kenya Certificate of Secondary Education, or KCSE. Unlike the primary certificate exam, which consisted of a long series of multiple-choice questions, the KCSE required students to write essays and short answers to questions in about ten subjects. These included Kiswahili, math, history-civics, biology, chemistry, business education, and physics. I had the option to drop two more subjects and replace them with others, and I decided to study history and CRE instead of geography and social science.

I studied in the refugee school from early morning until 8 p.m. The building grew very hot in the middle of the day, and drops of sweat rolled down my nose and along my spine as I studied. I pushed my friends to study, too, during the entire year of 12th grade. We took our bedding to the school compound to live there all the time, returning to our huts only to eat. We slept on the ground outside the school, except when it rained. I woke up at 4 a.m. and walked around the schoolyard, beating on a piece of tin with a stick. *Boom! Boom! Bopbopbop!* "Get up! Get up! Time to study!" As always, I liked history the most. I didn't much care for chemistry. The school didn't have qualified teachers in that subject, so mostly I just memorized the periodic table. I loved biology very much, along with business education, which taught about buying and selling.

Palath Thonchar: *I met John at school in Kakuma. We started talking and struck up a friendship in our second year of high school. We talked all the time, especially during our free time and after classes. We liked to tell stories. We even found out we had been in a lot of the same places at the same time.*

John and I studied together a lot in our third year. We took most of the same classes, and we both passed the graduation test. That was something. We knew only the camp and could go no other places, but we were tested about the world.

On June 13, 2001, I flew to Rochester, New York. I still live there, and I see John, when I have time.

I sat for the KCSE in 2000 and passed. A high school diploma marks a man as successful and highly skilled in Kenya, and

I thought I might make a career of running an organization, or maybe become a politician or a teacher.

When the boys in my circle got our grades, we threw a party. We pooled our money and rented a tape recorder-radio and some Congolese dance music cassettes from a thriving rental business in camp, and we shelled out a little more money to buy batteries. We could have listened to the BBC news programs on the radio if we had wanted to, but we would have considered that a waste of our rental fee. We wanted to dance and have a good time at our KCSE party, and we did just that. We also had a real treat: Some girls came to the party, and we walked right up to them and asked them to dance with us. No elaborate negotiations beforehand, just asking and dancing. When a song came up that I liked, I picked out a girl and held her hand while we danced.

HAVING FINISHED HIGH SCHOOL, I MOVED UP TO A PAYING JOB. For three years I had served in a voluntary, unpaid position as chairman of the Community Based Rehabilitation Committee in Zone 3, supervising unpaid, voluntary representatives who reported to me about people needing physical or mental health care. Some of the boys in camp suffered vision and hearing impairments, had lost limbs, or needed wheelchairs. Some had become deranged from years of wandering, privation, and violence. All told, about 1,200 people—just under a quarter of the zone's population—needed special care. As chairman I reported to a person known as a trainer. He earned $20 a month supervising the zone chairmen and collecting reports, which he passed up the chain of command, first to the head of all camp rehabilitation committees and then on to the camp manager. I gladly advanced to the job of trainer and started getting paid regularly for the first time in my life.

While studying for the KCSE, I learned a bit about America. I read about the separation of powers in the American government, and about the two houses of Congress. I learned about the country's military power and how it had won two world wars and the 1991 Persian Gulf War. I read about the White House, and somebody told me that every President after the first one lived there. Somehow in my mind I pictured all of the Presidents living together at the same time. The White House must be very big, like a city, I thought. I also remember reading in one of my books about Onandaga Lake in New York State and how badly it had been polluted by industrial waste. Clearly, not everything about America was perfect.

My interest grew keener when representatives of Church World Services and other relief organizations began telling the caretakers that the American government had approved the relocation of some of the Kakuma refugees to the United States. The approval process could take up to three years, they said. The caretakers began preparing boys for the possibility of traveling overseas to a strange new country. Everyone had the same questions: When would this happen? And what was America really like?

Church World Services caseworkers got a list of the camp residents and opened files on all of them. They took my picture, placed it in my file, and scheduled me for an interview. My name, John Bul Dau, appeared on my file, my ration card, and on all other documents in camp. That was a bit of good luck. Most of the Dinka refugees who had changed their names according to the Dinka traditions of dowry and marriage had conflicting documents with two different names on them and were denied permission to go to the United States. During my stay in Kakuma, if I had decided to call myself Dhieu Deng Leek, the name that my father had chosen for me and which I would have assumed by tradition once his marriage dowry had been settled, I might have been one of those prevented from entering America.

The processing followed a pattern. The caseworker for Church World Services asked the refugee to write his or her life story. Then the caseworker would read the account and ask questions to try to verify it or catch the author in a lie.

Some of the questions seemed rude and stupid.

"Do you have children?" my caseworker asked me.

"No."

"Do you have a wife?"

Now, why did he ask that? In the Dinka culture, if I had children then I had a wife, and if I had a wife then I had children. I did not know that the two did not necessarily go together in America. That idea still takes some getting used to.

Then the interviewer went over my statement to look for inconsistencies. I kept saying the same things, over and over, because those were the things that happened—the nighttime raid on Duk Payuel, my flight with Abraham, and my years in Pinyudu, southern Sudan, and Kenya. I said I knew of no living members of my immediate family, which the interviewers had made a condition for entry into America. Boys who told a variety of stories—because they wanted to hide facts about their families or their service in the SPLA—got rejected.

Having passed the interview, I moved on to get a physical checkup. A medic checked my blood for the AIDS virus, but I was clean. He also looked for evidence of malaria, which I had suffered continually since childhood. He said that would not keep me out of America. The medic also checked for evidence of drug use. A few of the Somalis in camp chewed leaves of the *khat* shrub, the euphoric stimulant of choice in East Africa, but I did not. Khat cost a lot, and I had neither the money to buy it nor the desire to chew it. In fact, I never heard of any Dinka using khat.

After the medical checkup, I headed for the final step, an interview with representatives of the U.S. Immigration and Naturalization Service. They used very big English words I had never heard before. Fortunately, they had a Dinka translator, so I could understand. They told me what would be expected of me if I traveled to America. I would have to be self-sufficient after 90 days, meaning I would have to have a job to pay for an apartment, groceries, and utilities...whatever they were. At the end of the interview, they told me I would receive word about my application in about two months. A letter would come to the Kakuma camp post office.

News traveled swiftly to every corner of Kakuma when a new batch of letters arrived. Resettlement candidates ran to the post office. I ran, too. I looked for my letter but didn't see it in the mountain of mail. I pretended to be someone in charge and began sorting a pile of letters that somebody had dumped from a sack. I handed out letter after letter while furiously scanning the pile of envelopes for my name. Near the bottom I saw it: "John Bul Dau." I stopped pretending to be a postal worker and dropped everything to open my letter.

My eyes landed on four words: "You have been accepted."

"Guys," I told the boys gathered around me, "I've got to go. I can't help you anymore." Someone else would have to distribute the rest of the letters.

Accepted to the United States. I was very, very happy. I jumped and skipped as I ran home. I didn't know when I would go, or what city I would fly to, but I didn't care. I put the letter in a prominent place in my hut, so I could look at it again and again. Of course, the boys who received letters of refusal felt very sad. A few went crazy. Others had a bad case of sour grapes. They told me that when I got to America, I would not get a very good job. I would have to cook for my wife—an embarrassment to a Dinka man—or maybe get a job cleaning up dog poop.

That was May 2001. I figured I had a couple of months to prepare.

A short time later, I began cultural orientation class to learn about life in America. A woman from the U.S. came and talked. It was a free country, she told us, and you will love having the freedom to make choices about your life, choices you would not have in Africa. But she didn't spend much time talking about the basic laws. I don't think she even mentioned freedom of speech, religion, or the press. Instead, in one of her first lessons, she did a funny thing. She showed my class a telephone and demonstrated how to dial 9-1-1. She said, if you are in trouble in America, people will come to help you if you can remember those three digits and punch them into the phone. She showed pictures of someone falling and making a phone call, followed by the arrival of an ambulance. I hoped I would not need to use that piece of knowledge any time soon.

Then, she talked about employment. The American government required refugees to work, she said. Each of us would be expected to hold down a job. We would have to go to work each day, on time, and work hard in order to earn a paycheck. We would need a steady source of money to pay our rent, utility bill, medical insurance, and other things.

In a later class, a male teacher told us about cold weather. It is very cold in America compared with Sudan and Kenya, he said. You will need to wear a lot of clothes, especially in winter. Then he said, "I will show you how cold it gets in America." He reached into a box and pulled out something that looked like a piece of glass, only rounded like a river rock.

"Feel this," he said, and he placed it in my hand. It felt so cold, yet it seemed to burn.

"Crush it," he said.

I tried to close my hand, but I could not crush it.

"That is water. It gets so cold in America that water sometimes turns hard. We call this an 'ice cube.' Feel it, and feel the cold in America."

I was amazed. How could people live in a land where water turned to stone?

The teachers taught us many practical things. They told us to be careful about crime in America, because there were people, especially in the big cities, who would try to rob us. They told us not to hold hands with our male friends when we walked in America, as we had all our lives in Africa, because people would think we were gay. I had to ask what "gay" meant.

The teachers told us many good things. No Muslims will try to kill you there, they said. You will be able to buy your own car and have your own apartment. You will have plenty to eat. Best of all, Americans valued education. Young boys and girls had to go to school; older boys and girls could choose to attend one of thousands of colleges or universities.

The teachers gave me a small, spiral-bound book titled *Welcome to the United States: A Guidebook for Refugees*. The introduction filled me with hope. In part, it said: "As a refugee, you may have lost everything, but in the United States you are offered a chance to start over and rebuild your life. Starting over may not be easy, but it can be done. Over a million refugees have come before you, and most have done well. You can succeed also. You bring the gifts of your special talents, your background and culture, and your courage."

The book offered advice from former refugees. It included the desirability of keeping an open mind, learning and speaking English, understanding American culture, and focusing on "how far you have come, not how far you have to go." It went on to talk about the importance of education: "In the United States, education is accessible to everyone, regardless of a person's age, race, religion or social class.... Most Americans view education as a way to qualify for more satisfying jobs and improve their standard of living."

IT SEEMED TOO GOOD TO BE TRUE, AND SOME OF THE REFUGEES decided it was just that. We talked about America every night after cultural orientation class. Somebody said it was okay to be lazy in America, and if you agreed to wear a green card on a string around your neck, you could eat free anywhere, any time. That horrified us because no self-respecting Dinka would disgrace his family's name through such voluntary abasement. Another boy said Americans killed black men all the time, without any reason or warning, so we would have to be constantly on our guard. Somebody else said the American military had the most guns and bombs in the world, and it could wipe out the entire planet in a minute if the President decided to do so. One boy said that American girls asked boys to go with them, and if the boys refused, the girls would see to it they never got another job. But if the boys gave in and married an American girl, they could never return to Africa, not even to visit.

Seeds of doubt began to be planted throughout the camp. I heard people saying maybe America wasn't such a good place after all. Others felt guilty about agreeing to leave Africa. Their elders had told them that if they went to America, they would never return to their homeland. Such thoughts weighed heavily on the minds of young Dinka men shaped by a culture that valued respect for family above all things.

An uncle on my mother's side, Bul, was one of those who had second thoughts. He had been accepted into America and booked on a flight. When the plane came, he ran and hid. My friends and I knew where he had hidden himself and told the Kenyan police where to find him. They dragged him, crying and screaming, and put him on the plane. Today he lives in Florida and says God has been good to him. He gives thanks we forced him to go.

The eldest refugees in Kakuma helped prepare me for America by reminding me of my Dinka heritage. We considered anyone married or a parent to be an elder. A few of them even had gray or white hair, making them like grandparents to the thousands of children in camp. They organized going-away parties for me and the other lucky ones. The men collected money and bought goats, and the women brewed millet wine in the Sudanese fashion.

At my send-off, several boys sat in a circle at the feet of the elders. A man with gray streaks in his hair carried a bucket of millet wine into the circle and put it on the ground. He made some brief remarks about the reason for the gathering then sat down. Someone pulled out a cup, and the elders started drinking while the young Dinkas, who didn't drink alcohol, watched. Plugs of tobacco appeared from shirt pockets and handkerchiefs, and smoke added to the atmosphere of silence and respect.

The elders began singing a song in the Dinka manner, having composed the lyrics and tune just for the occasion. You are going to a different world, they sang. You must have courage, just as if you were going to war. You must conduct yourself as a Dinka and remember your clan. You must find and marry a Dinka girl. You must come back to Africa for the wedding or send money to have a proper contract.

After the song, the male elders told us more stories about America and how different it would be from anything we had ever seen. They told us not to fear, for we would succeed as long as we remembered who we were.

"Some people say America is a place where you don't have to work," an old man said. "You go to a hotel, and in front of you are a lot of numbers, and you order your food by pushing a button next to the number. America is a place where you live in tall buildings. The higher you live in the building, the more important and rich you are. If you live in such a building, on the tenth floor, don't forget us just because you have become a wealthy man."

Another elder spoke up and said, "I heard something different. I heard America is a place where you have to work so, so hard. And the work is simple and repetitive."

And a third added, "This is true. It is so easy to be lazy in America. Don't be a lazy person. You would be letting down your tribe. Do not bring a bad name to the Dinka."

A fourth said, "America is so powerful. When you go there, learn how it became the most powerful nation in the world. Go to school; if you want, you can join the military. Learn about power so you can come back and teach us. You can come back to be governor and deliver us from the Arabs."

A fifth said, "Be a mechanic. Bring cars to Africa. Or be a pilot. The Arabs are pilots, and we should have pilots, too. That would be good. Relatives would boast, 'We have a pilot in our village.' Then we will bomb the Arabs and see how they like it."

If the messages had one theme, it was that going to America would not cut the cords of memory that connected us to our homeland. The elders urged us to help southern Sudan and its scattered peoples.

Then came the women's turn to speak. While the older ones talked, the younger ones kept an eye on the goat roasting over an open fire, out of sight from where we sat.

"You are my son," an old woman said to each boy in the circle. It was not literally true, but it got our attention. We knew she would give us the same advice our own mothers would have provided, if they had been there in the circle.

"Don't marry an American wife," she said. "They will not know how to respect the Dinka ways. If you bring an American wife here, I will run from you." We laughed. Running away is a bad thing for a Dinka.

The old woman continued: "We hear that in the United States, you don't know your brother, you don't know your cousin. You forget your family, and you will not send us money here. We have heard from those who have gone to America before you, and they have taken their money and bought fancy cars and put their money in the bank. They are not sending money back; they are not good Dinka."

Everyone nodded. I did too even though I did not know what a bank was. I thought it might be a place where you put extra money after you ran out of room to store cash in your house or in your pockets. In my mind, I saw rooms so full of money that the owners had to go to a new building, a bank, to stockpile whatever wouldn't fit.

The party went on for five hours. Every elder had the chance to speak and ask questions. A boy finishing his last classes in high school told the elders he did not need to go to classes anymore, because he had been accepted into America and had begun attending cultural orientation. One elder, a teacher, replied, "There has never been a better place than this for you to learn. You must continue to go to school here, before you go to America." It violated the Dinka way of life to refuse education, even when more education lay on the horizon. At the end of the party there was plenty of goat meat to go around, and I took some home to my hut.

Not long afterward, I was working with some of the disabled refugees when word came that a new set of names had been posted for flights to the United States. I grabbed a bicycle and I told one of my co-workers, "Let's go see whose name is out." I deliberately did not say anything about wanting to look for *my* name because I thought that might jinx it. My co-worker got his bike and we rode to the outpost of the Joint Voluntary Agency, the refugee-processing organization run by Church World Services in conjunction with the U.S. government.

A crowd of boys had gathered around an outdoor bulletin board. They scanned the list and leaped for joy when they saw their names or the name of friends. I wanted to get closer, so I could look for my name, but the crush of bodies kept me

Kakuma residents scan a bulletin board in August 2001 for the names of those accepted into the U.S. John Dau found his name on the list that day.

too far away. I saw a white man holding a big camera on his shoulder, a second man, darker skinned and carrying a small camera, and a third white man who looked as if he might be in charge. The first man filmed while the white man in charge asked questions of some of the boys standing in front of the board. The second man, the one with the darker skin, made me wonder. I didn't think he was black, because his skin wasn't nearly as dark as mine. And I couldn't tell his race from his hair, because he had shaved his head. I know now that most black American aren't literally "black," and that this camera-man was "African-American."

I circled around the back of the board and moved in sideways, pushing like the others to get closer. A few boys left, and finally I could look for my name.

I found it in a group of five on a piece of paper stuck to the board. The Immigration and Naturalization Service had accepted three in my group and rejected two. I was one of the lucky ones. Next to my name, the paper said, "Syracuse, N.Y." Andrew Ruach and Jacob Majok would go with me, and we would leave in one week.

Syracuse. I did not know how to pronounce it. "Sir-cuss," maybe. I knew something about New York, including its abbreviation. That had been in a booklet I had read at cultural orientation.

I told the boys around me, "There is my name!" I was so happy to be going to New York.

I turned to the white men. I thought they might be with the American government, and I wanted to talk to them.

"Hey, you," I said. "How are you?"

The white man who seemed to be in charge turned to me and introduced himself as Christopher Quinn. I kept talking, thinking he represented the INS.

"I am John Dau, and I am going to New York. Can you tell me why some guys are going to America and some are not? Will you come back and get them? Doesn't America know how bad the situation is here?"

The man replied, "I don't know. I am a journalist. I could try to talk to the government, but . . ."

At that point, when I realized he could not help the boys who had been denied entry to the United States, I started to make my apologies and leave. That's when Christopher said, "Wait. Can you answer our questions?" I agreed, and they interviewed me on camera about going to America. I answered everything they asked, and when I turned to go home, I let them follow me. They took pictures of my hut and my friends. They said they were making a documentary film to show in America. I figured talking to them could do no harm, and it might help spread news of the plight of the refugees of southern Sudan to an audience who could help us.

Over the next week, as I prepared to board the plane to America, Christopher and his film crew returned to my hut to shoot film and do interviews. One time they asked to be introduced to the funniest guy in my circle. I told them to talk to my friend Goi. He said some goofy things for the camera, and we all laughed.

The night before I was scheduled to leave Kakuma, my friends and I had a celebration amid our huts. We bought a lot of Dinka wine and good food. We sat around after dark, drinking the wine and singing songs. One of my best friends, Leek Gak, said, "John, let's sing our song."

As we sang it, everyone cried. We had made up a song about a saying among my people, "A human being can never be eaten." The song means the test of a man lies in the good or bad things he does, not in his physical body. A man who brings help to his community proves his worth. We sang other songs, too, all through the night, and told stories about our lives in Pinyudu and Pochala. Everyone in that circle of a dozen people told how they fled from violence and ended up in Kakuma. When we got to America, we said, violence would no longer find us. That was the morning of August 5, 2001.

I had to be at the section of the UN compound in Kakuma set aside for Americans by 8 a.m. I left my hut at daybreak. I wore blue jeans and a button-down shirt. In a little bag I had stowed a few photographs, some official documents, and 14 cassette recordings of the elders' advice from the big party where we roasted the goat. I had no tape player, but I figured I could get one in America. My pockets were completely empty; I did not even have a dime. I used my last money to buy the cassettes and make small gifts to my friends.

As I started to walk, people in my group formed a thick wall around me, and I could not go anywhere. They were my friends, come to say good-bye. "Go with peace," they said, and they reached out to hug me. The crowd was so dense I could not get through, and I felt afraid I might miss my plane. One of the elders grabbed my hand and pulled. "Let him go," he told the crowd, and he cleared a space for me. It took about an hour for me to say all of my good-byes and work myself free. All the time, people cried. I cried.

I continued by foot to the door of the U.S. compound. A small group had congregated there, waiting to get in. A security guard opened the door and directed everyone inside. I sat down and someone handed me a cup of sweet milk tea. I surrendered my ration card to be canceled. Now I felt completely on my own.

Our airplane arrived a few hours later, at midday. Several UN cars pulled up to the compound. I climbed into a car and folded my body to fit in the middle of the back seat. Five more passengers and the driver jammed in. The back of my head pushed against the ceiling, forcing my chin down. I looked at the floor, where I had stowed my bag. Drops of sweat rolled off my face and plinked next to my sandals. My legs were so long I could not point my knees straight ahead but rather pushed them to the side. It was quite uncomfortable and a little scary. Fortunately, the drive to the airstrip did not take long.

The car stopped, and I got out next to the plane. It was smaller than the planes that dropped food during our walk from Ethiopia to Kenya. A cool breeze stirred the airfield and dried the moisture on my forehead. Far away I saw a barbed-wire fence and rows of black faces, four or five deep, lining the other side. They were too far away to see faces, but they waved. I waved back. I recognized a couple of people by the color and pattern of their shirts.

The officials at the compound called our names and put us in a line. They asked us to show our approval letters and certificates, which we had been given at cultural orientation. The documents had our pictures at the top of the first page. A man walked down the line, and when he came to me he checked to see that my face matched the picture on the paper.

The line moved forward. I stepped onto the open door hanging down at the tail of the plane and turned to look at Kakuma. This might be the last time I would see my African friends, I thought. I waved one last time, turned, and walked into the plane.

I HAD NEVER BEEN IN A PLANE BEFORE. I PICKED OUT A WINDOW seat on the right side near the front and sat down. One of the crew showed me how to buckle. I heard belts clicking all around me and nervous chatter, but I said nothing. The space felt hot and confining. Again I had to sit sideways, my knees to one side, in order to fit. I rapped, *ting-ting,* with my knuckles on the interior walls. How could anything made of metal get off the ground? And would it go *bump* when it hit a cloud?

The noise in the cabin grew louder. The tail closed slowly with a whine, and the propellers started to turn as the engines warmed up. Clouds of reddish dust, the same that greeted me when I first came to Kakuma, rose all around. The plane began to move forward, slowly gathering speed. With a strange *whooshing* feeling in my stomach, the plane lifted off the ground. We banked to the right,

*John Dau waves good-bye to his Kakuma friends after entering the
UN compound to await his flight. A security guard closes the gate.*

and I looked out my window at the ground directly beneath me. I
felt weightless and scared and exhilarated, all at the same time. We
rose into the blue sky of a clear and sunny day and headed for Nairobi. Despite the bumps, as the plane jumped up and down in the
air, I fell asleep. I had been up all night.

At the Nairobi airport, I got out of the plane and onto one
of two buses. We drove to the GOAL Accommodation Center in Nairobi. GOAL, an international relief agency, served the
poorest of the poor and aimed to relieve suffering. The agency's
service to us included meals of bread and soup, nights spent in
dormitory bunk beds stacked three high, and lessons in hygiene
and dealing with long-distance flights. The orientation instruc-
tors told us we would fly to Belgium. I couldn't wait to see it and
the people who had colonized the Belgian Congo, which I had

read about at Kakuma. They told us somebody would meet us in Brussels and split us into flights going to American cities. If we could not find our connecting flight, we were told to ask directions. Everyone would be helpful, they said.

They gave us medicine for malaria. It was very powerful. I swallowed the tablets and felt very sick.

They also handed out a sort of uniform. Everyone got a new pair of pants and a T-shirt printed with the letters UNHCR. We also got soft brown shoes. I put my old clothes in my bag. After we had all put on our new clothes, we returned to our rooms. I found the bathroom and threw up. I think it was a reaction to the malaria medicine, but also I might have been stressed from excitement.

I spent two more days at the GOAL office waiting for my plane. I talked with the other boys about America, and we shared more of our hopes and concerns. In addition, an American woman who had served as a Catholic relief worker in Kenya for many years came to give us final words of advice. She said her name was Sister Maureen.

"When you get to America, don't send money to Africa," she said. "Make sure you take care of yourself first." The moment she said that, I remembered the words of the elders in Kakuma: Americans do not act as if they have extended families; they only watch out for themselves. Their words already seemed to be coming true, and we had not even left Nairobi.

She also said life would take some getting used to in America. Women and men were equal there, she said, and it was against the law to beat a wife or child. Crime would be a problem in America beyond anything we knew in Sudan, she said.

"Sister Maureen," I said, "I am going to New York. What advice can you give me?"

She said, "Well, you are tall. You will do very well in New York. It is a very busy place, and you will have an advantage there. Because you are tall, you can move very fast. People move very fast in New York."

A boy asked another question, not looking Sister Maureen in the face as he spoke. She ignored the question. "You can't do that in America! Look me in the eye when you talk to me," she said.

IT CAME TIME TO GO TO OUR PLANE. ABOUT 50 OF US GOT ON the buses and rode to Jomo Kenyatta International Airport. I still felt nauseated and cold from the malaria medicine and feared I might throw up at any moment. We formed a line and worked our way through the check-in. While I stood in line, I became aware of people staring at us. We were all very tall, very black, and dressed alike.

"Is that a basketball team?" I heard someone say.

"No," a man replied. "Those are the 'Lost Boys.'"

The what? I had never heard that term before. What did that mean? Nobody explained it to me, but over the next few days and weeks I kept hearing it again and again. Years passed before I learned that Western journalists and aid workers in Africa had named us after the boys in *Peter Pan* who had no families and who never grew up.

Our guides kept us together until our plane arrived at Kenyatta in the middle of the night. They told us to board the plane and to be sure we had our special envelopes. During cultural orientation, the teachers handed us envelopes containing our immigration papers. They told us never to lose them or open them, because if we did we would not be allowed into America. I checked to see that I still had the envelope and got on the plane.

The airline was KLM, Dutch. I sat in a middle seat, next to a white woman heading to America. The flight attendants gave us many instructions, more than I could digest. Screens popped down from overhead and showed moving pictures. The attendants showed me how to plug in my earphones if I wanted to listen to music.

The plane pushed back from the gate and taxied down the runway. It was much bigger than the plane from Kakuma, and it rose smoothly into the air. After a while, a voice seemed to come from everywhere at once, telling us we could get up and move around if we wanted to. One of the attendants demonstrated how to work the bathroom door. When you are inside, she said, just push the latch closed until it says "occupied." That will lock the door and let people know you are inside. One of the Lost Boys must not have understood. When somebody else pulled on the door to use the bathroom, there he was, sitting on the toilet.

Christopher Quinn and his crew also were on the flight. They worked all day taking pictures. I wondered why they never seemed to get tired.

I knew the plane would have to cross over Sudan on its way to Belgium, and I wondered whether the djellabas would try to shoot it down. If I made it safely out of Africa, I thought, they would never be able to shoot at me again.

The attendants began going down the aisle with food. In our cultural orientation class, the teacher said that if we were ever asked to order food but did not know the menu, we should just ask for chicken or beef. I asked for chicken. It came on a little tray, covered in plastic. The white woman in the next seat looked at me and noted how I struggled with the food. She showed me how to pull down the back of the seat ahead of me and remove the dinner's plastic cover. The food came with a knife and fork, which I had never used before. All I knew was the spoon, and it was no use on the chicken. I picked it up with my fingers to eat. There were other things on my plate, but I did not know what they were so I did not eat them. Something green and leafy. Something green and bumpy. Boy, I did not like the look of them. Other boys opened their mayonnaise packages and licked the contents, but I did not. I had no idea what that white stuff was.

I tried the brown drink in my glass. The attendant said it was tea, but it tasted so bitter, not like African tea at all. I put the glass down. The woman beside me asked if I needed sugar, and I said yes. That made it taste much better.

The chicken nearly burned my tongue. Strangely, I could see no cooking fire on the plane. I may have learned the word "microwave" during secondary school, but I had no idea how it worked or what it did.

I fell asleep for a few hours. When I woke up, the plane was over Europe. We touched down at about 6 a.m. in Brussels. The Lost Boys filed off the plane and entered the terminal. People standing around saw us emerge from the Jetway and started clapping and cheering. I guess they knew who we were. I ate a sandwich and waited for my plane to America. I looked outside and had a notion of what the triangle trade really meant. Goods from America came to Europe, and then goods moved from Europe to Africa, but everything depended on Western civilization first importing enough African slaves to do the dirty work. Look at all those buildings, I thought. These guys are rich partly because they stole people from my part of the world.

I had finished only my second flight, yet already I was becoming accustomed to the routine of flying. I boarded a plane bound for JFK Airport in New York City, found my seat, and buckled myself in like a veteran of the air. Soon the plane left the land behind and soared over the Atlantic Ocean. I had heard in school that it was a big body of water, but I had never imagined how big it was, or what a thrill I found in looking out the window and seeing nothing but water in every direction. I remembered my lessons about aquatic life and about American submarines patrolling, invisibly, somewhere beneath me.

I felt tired when the plane landed at JFK. It was about 2 p.m. on August 9. The airport hummed with so much activity, so many people moving so fast in so many directions. My first look at Americans in America, I thought. What do they look like? So many of them were short by Dinka standards, and they walked like crazy, almost as if they were running. They seemed to all be in a hurry. The woman behind the immigration desk asked for papers by saying, "Next." That was all she said. "Next. Next. Next." I gave her my precious, sealed envelope. She opened it and looked it over. She signed my name to some document and gave me more papers. Then she motioned me through, very fast. "Next," she said.

I had questions about how to find the waiting area. Sometimes, busy Americans didn't even speak to answer. They just pointed. *Point. Point. Point.*

I came to the waiting area by the baggage claim. Andrew and Jacob joined me. Nobody said a word. We were hungry and tired, and I still felt sick from the malaria medicine. After a while, a tall, white man walked by, calling names. "Dau, Dau," he said. I did not recognize it as my name because I am supposed to be called John. He kept calling the name, and it finally dawned on me. I stood up and introduced myself. He took me and the other two boys to a van outside, and we got in. Then he did a very strange thing: He got behind the wheel. In Africa, a white man never drove a car—or, at least, I had never seen a white man drive. That was the job of a poor man, a black man. But here he was, white and driving us. He took us to LaGuardia Airport and showed us where to wait for our plane.

At LaGuardia I had to urinate. I asked somebody where I could do that. He did not understand me. I tried again. "Where is the latrine?" I asked. He still did not understand, but a man standing next to him said, "He wants the bathroom." They showed me where to go.

I walked into the men's room at LaGuardia and saw the toilets and fancy sinks. I had seen pictures of them at orientation, but they still seemed strange. I had watched a lesson on how to work a toilet, and I used it without incident. But the sink was another matter. It had no faucets. I needed to wash my hands, but the sink had no handles. I tried gripping parts of the porcelain and steel to see if the sink had a hidden lever. Without warning, when I moved my hands in front of the tap, the water came on by itself. This is a magic country, I thought, and white people— that's how I thought of Americans—are so cunning. They make things easy for themselves; they make things work for them. I wondered if that made it tempting to be lazy.

A very small plane arrived at the gate to take Jacob, Andrew, and me to Syracuse. It was a short flight, right at sunset, and we never got very high off the ground. I looked out the window and saw rivers and oceans of light below me. I didn't believe there could be that much electricity in one place, so I figured the country must be full of forests, and all of them on fire. It almost looked like a picture I saw in a book in Kenya: lava flowing in streaks from the mouth of a volcano. I did not realize until after I landed that, yes, American cities burned with artificial fires that never consumed them.

I got off the plane and made my way through the terminal toward the baggage claim area. I had no bags, but that was where I was told I would meet the people who would take me into town.

I stepped into a brightly lit room and spotted three former Lost Boys, now Sudanese Americans, who had come to greet me. They were with some white people, including a woman and her son. They stood a short distance away, more reserved than Africans, as another white woman walked up to me and said, "Are you John? Oh, John, I was waiting for you."

I said hello, and she hugged me. It was like a signal to the others, and they all crowded around to shake my hand and pat me on the shoulder. They did the same with Jacob and Andrew.

"Welcome," said the woman who first greeted me, and everyone joined in.

Welcome to Syracuse. Welcome to America. Welcome.

5

THE U.S. STATE DEPARTMENT DECIDED IN 1999 TO BEGIN *allowing refugees from the Sudanese civil war to immigrate, making America the only nation to accept Sudanese children from the camps. The United Nations High Commissioner for Refugees endorsed the decision, having determined that parentless children uprooted by war could not be safely repatriated to Sudan. Interviewers working for social service agencies and the UNHCR determined who got to go to America and who didn't. They sometimes decided that refugees with relatives in Africa would best be served by not resettling in America. About 3,600 Sudanese refugees from Kakuma, all males except for 100 females, made the final cut. Of the total approved for resettlement, those younger than 18 numbered 500, making them the largest group of unaccompanied children ever resettled in America.*

Various social service agencies, often affiliated with churches, worked with the American government to place these children in foster homes throughout the U.S. The Office of Refugee Resettlement, a part of the State Department, oversaw the adults, resettling 3,100 refugees in American apartments and providing initial cash payments for rent, utilities, and other necessities.

From left, Jacob Majok, John Dau, and Andrew Ruach
arrive at the Syracuse airport in August 2001.

Ten volunteer agencies worked with the federal office to ease the adults' transition to an independent lifestyle. Resettlement of the Lost Boys halted after the terrorist attacks of September 11, 2001, when America set a tougher watch on its borders and reduced by two-thirds the number of immigrants it accepted from all over the world.

Sudanese approved for resettlement dreamed of getting an American education. Julianne Duncan, a Catholic Conference worker who spent a year interviewing refugees in Kakuma to assess their chances of success in America, said children who placed their hopes in a Western-style education exhibited a healthy response to the trauma that had plagued them for so many years. "Because they could see a way forward for themselves, they didn't lose hope," she said.

ONE OF THE FIRST THINGS I LEARNED IN SYRACUSE STUNNED ME: America was such a rich country that nearly everyone owned a car.

My caseworker's name was Brandy Blackman. She drove to Syracuse's Hancock International Airport to welcome Jacob, Andrew, and me at the baggage claim area, and she brought along three Lost Boys—Kur Achiek, Matiop Kuol, and Ajak Bol. They had immigrated before me and were there to help with questions and to make the transition from Africa to America a little smoother. Susan Meyer and others from our sponsoring church, First Presbyterian of Skaneateles, New York, also greeted us as we emerged from the terminal corridors into the public reception area. I greeted the Lost Boys in Dinka, and we talked a bit as we walked toward the parking lot. There was no need to wait at the baggage claim conveyor belt. We had traveled halfway around the world without any checked luggage. We wore or carried everything we owned.

Susan Meyer: *One of the things that surprised me at the airport was that when John and the others came off the plane, I expected them to look confused, lost, or frightened. And they were none of those things. When I step off a plane in a foreign city, I stop, look around, and try to get my bearings. They walked off, went right past us—we were holding signs—and looked as if they would have kept on walking. We practically had to go up to them and say, "Hi, you must be the Sudanese guys."*

When we got to the parking lot, Brandy took us to her car. I asked Kur, one of the Dinka who greeted us, whether the car belonged to Brandy's company. He told me no, she owned the car all by herself. Two shocks: that a woman would drive, which I had never seen in Africa, and that she personally owned the car.

"John, you come with me," Brandy said. Andrew and Jacob got in Susan's car, and the Lost Boys who greeted us divided themselves between the two vehicles. I got in the passenger side of the front seat. When Kur and Brandy told me to buckle my seat belt, I watched Brandy closely as she pulled a strap and clicked two halves of a metal clasp together. I imitated everything she did, nervously buckling and adjusting my seat belt. Brandy asked how I felt, and I mumbled something. She said something else after that, but I couldn't understand it. Her voice floated high and soft into my ears, and I couldn't make out the words. I didn't want to ask her to repeat herself, because that would be rude, so I kept quiet. She kept asking questions, and I finally made out the word "tired." Yes, I told her, I was very tired, and the malaria medicine I had swallowed in Kenya still made me feel nauseated and feverish.

I remember every detail of the ride into town that night. I had never seen a highway like the one we took from the airport south toward Syracuse. I had only seen city streets in Kenya, bumpy with potholes that jolted cars and slowed the patterns of traffic. And southern Sudan had only dirt paths between the villages. They looked nothing like the wide, velvet black ribbons that curled and ducked and flowed as far as I could see, unbroken by intersections and policemen directing traffic, yet flanked by giant advertisements for stores and restaurants. As we zoomed along—oddly, in the right lane—I tried to comprehend everything. Green signs with white letters, zipping by the windows at incredible speed. Cars approaching and overtaking us from behind, their headlights like twin shafts of fire, their drivers making slight adjustments to the steering and brakes as if doing so automatically, without thinking. Lights blinking on an ambulance as it roared past our car toward the city. Twinkling lights in the distance, apparently the cooking fires of a hundred thousand homes. Lights overhead, too, blinking red as airplanes descended toward the airport. In cultural orientation, the teachers had said America was crowded with traffic, even in the air.

It was all overwhelming and confusing. I concluded that Syracuse must be a big, fast village, and it would take a long time to figure everything out.

The lights along Interstate 81—how could anyone explain them? Why did Americans put up lights in the middle of nowhere, where nobody lived, when cars had their own headlights? It seemed so wasteful. Americans must be wealthy, since they could spend so much, so freely, to light the empty darkness. The highway signs seemed extravagant, too. What good were such signs to the many people who could not read? As many as nine in ten people in Kakuma could not read such signs. As with car ownership, the extent of literacy in America was something I did not yet comprehend.

We passed under Interstate 90, with Susan's car behind us. Our road passed under a bridge that carried traffic of its own. It frightened me, looking up and seeing cars *above* us. Brandy and the Lost Boys asked me a few more questions, but I said little in response. I kept thinking, "Oh, man. This is a lot to see."

As we got close to downtown, I saw the lights of high-rise office buildings. I hoped Brandy would turn off the highway and that I would be living in one of those. The elders in Kakuma had told me that Americans preferred to live in tall buildings, as a sign of their wealth and power. But she passed the edge of Onandaga Lake and kept moving east. Downtown disappeared in the rearview mirror. The buildings got shorter and shorter the farther we drove. Oh, great, I thought. I will live in the smallest building in town, and people will treat me as if I were nothing. Brandy pulled up to a stoplight and turned left. I looked around and tried to remember how we had gotten here from the airport. So many turns. I wondered if I could ever learn my way around. If not, I would be in trouble if things didn't work out in Syracuse and I tried to run away. I asked about the stoplight; I had not seen one before, and I wondered what the yellow light meant. Major intersections in Kenya had policemen on hand to direct traffic, and, of course, we had no such intersections in southern Sudan.

It was a warm August night. A few people stood along Teall Avenue and by the highway off-ramp. One man held a sign identifying himself as homeless and asking for help. I had seen street people in Kenya but never in southern Sudan. In my homeland, nobody could ever be homeless, because even strangers could find a haven in Sudanese homes. Dinka like to have people living with them, to have the companionship and to live the gospel. In the Bible, Jesus says, "I was a stranger and you took me in; I was naked and you clothed me." The Dinka literally believe that those who perform such actions for the least of God's people do so for Christ.

At last, we turned into a collection of two-story brick buildings set amid green lawns and broad, leafy maple trees. The cars pulled into a parking lot, and we stopped. Andrew, Jacob, and I split up to spend our first night in the apartments of the Lost Boys who greeted us at the airport. It was getting late, and we promised to see each other in the morning. I slept that night in the apartment where a Lost Boy named Majer Anyang lived. He and I recognized each other from Kakuma, but we hadn't really known each other there. He had come to America in 2000. We made small talk in Dinka about life in Kakuma and in New York. We ate a little bit then fell asleep. The window air conditioner blew all night, but it did little to relieve the heat in the apartment.

THE NEXT MORNING, MY FIRST FULL DAY IN THE U.S., I GOT A lesson in American wealth and hospitality.

Jacob, Andrew, and I got our own apartment at the Grant Village complex, where the other Lost Boys lived. We knew we would have our rent, utilities, and food provided for us for 90 days, and then we would have to be self-sufficient. Volunteers from the First Presbyterian Church in Skaneateles showed up early in the morning. They backed a truck up to my new apartment and unloaded beds, chairs, towels, utensils—everything they thought we might need to live comfortably in Syracuse. Then they showed us how things worked. They took us around the apartment, flipping light switches to demonstrate how to turn on the lamps, opening the oven and twisting knobs to show us how to cook without fire, and taking us into the bathroom to twist the knobs in the shower. Water from overhead—delightful!

Susan Meyer: *At one point I was in the bathroom with the three guys, and I showed them how to turn on the faucet in the bathtub and then how to press the button to start the shower. Every one of them made this openmouthed look at the water from the showerhead, and they laughed and laughed. Each of them had to have a turn, turning on the faucet in the tub and then starting the shower. And they laughed again when the water came down. The vacuum cleaner was a wonder. We showed them how to use it. I think they couldn't figure it out. They looked at me as if to say, "And the purpose of this is...?"*

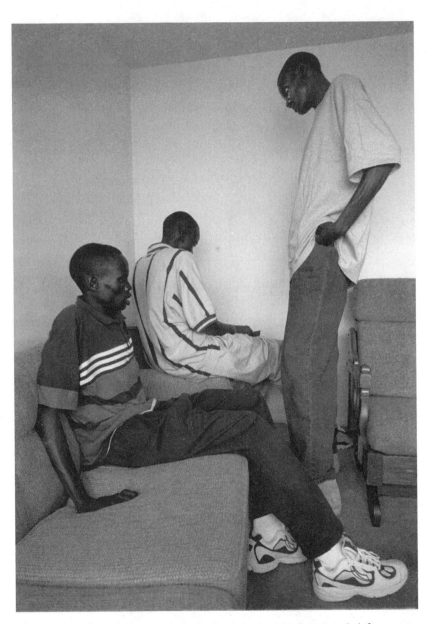

After arriving in Syracuse, John Dau, standing, Andrew Ruach, left, and Jacob Majok learn it takes time to adjust to apartment life.

The three of us helped unload the furniture. We discovered that the beds were too short for me if I lay straight on them, but if I stretched out diagonally I could fit. After three hours of unloading and arranging furniture, they told us they would buy us lunch. One of the women dialed the phone and ordered pizza. That was my first American food. I took one slice and tried to figure out how to eat it. I grabbed a knife and started to cut it into little pieces until Stephen, Susan's 14-year-old son, showed me what to do. You hold the triangle at the wide end, he said, and put the narrow part in your mouth.

After that, some of the volunteers left. Susan and Stephen Meyer and Penny Allyn from the Skaneateles church stayed. They announced they wanted to take us grocery shopping at Shop City. I did not know what "groceries" were, but I was willing to go along. They drove us a short distance down Grant to several acres of blacktop parking lot flanked by a line of low buildings. One of them had a sign on top that said "Peters." We headed that way.

We walked through a door that opened on its own as we approached. The interior of the building stretched away in three directions in front of us, all of the space crammed with food. I had never seen so much to eat in my life. Jacob, Andrew, and I must have stood with our mouths open, while Susan and Penny got two shopping carts and tried to herd us to the right side of the store, toward the displays of vegetables.

Susan asked if I wanted some lettuce. I did not know what that was, but it looked as if she were pointing at a bag of leaves, the kind I fed to the farm animals in Duk Payuel. I saw something labeled "cucumber" and asked Susan about it. She said it was a good vegetable; it could be sliced and put in salads. It looked like what I fed the goats. I recognized bananas, though. We had those in Africa.

Susan and Penny took us to every counter in the store and asked the workers if we could have samples. The butcher cut a tiny slice of pink flesh.

"What is this?" I asked.

"It is ham."

"What is ham?"

"It's meat. It comes from a pig."

Meat is not meat unless it comes from a cow, I thought. Clams, lobsters, shrimp—do people eat such things? Yes? I didn't want to criticize, but they did not look like anything good to eat. Lobsters and shrimp looked like big bugs. Someone asked if I liked fish. I said no. That wasn't true; I do eat fish. But I didn't want to eat anything that came from the counter next to the giant insects. Not far away I saw lots of chicken roasting on skewers. I wanted to eat those chickens.

One of the grocery store workers handed out doughnuts. I took one but didn't want to eat it in the store. Dinka culture dictated that I go back to the apartment, go inside, and eat. You don't eat in front of other people, not even to peel an orange. Mealtime is separate. And small, sweet foods are inappropriate for grown men, who should eat beef and milk. Popcorn, cookies, sweets—those are for small children. If a baby cries while waiting for dinner, it is okay to drop a kernel of corn near the fire, grab it as it pops, and give it to the child. But it is an insult to offer a trifle such as popcorn or candy to a man.

We came to a counter where I saw stacks of beef, cut into small portions and covered in something clear and thin.

"Where are the cows?" I asked. I didn't see any anywhere. The store owners had to have cows grazing outside in order to have freshly butchered meat inside. But there were no cows on the pavement where we parked the car, and none near the homes that surrounded Shop City.

"They lived on ranches far away," someone said. "The meat was butchered and shipped here on a truck."

It was strange to think of cows being raised in one place, butchered in a second, and eaten in a third. But the system must have worked. The store had enough beef to feed an entire Dinka village for a month.

Susan asked me what kind of food I wanted. Milk, I said. We put three gallons in one of the carts for the three of us. That ought to last a day or two, I thought. I recognized chicken eggs, too, and we got some of those. I could boil those on the stove and remove the shells. We also grabbed some sodas. I think I drank a total of five sodas while I lived in Kakuma, where everyone considered them a special treat. The amazing volume of soda on the shelves, coupled with the variety of flavors and the array of brand names, overwhelmed me. I remember seeing the red-and-white swoosh of Coca-cola and the blue-green Sprite label in Kenya; I thought they were the names of flavors, like chocolate and vanilla. The other Lost Boys must have thought the same. That's why Panther Bior, one of the Lost Boys interviewed in Christopher Quinn's movie, got confused when he drank a bottle of Pepsi for the first time. He told Christopher he had tried the same thing in Africa, where everyone called it "Coke."

Susan and Penny warned us not to drink too much soda, because it would damage our health. Later, when they were not around, we bought a lot and drank it anyway. It was a short, sweet affair. We got sick of it pretty quick and went back to drinking milk.

I had my biggest shock when we passed the aisle beneath the sign that said "dog food" and "cat food." My family had dogs in Duk Payuel. We gave them a little food from our dinner. If I wanted to feed the dog, I put a scoop of boiled maize on the floor and continued eating. My dog knew to wait until I had finished and left the room before advancing to eat what I had given him. And later, during the civil war in Sudan, my countrymen starved every day, and tens of thousands went hungry in the dark days in refugee camps, while in America dogs had special meals prepared just for them. Forty-pound bags of dog food took up an entire aisle of the store. An entire industry had sprung up around the need to feed the family pet.

We spent a couple of hours in the store. It took that long, because Susan, Stephen, Penny, and the store workers had to explain everything to us. Mouthwash? What do you do with that? Toothbrushes? We used an achuil stick to clean our teeth. Turkey? It looks too ugly to eat. Shaving cream? My beard never grew in Kakuma. It started to sprout only later, after I started eating regularly.

We left the store with meat and eggs, milk and soda, and "corn on the cob"—maize, raw and recently picked. We knew how to boil it, and that it would make a good dinner. We bought dry beans, too. The only thing we wanted but did not see was pumpkin. We found some later at a farmers' market, but it did not taste sweet like an African pumpkin.

When we checked out, Susan and Penny paid for everything. I had no money. We put the groceries in their car and drove home to our apartment. They said they would cook for us. They prepared the beef and beans and set it on our table at 6 p.m. We thanked them, and they left. We ate hardly any at all. It was too early in the day. In Sudan, we waited until around nine o'clock to eat. Also, the food had an odd smell. We drank milk instead.

We didn't want to be ungrateful, but most of the food we ate in America tasted salty or sweet or had an odor that we found unpleasant. We threw the beef and beans away in the morning, but we never said anything to Susan and Penny.

SUSAN SET UP A SCHEDULE FOR PEOPLE FROM THE SKANEATELES church to come to our apartment every day for the first week or so. They brought a new food each day and showed us how to cook it. Baked potatoes were good. Spaghetti too, was good, although it had been strictly a celebration food in Kakuma. Eating it frequently would take some getting used to.

Every morning we warmed milk on the stovetop for breakfast. When it boiled, we added sugar and then let it cool. For two or three days, we drank a lot of sweet milk and ate doughnuts from the grocery store. After a while the doughnut smell got to me. I couldn't stand the odor and never ate them again. Not long after that, volunteers from Living Word, a church much closer to our apartment, gave us cookies as a treat. Cookies! We took them and laughed after the volunteers left. I pointed at Jacob and said, "Jacob got a cookie!" It was so funny, big men being offered baby food.

According to Susan's schedule, members of her church picked us up at our apartment and drove us 45 minutes down the highway every Sunday for worship service. She arranged it so that we always had a host family, who would take us out to eat afterward or invite us into their home for a meal. They had the best intentions, but they confused us. In Sudan, families and friends gathered in each other's homes for the joy of being together. Hosts brought out food if it happened to be a mealtime; nobody ever said, "Let's get together for dinner." We never ate with casual acquaintances and never made eating the reason for sharing time together.

"Is it a good thing to be invited to eat with people?" I asked the women of my church. They said yes, it was an honorable thing. If a person invites you to lunch, they said, it means the person likes you, and it would be an insult to refuse. So, I got used to accepting invitations, despite my cultural conditioning.

Generally, Dinka shy away from new things. Andrew, Jacob, and I struggled with the dilemma of loosening our grip on our Dinka ways or insulting the people who sponsored us in America and meant us no harm. We decided to do what our fellow church members asked of us if it seemed a reasonable American request. We ate the food they offered, played games with their children, and talked about life in Africa and America. Every week, someone new took us in.

Once in a while, we just couldn't do as they wished. Some church volunteers brought us secondhand clothes. One of the donors told me I was getting the clothes of his grandfather. I accepted the gift but threw it in the garbage after everyone had gone. Taking clothes that belonged to people who have died is taboo. I could not wear them, ever. I did not refuse to take them, though, because the donors offered them in a good spirit. I wondered if they ever suspected something was wrong, because they never saw me wearing anything they gave me.

ANDREW, JACOB, AND I STARTED TO GET USED TO THE RULES and the rhythms of life in America. We went to a center in Syracuse designed to acclimate new refugees. I watched movies there, about how to get a job, keep a job, and not break the law. I knew I had to have a steady paycheck within three months, so I tried to learn all I could.

I was there, outside the center on a Tuesday morning in September, when a woman came out to say America had been attacked. She was so emotional that we had trouble understanding what she was saying. Other people began to come out, too, saying New York City had been hit by rockets, stories like that. They closed the refugee center and sent us home. I had no car, so it took awhile to get back to my apartment. Andrew, Jacob, and I watched on our television as the World Trade Center burned and crumbled to the ground, and hundreds of people ran in the smoke-filled streets of Lower Manhattan. The commentators on the news said somebody had flown airplanes into the towers, and that another building in Washington had been hit. Firefighters and police, dust and tears, confusion everywhere—this was America one month after I arrived.

As the news unfolded over the next couple of days, people on television started talking about Islamic fundamentalist Osama bin Laden as having masterminded the attacks. That was the worst possible news to the Lost Boys. I had never heard the name bin Laden before coming to America, but I knew all about the embassy car bombings carried out by his organization in Kenya and Tanzania in 1998. He had resorted to terrorism in Africa to further his political causes, and it made sense that he would choose to do so in America as well.

I feared repercussions from Americans unfamiliar with the Sudanese civil war. They heard on the news that Sudan had harbored bin Laden during the 1990s, and I wondered whether they would retaliate against all Sudanese. I wanted to tell them I did not support the Khartoum government that had given sanctuary to the madman, bin Laden. In fact, I had fled from that very government for the same reasons that Americans found the most extreme form of Islam distasteful: the enforcement of sharia, the subjugation of non-Muslim citizens, and the open violence against innocent people. I had escaped these things and come to America thinking I would find peace and security. Apparently, the world no longer offered such perfect sanctuary.

Some of the Lost Boys whom I knew in New York State blamed themselves for the attacks, as if bad luck followed us from place to place. They reasoned that they had lived quietly in their villages in southern Sudan, only to have their homes attacked. They had fled to Ethiopia and lived peacefully, only to be attacked. Now they had come halfway around the world to find a better life than the one they left behind, only to have their new home attacked again. They thought the unluckiness of the Dinka had cursed America for taking them in.

Nothing came of their fears, or mine, however. Americans turned their attention to those who planned the attacks of September 11, 2001. Their focus on Muslims and Arabs excluded the black Christians of Sudan.

My heart felt heavy the next morning as I took a bus back to the refugee center. The attacks gave Americans a taste of something I had lived with for many years. I knew they would learn and respond just as the Dinka had done to the terror of djellaba attacks—not only with a military response but also with adjustments to their lives to take account of threats from their new enemy. First, however, Americans had to deal with the immediacy of their grief. Everyone cried at the refugee center. Not just the

During his last interview for the film God Grew Tired of Us,
John Dau pauses in thought in downtown Syracuse.

students but the teachers too. It was terrible to see so many tears
on the faces of adults.

A woman asked the class, "Where is God?" That prompted a
discussion among the people in class about God's relationship to
the world. I told the woman to read the Book of Job. You see, I
told her, Job never did anything wrong, and he loved God. Yet
Job lost his family and his property, and he almost died. Job realized that just loving God did not mean that God would do good
things in return.

We also talked about the differences between September 11
and what happened in Sudan. The way I saw it, it was like a
philosophy question I had heard: If a tree falls in a forest and
nobody is there to hear it, does it make a sound? The villages of

southern Sudan had been attacked again and again, and hundreds of thousands of people had died at the hands of the djellabas. I could see two main differences between that war and the one carried out by bin Laden. First, the villages of southern Sudan had no tall buildings to fall down. And second, no journalists with television cameras captured and shared the news of my homeland's destruction with the world. By making such a public display of violence in America, bin Laden hoped to horrify the world and change things to his advantage. In reality, he merely exposed his evil in such a way that nobody with a brain or a heart could doubt it. If only the world had seen what had been done to southern Sudan in the name of Allah, it might have been better prepared for a terrorist organization like al-Qaeda attacking the West.

Even though I was not a citizen, I tried to help my adopted country. With the assistance of a *Syracuse Post-Standard* reporter who had interviewed me once, I drafted letters after America invaded Afghanistan. The reporter suggested I mail them to New York Gov. George Pataki and President George W. Bush. That made sense, so I did.

Dear Mr. President,

I am writing to tell you how sorry I feel about the terrorist attacks on the United States. But I also think it is not enough to say you are sorry; one must do something as well. Everybody must do something, even me. Although I am a refugee from the Sudan...I want to help....If given a chance, I will go to fight for this country. It is not that I want to fight, that I am eager for blood; but I want to defend this territory. I am living in America now and must defend it. I would fight to protect my place, to protect my brothers, my friends.

The United States government has done a very important thing. It has helped us when we were in trouble. Americans help because they are humanitarians. They help me, so I must help them.

I write also to urge you to continue your fight against terrorism, against Osama bin Laden, against the Taliban. As a leader, you must always do what is right, what is necessary, even when not everyone agrees with you. In Dinka we say, 'If you are a leader, there will be ten who love you and ten who dislike you.' When Moses led the Jews out of slavery in Egypt, there were those who cried and wanted to go back, because they were afraid. When the soldiers chased them, and they came to the Red Sea, they cried, 'Oh, Moses, why did you bring us here?' So many people, those who cannot see far, those who are shortsighted, they panic and complain. But Moses, the leader, he trusted in God, and laid down his staff, and the waters stood apart for the Jews to pass, then closed on those who chased them.

As President, you have to see far. The weak ones, who cannot see far, they may cast obstacles in your way, but you must continue. I urge you to go ahead, to go ahead with the fight. Terrorism, religious war—it is what is now in Sudan, and has been these 18 years of war. They are killing people in southern Sudan. Terrorism—this is our common enemy. The tragedy in New York and in Washington, D.C., was not so strange to us, we who are from the Sudan. We have been living with this for a long time.... The war in Sudan is everywhere. We are people in the same situation. Osama bin Laden had a headquarters in Sudan. We are in the same boat, and we must stick together.

This is my message to you. This is what I want to say.
God bless you.

I sent the letters off expecting to hear back from the President and the governor, but I got no replies. My offer still stands. If my new country needs me, I will answer its call. I was not born in America. Instead, I *chose* to live in America. I would fight to defend my new, wonderful homeland, just as if it had been my native country. It would be my privilege.

AT ABOUT THIS TIME SOME OF THE OTHER LOST BOYS INVITED Andrew, Jacob, and me to check out Living Word Church in Syracuse. It offered a style of worship much like what I had experienced in Kakuma's "synagogues," and it had midweek services at night. When I walked through the door, Brother Bob, one of the pastors, asked me my name and shook my hand.

"My name is John," I answered.

Then I added, "Do you like Jesus Christ?"

He smiled and clapped me on the shoulder. He told me, "That's what we like to hear."

The church services lacked the formal structure of the Presbyterians, but their flexibility allowed praise, singing, and worship whenever and wherever the hearts of the congregation led. Americans called the church's style "full gospel," meaning it embraced the gifts of the Holy Spirit such as speaking in tongues. The words and actions of worship flowed back and forth between the pastors and the members. People clapped their hands and said "Amen." I clapped my hands and said "Amen." I put my arms around other people during worship, knelt when the spirit moved me, and offered up my own prayers for the security of America and my circle of loved ones in New York and in Africa.

I decided to introduce the Living Word congregation to the Dinka style of worship. My friends and I brought about three dozen Sudanese to a Wednesday night service, and we gathered on stage to sing hymns of praise in our native language. One of my friends translated the words, so everyone knew what we sang. The worshippers tried to join us, in Dinka, as best they could.

On stage, we moved about in unison as we sang, and the audience followed along. Then we sang a hymn we learned in English at our Kakuma synagogue: The lyrics included a line that said, "Even Muhammad bows before him." We sang that too, at Living Word. I realized later that some Americans would not see the phrase as being "politically correct," because we sang about the founder of Islam kneeling before the Christian God. Nevertheless, that was how we felt: God is God, Jesus is Jesus, and there is no other truth. We Dinka take the Gospels very seriously.

The congregation seemed to enjoy our leading them through the songs. When I saw white faces and black faces together, united in praise, without differences, I felt I had found a good second home in which to praise the Lord.

One time I gave my testimony to Brother Bryan, an associate pastor, about my journey from Africa. I told him how passionately I felt—particularly after the attacks of September 11—about the ongoing conflicts in the Middle East. There is true evil in the world, I said. I have seen it.

"I would never presume to tell you what to think or do, John, because you have such a deep and personal experience," Brother Bryan told me. "But you should know, we all have dual citizenship. We are citizens of this world, like citizens of the United States, and we also have citizenship in heaven. So we always have this tension, these divided loyalties, to heaven and to our earthly countries. It's not easy to hold both."

One of our citizenships, on Earth or in heaven, has to take precedence, he said. I know which one is most important for me, and I have struggled, I continue to struggle, to discern the will of God in the tragedies that have befallen America. God wants the killing to stop. Of that I am certain. The path to peace, however, is dark and difficult. I have come to believe America will best be served by strength and resolve, just as those tools have served the peoples of southern Sudan in their long struggle. The terrorist attacks of 2001 have worked, in time, to renew my faith, just as they have done for many native-born Americans.

MANY THINGS HAPPENED QUICKLY THAT FALL. I LEARNED HOW to drive. I got the first in a series of jobs. I saw snow for the first time. With each new experience, I embraced my new life in America.

I knew I had to learn to drive in order to have the same freedom as other Americans. In this country, you cannot go where you want to go, when you want to go, unless you drive a car. Until I gained control over my ability to travel, I knew I would be at a disadvantage competing for jobs and a better education. Public transportation and the generosity of church friends who offered me a lift only went so far, and I had to budget hours of extra time whenever I wanted to go anywhere. My own car, and the license to operate it, spelled independence.

A lot of people took turns teaching me to drive. Church volunteers from Skaneateles drove to Syracuse to give me lessons. Susan Meyer, who had taught me about grocery stores, helped. So did Jack Howard, my "grandfather" at the Presbyterian church. I called him that because he was like a Dinka elder, in his 80s and wise. I turned to him for advice.

Cynthia Dietz from the Skaneateles church sometimes drove me around Syracuse and let me handle her car. I circled many empty parking lots and drove along many two-lane highways. The pavement seemed to get narrower whenever another car approached from up ahead. I also hired a professional driving teacher, a Vietnamese immigrant named Mr. Nguyen, to prepare me for the road test exam. He hardly ever said anything as he sat beside me in the front seat. All he did was point. *Point left.* I turned. *Point right.* I turned. *Point left again.* My driving improved with Mr. Nguyen, but I never learned any Vietnamese, and he never learned any Dinka.

My friends at the refugee center kept asking me, "How long have you been in America?" I told them I had arrived in August. This was the middle of September. They said, "Do you know snow?" I replied that I did not.

"My God," someone said. "You are going to die."

Syracuse lies east of the Great Lakes, they said, and the city gets hammered every winter with huge amounts of snow. My church friends from Skaneateles First Presbyterian and Living Word started donating blankets, gloves, and coats, and they took me and my roommates to the store to buy heavy socks. I finally had to say, "Please stop."

When I heard snow had fallen east of town on October 21, I had to see it. Cynthia came to my apartment that day to give me another driving lesson. We drove out of the city along the highway, until the buildings fell away on both sides and we came to the edge of a quiet cemetery in East Syracuse. An inch of white powder blanketed the trees, the grass, and the sides of the road.

"Everything is so white," I said. "Is this snow?"

"Yes," she said. "This is snow."

We parked the car and got out. I couldn't wait to touch it. I grabbed a double handful and held it up to the sky. Water trickled through my fingers. As I watched, and as my hands grew numb, drops ran down my arms to the elbows. I focused my attention on the miracle of frozen flakes of water.

Smack! Something cold and hard hit me in the back. Cynthia had pasted me with a snowball. I packed the snow in my hands into a ball and threw it at her. For ten minutes, we had a snowball fight at the edge of the cemetery. I think I grinned the entire time.

Finally, Cynthia said, "John, we have to go."

I felt reluctant to leave the snow behind. I wanted Jacob and Andrew to see it. So I packed some snow into a globe the size of a bowling ball and put it in the trunk of Cynthia's car. I got in the front seat, and she drove us back to Syracuse.

When we arrived outside my apartment building, I called to my roommates to come out and see what I had brought them. It still hadn't snowed in Syracuse. Andrew and Jacob walked to the car, and I opened the trunk. They looked at the white ball. They touched it with their fingers. They caressed it as if it had been the rarest object on Earth—a sphere of the finest ivory or a gemstone from some jungle mine.

"Let's put it in our apartment," I said.

We took the snowball inside and placed it on our living room table. We sat and looked at it. Cynthia went home. We brought food to the table and ate, staring at the snowball. After a few minutes, it formed a puddle of water on the table, and we knew it soon would melt. I moved it to the kitchen sink, where it wouldn't soak the floor.

I have seen many snows since that day, but none has ever been as magical.

I GOT MY FIRST JOB NOVEMBER 1, 2001, BEFORE I EARNED A driver's license. Volunteers picked me up at my apartment and took me to work for the 2:30 to 11 p.m. shift; at the end of the day they took me home again. The company that hired me,

General Super Plating, produced materials used in the construction of men's razor blades. I loaded heavy boxes into racks for seven dollars an hour. I had to pick up the boxes with my hands and move them around the factory. The boxes weighed a lot, and lifting them all day hurt my back. I lay on the floor at night when I got home from work. A woman from Living Word gave me some lotion to rub on my back to take the pain away, and it helped a little. I kept that job for three months, until I had surgery to fix the blindness in my left eye resulting from a childhood accident. Now I can see a bit out of my repaired lens.

While working at my first job, I got an introduction to the complexity of relationships between American men and women. For the first time in my life, a woman called me her friend. It happened while I was going through orientation at General Super Plating. New employees gathered for training, and I met some people who would become my co-workers. A woman at the orientation whom I had just met introduced me to someone else as her new friend, John.

"I am not your friend," I told her.

In the Dinka culture, a woman and a man do not call each other friends. That would imply a degree of familiarity that did not exist between us. Dinka men simply do not have female friends.

Her face fell. I could tell I had injured her feelings, and that bothered me. I realized she was trying to be nice by claiming to be my friend, and I had obviously embarrassed her. But she recovered nicely. She figured out that I must have spoken out of my ignorance of our cultural differences.

"John," she said, "because I know you, I call you my friend." She explained that she meant nothing more by the word, and

Finding the job easier than collecting fallen tree limbs in Sudan to make a fire, John hauls firewood for Kim and Dick Poppa, friends from church.

that it was a common term among acquaintances in America. I filed away that thought and listened for the word "friend," eavesdropping on other conversations over the next few days. The woman was right. Americans claim nearly everyone and everybody as their friend. Now I do too—even women. It just took a little time to get used to it.

As my first Christmas in America approached, people in the Skaneateles church asked me how the Dinka celebrated. We told them about our rituals of feasting and parading from village to village to announce the birth of Jesus. Susan Meyer filled me in on the American customs. She invited Jacob, Andrew, and me, along with our new roommate, Santino Atak, who arrived in the United States shortly after the terrorist attacks of September 11, 2001, to the Meyer house on Christmas Eve for a celebration.

We dressed up in our gold-colored robes and entered the Meyer home, which the family had brightened with lights and decorations. A tree with tiny, sharp needles and branches covered with candy stood in the corner. What did such things have to do with the birth of Jesus, I wondered. Were there trees and candies in Bethlehem 2,000 years ago? I didn't recall reading about them in the Bible. Or Santa Claus, for that matter. Where was he in the New Testament?

I'm afraid I may have come off a bit reserved at the Meyers' family party. I played some foosball in the basement and drank some soda, but mainly I thought about the coming of midnight and tried to pray. My spirits stayed a bit down the next day. Someone from Living Word Church sent a tree to our apartment. I didn't feel ready to embrace American Christmas customs, so I ignored it. Andrew set it up without my help.

I didn't understand the tradition associated with Santa Claus, the giving of gifts to one another. Even now, when I know the custom better, it still seems greedy. Americans ask each other what they want for Christmas. That doesn't seem to be in harmony with the spirit of the free gifts we get but do not deserve from God—such as the gift of his son, Jesus. If you ask for something and someone feels obligated to give it, then you cannot call the thing a gift. Presents must be given from the heart, and they must be surprises. When the three elders came to the manger in Bethlehem from the east, they brought what they had. They didn't ask Mary and Joseph, "What should we get the baby?"

Since that first Christmas in my new homeland, I've adapted enough to American culture to give and receive gifts. But I still don't want to tell anyone what to get for me, and I don't want them to ask me. Let us both be surprised.

I got my first paycheck shortly before Christmas. I remembered the nun at Kenyatta Airport in Nairobi, who warned me not to send money to Africa. *Ha!* The very first money I earned in America I wired to my friends in Kakuma through a Somali agent in Syracuse named Muhammad. The paycheck deposit put $1,010 in my savings account at the bank. The government had paid my apartment rent for a while longer, so I took all but $10 and sent it overseas. I tried to spread the money around. I gave people anywhere from $20 to $50. I hoped the Lost Boys would spend the money on new clothes and beef to celebrate. I wanted them to eat until they could eat no more, so they would never forget the feast.

From then on, I sent money back each month. Our rent came to $600 a month. Split four ways that cost us only $150 per person. I always had plenty to spare, even after I became totally self-sufficient at the end of 2001. Not surprisingly, Lost Boys in Africa began calling me to ask for money. On the busiest days I got 50 phone calls in my apartment. Some of the callers didn't know me. "Who are you?" I asked them. They told me odd stories —"I helped this guy who knows your friend, and he said you would send me money if I needed it, so I'm calling." They got upset when I didn't answer the phone in person, and they had to leave a message on voice mail. It is unlike a Dinka to say no to a fellow Dinka in need, but I am starting to learn how to handle the many requests. On those days when the phone rings and rings, I pick it up and tell the Lost Boys on the other end of the line, "How can I earn money if you don't stop calling so I can go to work?" If they persist, I put their name on a list and tell them they will have to wait their turn.

I started two new jobs in February 2002. While I recovered from my eye surgery and couldn't work at General Super Plating, a member of the Skaneateles church offered to set me up with a new job at a company he co-founded called XTO. The man, Donald Krieger, also hired Andrew, Jacob, and Santino. I took the new job and quit the old one.

XTO made die-cut gaskets, tapes, and adhesives. I inspected plastic gaskets Monday through Friday. I counted them, cleaned them, and made sure they met the manufacturing specifications. My shift worked from 7 a.m. until 4 p.m. Afterward, Santino and I worked second jobs at McDonald's. The night shift started at 6 p.m. and ended at midnight.

FOR MONTHS, I LIVED A MOST EXHAUSTING SCHEDULE. A RIDE-share program operated by the city of Syracuse arranged to pick us up at our apartment, take us from XTO to McDonald's in the evening, and return us home at night. Unfortunately, we could not get paired up with other workers who shared our exact hours. The car pool arrived every weekday morning outside our apartment at 5 a.m., and the driver blew the horn to summon us to the parking lot. That meant we had to get up at 4 a.m. to eat breakfast, shower, and dress for work. The car dropped us at XTO a little after 5, when it was still dark. The arrangement wasn't too bad for Santino and Jacob, because they worked in a building that opened early. Andrew and I had no such luck. We waited outdoors, on a bench under a tree, for two hours un-til our building opened for the day. When the weather got cold that fall, we put heavy coats over our heads. Sometimes it rained or snowed, and we shivered and got soaked. If we were lucky, we managed to fall asleep for two hours. Otherwise, we tried to keep warm and stared at the blank wall of the factory across the street. When the weather turned very cold, the waiting became extremely uncomfortable. We started wearing a lot of the heavy winter clothes our church friends had given us and changed into lighter, drier clothes once the factory opened. The work included repetitive tasks, but at least it didn't involve heavy lifting like the job at General Super Plating.

After 4 p.m., our ride came to take us to McDonald's. I changed into my uniform and cooked hamburgers for six hours over a steaming-hot grill. So, I froze in the morning and sweated at night. No wonder I got sick.

After the restaurant closed at midnight, Santino and I had to wait outside for an hour for another car pool to pick us up and take us home. We usually got back to the apartment around 1 a.m. and fell asleep around 2. Two hours later, the alarm went off and we started the cycle over again. By Saturday, I felt like the walking dead. My eyes burned from lack of sleep, and I couldn't think straight.

In June, I quit the McDonald's job and began working as an inspector for UPS. I placed packages on a scale to make sure they had been shipped at the correct weight. Sometimes they weighed more than the posted number, and I had to refigure the shipping costs. I wrote the correct numbers on a form and turned it in to my supervisor at the end of my shift. Syracuse serves as a redistribution point for deliveries, so I also loaded trucks with packages.

The office that arranged for my rides to work stopped providing the service, and I had to arrange for a substitute to take me home from UPS in the middle of the night. Many people stepped forward with offers of assistance. A Ghanian named Patrick Kwame, who worked with me at XTO, dropped me at UPS in the evening and sometimes took me home later. I also called on my fellow church members from Living Word for rides home. One in particular, Jim Hockenbery, helped me even when I called in the middle of the night. When I rang his home phone at midnight, as my shift ended, he cheerfully said he would pick me up. I had no idea at the time that calling a person's home so late violated the rules of good behavior. There was no way I could have guessed, because he acted so glad to help me. "John, how are you?" Jim said as I hopped into his car in the darkest part of the night. Amazing, these Americans.

Patrick's car broke down every once in a while, including in the middle of the highway. One time he simply could not pick me up after my job at UPS, and I had no luck with my friends at Living Word. I called home and got Andrew on the line. He was the first among the four of us in the apartment to buy his own car. However, at the time I called, Andrew had only a learner's permit, not a driver's license. "Patrick's not coming. Can you pick me up?" I asked. Andrew didn't hesitate. He jumped in his car and took off down the road—without remembering to turn on his headlights. Andrew got as far as the highway before an officer in a Syracuse police car spotted him and made him pull over. The officer asked to see Andrew's license. All Andrew had was a learner's permit, and he expected deep, deep trouble. Surely the officer would arrest him or, like the Kenyan police we knew in Kakuma, shake him down for a bribe. Surprisingly, neither happened. The policeman questioned Andrew, who said he realized he had broken the law but knew of no other way to get me home safely that night. The officer ordered Andrew to put on his lights and escorted him, slowly, to UPS. I got in the car, and the officer followed us home to Grant Village. When we got to our parking lot, the officer gave Andrew a lecture that concluded, "Don't drive without a license again."

"Yes, sir," Andrew said.

And that was that. No arrest. No ticket. No bribe.

This is a good man, I thought. Now I know the Americans are good people, because even the police are good.

At the end of the summer of 2002, XTO fired the Lost Boys. The supervisor told me we had taken too much time off for medical leave, and we also had begged off too many shifts so we could attend classes at the start of the fall semester. I could tell the company managers worried about how losing the jobs would affect us, but I told everyone not to worry. I didn't want the company to lose money because of me, and I knew I could find other options in Syracuse. In fact, I quit my job at UPS at about the same time. I already had begun thinking about better options for my future.

I KNEW I DIDN'T WANT TO WORK TWO JOBS FOR THE REST OF my life, so I decided in the fall of 2002 to go back to college. American colleges welcome students who want to learn and who work hard. I wanted to be an educated person; I didn't want to be left out of the good things in life. If I got a college education, I would fulfill the expectations of the elders in Kakuma. Education would indeed become my new mother and father.

Jacob and I sat for an entrance examination that tested our English and math skills. We passed and got accepted to Onandaga Community College in Syracuse. I signed up for 12 credits my first semester. My classes included English as a Second Language, anthropology, and sociology. Sitting with American students at an American college felt wonderful, but I couldn't help remarking on the friendly relationships between teachers and students and the ease with which students passed the tests. There were no disciplinarians like the ones I had in Kakuma. Everyone acted so polite; it was like a party compared with what I experienced in Africa. The students had lots of books and supplementary materials to make studying easier, yet they still wanted to know what would appear on their tests and complained about their grades.

I took more classes to make progress toward an associate's degree. Meteorology, philosophy...I studied a lot of subjects to try to get a well-rounded education. I learned about America from listening to my teachers and fellow students, and I think they learned a bit about Africa from listening to me. A philosophy of ethics class in the fall of 2004 provided this kind of two-way exchange. A class assignment focused on whether anyone has the right to die. If someone is in great pain or great despair, can others permit that person to put an end to life? There was much discussion, as if both sides of the question carried equal weight. I did not see it that way. The answer was obvious.

The professor presented a case study. He said it was a true story, and it illustrated the complexity of the question. There was a man, he said, who pulled his car into a service station to fill the gas tank. The pump exploded, and flaming gasoline doused his body. He was badly burned; he lost much of his face and, I think, both of his legs. An ambulance rushed the man to the hospital, and the doctors and nurses tried to save him. They tended to the man's wounds very carefully. They kept putting paper on his skin to protect him from infections, but every time they removed the old paper, it came off bloody. The pain and disfigurement tormented the poor man. "Kill me, kill me!" he begged. But the doctors and nurses refused to do so.

The professor asked: What is the need, what is the reason, to keep this man alive? Should he be allowed to die rather than go through agony? Make a decision and defend it, explaining why you would let the man die or struggle to keep him alive.

There were those in class who favored killing the man. I strongly disagreed. This man is not rational, I said. He is in such pain that he cannot be expected to make a wise decision. We must use every resource to bring him back to appreciate the life that God gave him, the life that God would not want him to throw away. Give the man some time, I said, and he will be okay. I said I remembered my mother telling me when I was a young boy in Duk Payuel that everything in life goes around and comes around again. When times are very good, she said, remember that hardship always returns. When times are very bad, remember God will send you joy again, and so be patient. Someday, when the burned man has emerged from his pain, he may come to love his life, I said.

I was in a student group that put together a class presentation. One of our group members decided to try to find out what happened to the burned man. The student managed to track the man down, using only a few clues in the professor's assignment, and the man is all right now. We called him at home during class time, when we were giving our presentation. His body is covered with scars and disfigured, but he is glad to be alive.

We asked him, "Did you regret what you told the doctors and nurses when you were in pain?"

"Oh, yes," he said. "It was something I should not have said."

I feel my group won the discussion that day.

As our group prepared the presentation, I thought about my own life and how it influenced my opinions. My life story is so long, I told the class, but if I tell it to you, you will come around to my point of view.

"Look at me," I said. "I am a Lost Boy of Sudan. I have seen my share of death. When I lived in a refugee camp in Ethiopia, the hyenas came at night to feed on the bodies of the friends I had buried during the day. I have seen my village burned by armed invaders. I have been so hungry and thirsty in the dusty plains of Africa that I consumed things I would rather forget. I spent many nights wondering whether my family was alive or dead. I have crossed a crocodile-infested river while being shelled and shot at. I have walked until I thought I could walk no more and surely would die.

"But I am still here. I have a job, an apartment, and a wonderful new country to call home. I am sitting here in a classroom in Syracuse, New York, and life is good. They say I am a Lost Boy, but God has found me.

"Do not give up hope when times are bad. Hope is never lost."

Community college classes ended in the early afternoon. That left plenty of time to earn a living. I figured that if I got a job as a security guard, I could read my textbooks at work during my down time.

So I took security training and got hired as a guard at a building in downtown Syracuse. I worked in the building's parking garage from 2:30 p.m. until midnight, when the garage closed, and went to classes in the mornings. That job paid six dollars an hour, which wasn't much, but it allowed me time to read and do my homework while waiting for cars to check in and out.

I figured that I would have to have my own car if I worked late hours downtown, so in fall 2002, as I started classes at Onandaga, I took the driver's license exam. I failed. The examiner said I entered an intersection too quickly, having forgotten to wait long enough for oncoming traffic. I rescheduled and took the exam a second time. Again I failed; the examiner said I did not parallel park correctly. The third time, I went with Grandfather Jack from church, and I got my license. There was something about him, like a good luck charm. Andrew failed the driver's exam many times, and when he went with Jack, he got it. The same with Santino and the same with Jacob. Maybe it's just coincidence, but whenever Jack drove one of us to the license bureau, we passed.

I bought a 1995 Mercury Sable. Richard Way, a friend from the Skaneateles church, went with me to the dealer's used car lot to negotiate the price. The car had more than 100,000 miles on it, but it ran well. When I slid behind the steering wheel, it felt as if I were taking control of my life. I paid cash—$1,700, which I had saved from my various jobs. That's a lot of money when you get paid six dollars an hour. I had been frugal with expenses at my apartment and managed to save enough to send money to my friends in Kakuma and buy a car, too.

The first time I drove myself to the office building where I worked, I felt so happy to be in my own car that I circled a few laps inside the parking garage, going around and around, up and down, through the levels. Obviously, I had nowhere to go; a parking space on the bottom floor was as good as a parking space on the top. It didn't matter. All I wanted to do was enjoy the sensation of driving wherever I felt like going.

Everyone loves their first car. Mine was a good one. I drove extra carefully. The police never pulled me over for speeding or any other violation. So I felt terrible about getting in a wreck in the summer of 2003. I was driving on Route 11 to a place that sold batteries for mobile telephones. The highway had only two lanes, one going and one coming, and there weren't a lot of buildings next to the pavement. I drove and drove, and finally decided I must have passed the address. I put on my turn signal and started to go left into a driveway so I could turn around. Another car, coming up from behind, clipped my car on the driver's side. The police gave me a ticket, but I still don't believe the accident was my fault.

Although it still ran well, my Mercury Sable had a big dent in it. All that winter I drove my dinged-up car. Then the heater failed. It was a cold winter, and I needed heat. For two months I tried to tough it out, then gave up. I traded in the Sable and with an extra thousand dollars bought a Jeep Liberty with only 18,000 miles on it. I put a "Smile—God Loves You" bumper sticker and an American flag decal on the back.

AS I GREW MORE INDEPENDENT, I MET MANY AMERICANS WHO celebrated my successes with me. My church friends complimented me and shook my hand with every step I took. However, not everyone looked upon the Lost Boys with such kindness. Seven of my friends, all Lost Boys, lived in an apartment on East Fayette Street. They worked hard, saved their paychecks, and paid cash to buy their own cars about eight months after they arrived in America. Some of their neighbors watched them and felt jealous. They knew that the government had initially paid their rent, utilities, and groceries, and they believed, wrongly, that the government gave them the cars for free. One day, a Lost Boy named Jok parked his car in front of his apartment and ran inside to get

something. He left the keys in the ignition and the engine running. While he was inside the apartment, a neighbor jumped in
the car and drove away. Jok came out, discovered his car missing,
and started making calls. His friends at Living Word told him to
call the police, so he did. The police recovered the car, but not
the keys. Jok figured out who had stolen the car and confronted
the thief, a man who appeared to be in his early 20s, just like Jok.
The thief acknowledged that he had the keys yet refused to give
them back until Jok paid him something.

"Our government is giving you money to help you buy a car,"
the thief said. "Give me some of that money, and you can have
your keys back."

"No, that's not what happened. I worked hard to buy that
car," Jok said.

They argued and argued, and a fight broke out between the
Lost Boys and some of the native-born residents of the apartment complex. Car and apartment windows got smashed, and
the police came to halt the violence. They arrested the thief and
returned the keys to Jok. I told him he had to move away or face
retaliation from the thief's friends. He agreed to move closer to
me and the other Lost Boys in our apartment complex. It was
a shame that he had his property destroyed because of jealousy
and misunderstanding. That was a hard lesson.

I encountered more hard feelings in the fall of 2003, when
I got fired over a couple of incidents at the building where I
worked security. One involved my wages. My paycheck kept
coming up short of what I thought I should have earned. I
pointed out the disparity first to my boss, then to my boss's supervisor. The supervisor asked my boss for an explanation. That
seemed to put my boss in an awkward spot. He tried to blame

the shortfall on this and that, but he never answered the question to my satisfaction.

The second dispute involved a report I filed at the end of a particular shift. The building's rules prohibited smoking indoors, which included the parking garage. I always go by the rules. One day, I saw two women from an insurance company smoking at the gate. My report that night said that someone had smoked. I didn't name anyone. However, one of my fellow workers, a long-time employee of the security company who smoked at the office in violation of the rules, suspected I had ratted on her or soon would do so.

Thus, in a short period of time, I had crossed swords with two key people, my boss and an employee who had worked in security for a long time. I can't be sure, but I suspect that those conflicts resulted my being branded a troublemaker.

One night, I got called into the office of the boss who had struggled to explain the problem with my paycheck.

He said, "John, I am sorry, but you are not working with us anymore."

"Why?"

"Well, because you are not doing your job," the boss said.

"What is the problem?"

"John, sign this paper," he said, "and if you need anything filed, we will help you file for unemployment. And if you are referred to me, I will give you a recommendation."

The news stunned me. I showed up for work on time, did what I was asked to do, and tried to follow all the rules. I pressed for more information but got nowhere. I refused to sign the paper the boss held out to me. He made a note of my refusal, and that was the end of it. I went home.

Despite being angry and confused, I shook off my dismissal. I have survived slow starvation, crocodiles, and djellaba bullets. Being fired from a six dollar-an-hour job paled in comparison. I filed for unemployment compensation and collected it for one month.

In January 2004, I started working as a security guard at St. Joseph's Hospital in downtown Syracuse. The hospital offers a broad range of health care services, including its Comprehensive Psychiatric Emergency Program, a sort of emergency room serving the mentally ill. The work has been great, and my employers and I appreciate each other. I work plenty of overtime, meet lots of people, and take home a good paycheck.

Joseph Scicchitano, director of facilities services at St. Joseph's Hospital, on the first time he saw John: *John got off the elevator, and I saw this big guy standing there, ducking to get out. I walked up and said, "You must be John," and he said, "Yes, you must be Joe." I go to shake his hand, and he has such a nice, firm handshake. He got the job, and after spending a few minutes, we knew right from the get-go that he was going to provide a boost for us here.*

Why did I think he was a good potential hire? Well, I learned during the interview process a little bit about his background. And the thing that impressed me most about John is his appreciation for living in this country and having the opportunity to work. Nothing beyond that. We talked about that in the interview. He was so happy to come to the hospital to provide a service we need and just to have a job. He's glowing with a big smile. That's what we were looking for at the time, because we can train for technical expertise.

You cannot work around this guy and stay "down." Everything about John is forward, forward-thinking. He has used those things that happened to him in the past as building blocks to the future. There's a lot on my plate. I'm stressed out. I come in here for eight hours, I forget about my family, my faith, but when I see him, it all comes back. He just buries my hand with that giant hand of his. He's a unique guy, the kind we don't see in these parts very much.

My job is to detect and deter. I detect and report problems, and I deter them by patrolling in my uniform of blue shirt and black pants. I issue visitors' passes, and I arrange for friends and family to visit patients. I keep an eye out for intruders and trespassers; the hospital's neighborhood has deteriorated over the last few decades, and I help the hospital workers and visitors who need escorts. And every once in a while I help restrain patients who threaten violence to themselves or to others.

I got a taste of the job's potential danger shortly after I started. A patient being interviewed in the Comprehensive Psychiatric Emergency Program building sat with a counselor in a small room. As they talked, I watched and listened. Suddenly, the two men rushed out and wrestled on the floor. I called for help. I learned in training not to take on somebody dangerous all by myself. Three other security officers arrived, and we took the patient back to the interview room. The doctors wanted to medicate the man to keep him calm, but he refused to take the tranquilizers. The patient barricaded himself in his room. He yelled that he had been a marine, and he would fight to the death if anyone tried to force him to take medication. The nurse and the doctor said the man would either take the medicine voluntarily, or he would be restrained and forced to take an injection. The patient refused to listen. So the doctor called on the security team to hold the man down.

I moved forward at the front of the security team. As we approached, the patient slowly backed away. When I got within an arm's length—and I have very long arms—the man reached out and grabbed my hand. He was very strong, and he pulled me

just as I began pulling him. He put me in some kind of wrestling hold. Fortunately, that kept him occupied while the other
security officers moved forward and put him on the floor so
the nurse could give him the shot. As I went down, the patient
yanked and pulled at my back, and poked me in the ribs. I also
banged my feet against the edge of a metal bed frame and broke
the riveted hooks at the top of my right work boot. I didn't have
the money to fix the busted hooks or replace the shoes, so I wore
the boot half-laced for the next two years.

I loved my job and had been at it for only six weeks when I
got injured in my scrap with the mental patient, so I decided not
to say anything to my boss or ask for any time off. I didn't want
to jeopardize a good thing. But my back kept hurting, and after
a couple of days the pain became unbearable. I finally told my
supervisor. He was very understanding, and he arranged for me
to get medical treatment. It helped some, but the discomfort still
lingers. When I sit for hours at a time, my back aches and I have
to take medicine for the pain.

Since that time, I've been called upon from time to time to
physically restrain other patients. It's funny, but I have found a
way to bring my Dinka heritage to bear on the duties of my new
job. I'm an important wrestler now, just like my father.

I prefer the other aspects of working security, though. I appreciate my co-workers. They are very nice, very friendly. I look forward
to going to work each day. I try to treat people with dignity and respect, as I was taught in Duk Payuel. However, some people never
seem to reciprocate. Some Americans are so busy and so angry at
the world they just don't appreciate the country they live in.

For example, during the summer of 2006, St. Joseph's Hospital blocked its main entrance for construction of an expanded

*John, right, and Peter Bior enjoy the New York City sights on a trip
arranged by the family of Andrew Heyward, President of CBS News.*

entrance and pedestrian bridge. The work complemented a plan
to improve parking and access for patients and visitors. In the
long run, the construction will make the hospital a better place
for everyone. Yet the construction made some people angry in
the short run. The hospital had a rule that nobody could park in
the temporary entrance during construction. That made sense
to me, because the space had to be kept open for emergency vehicles. One night while I was on duty, a woman drove up with
a passenger and stopped in the emergency entrance. I told her
she could stay only for two or three minutes to drop off a patient. She told me she wanted to park because her passenger had
a handicap. I told her where to drop off the handicapped patient,
whom I said I would be happy to help, and I asked her to park a

short distance away and come back. To make a long story short, she insisted on parking in the restricted zone.

"I respect you," I told her, "but you must drop your patient and park your car elsewhere."

She put the car in park and turned off the ignition. She must have heard my accent and figured I came from Africa.

"Who are you? Who brought you here?" she shouted. "Go back to your f------ country! You are stupid. This is America, and you cannot tell me what to do!"

I called my supervisor.

"Come and rescue me," I said.

We made the woman move her car. When she came back, she had a terribly foul mouth.

"Ma'am, this is my job," I told her. "I always go by the book. You are a healthy person; you can walk." The woman and her passenger walked into the hospital. I noticed their car had no handicapped tag hanging from the rearview mirror. It's possible the passenger had a legitimate handicap. More likely, I think, the two women had tried to circumvent the parking rules and get a spot close to the front door. But even if the passenger had been handicapped, they would have had no right to block the entrance for people who needed emergency medical attention. And they had no right to treat me with such disrespect. Instead of being happy about having to take a short walk to get excellent medical care, they complained about the inconvenience. I have found their attitude to be surprisingly common. Americans have so much, but they insist on seeing the glass as half empty instead of half full. To extend the metaphor a bit, when I lived in Kakuma I didn't even have a glass.

The other side of my experience with Americans is that so many of them act so generously. They have no expectation of gain, yet they freely give to help a stranger. In this way, Americans share many of the qualities and blessings of the Dinka.

Many times during my first months in Syracuse, total strangers went out of their way to help me and the other Lost Boys. I felt grateful toward my friends from church, who worked hard to furnish the apartment for Jacob, Andrew, Santino, and me. I loved how they drove each Sunday to take us to church in Skaneateles and fed us afterward. I appreciated how the car pool volunteers in Syracuse picked us up in the middle of the night so we could go to work and come home. In particular, I was stunned with gratitude when a woman from Ovid, New York, read about me in a newspaper in the fall of 2001 and sent me and my roommates a bag of winter clothes. She did not want to be thanked; the package came with no return address. "We know you came from somewhere with no winter," she wrote in a note, "and you need winter clothes."

I had two encounters in the local grocery store that illustrated the bright and dark sides of American character. One time, I saw a boy about nine years old shopping with his mother. He saw Andrew, Santino, and me shopping for food. The boy asked his mother for some money, and she gave him a few dollar bills. He walked up to us and handed each of us a dollar, no questions asked. The boy said he could see we had come recently from Africa, and he wanted to show us how welcome we were in the United States. I thanked him very kindly and took the dollar. His mother's jaw dropped open in surprise. I compared that with another time I saw a young boy in the store. Dinka tradition considers it a virtue for adults to give things to children. I bought a piece of candy and handed it to a little boy who was wandering the aisles. His mother spotted me and gave me the strangest look. She grabbed her son, said, "Come on over here," and pulled him out the door. What she thought of me I can only imagine.

I think about such things and wonder: Which America, bright or dark, is the truer one? Will America be governed by its principles of loving and helping one another, or by its moments of suspicion and cynicism?

I cannot say. All I know is, I have seen a great deal of the best, and some of the worst, of America. As a new American, I must do my part to make things better.

6

ACCULTURATION CAME EASIER FOR SOME LOST BOYS IN AMERICA *than for others. A* New York Times *reporter watching the arrival of a group of Lost Boys in Boston said one screamed and fled in fear at the sight of an escalator. Another rode in a car through the woods to get to his new home and asked the driver, "Are there lions in the bush?" Similarly, John Dau and his roommates hesitated to swim in blue-green Skaneateles Lake until they received assurance that it held no crocodiles or hippos.*

"For them, everything is new," a letter from the Skaneateles First Presbyterian mission committee explained to the church congregation. "They are wide-eyed and full of wonder. They are like sponges in this new environment. They are almost childlike, most never having had a childhood. They need parenting and guidance, and [they] accept their sponsors in this role. They are very polite and respectful. Dating and marriage is of great concern to them, and they have had no education in these areas. Their cultural background is very different from ours.... When you meet them, you will feel you have been given a gift that you would not receive upon meeting another American."

One of the biggest transitions for many Lost Boys centered on the sudden freedom and self-sufficiency. Refugees in Kakuma had been handed many of life's necessities. In America, a totally foreign land where water, the most basic requirement of life, had to be purchased before it flowed from faucets, rained down from showerheads, and froze solid in boxy kitchen appliances, the Lost Boys needed to find jobs as soon as possible. Many started out doing menial tasks in factories and fast-food restaurants.

Health insurance, Social Security deductions, income taxes, traffic regulations...the rules that governed basic survival overwhelmed the newcomers. Beyond them lay the folkways and mores, some subtle and some not so subtle, that made social life pleasant or uncomfortable. How often do Americans bathe? How should men treat women at the workplace? How do Americans handle the issue of race? How could Lost Boys make new friends? And why do Americans stay all by themselves in their rooms at night, instead of gathering for time together? Lost Boys often learned lessons the hard way. Two of them in Kentucky chatted with an American woman who had been married for seven years but did not have children. One of the Lost Boys asked, "What is wrong with you that you do not have a child? Is it your problem or is it your husband's problem?" The other Lost Boy, more worldly than his companion, admonished him that the reason a married couple did or did not have children was a delicate subject in America.

Lost Boys occasionally got into trouble with the law. Most scraps were minor, but Boston authorities charged one resettled Sudanese with rape. Lost Boys also became victims. One died in Atlanta in a drunken dispute over ten dollars that resulted in charges being filed against another Lost Boy. Others suffered violent deaths in Nashville and Louisville. In 2006, Lost Boy David Agar was shot to death in a scuffle with an armed robber outside a bar in Pittsburgh, five years after he arrived in America as a teenager. According to the Pittsburgh Post-Dispatch, Agar planned a career in video production and a reunion in America with his mother, who had turned up in a refugee camp after he arrived in America. "By all rights," the paper said, "Mr. Agar's first 18 years of life should have granted him immunity from such senselessness." Friends described Agar as quiet, gentle, friendly, religious, and profoundly keen about the fortunes of the Pittsburgh Steelers football team. In short, not so different from a lot of Americans.

I DREAM OF AFRICA ALMOST EVERY DAY.

Sometimes I dream at night that I am back at Kakuma or walking with Abraham along the path from Duk Payuel. Sometimes my mind wanders while I work at the hospital, and I see things that are not really there. For some seconds, I do not remember where I am. Then I snap out of it, and I am back in Syracuse.

Over and over I have variations of the same dream. Soldiers want to kill me. Lions want to eat me. I shake and wake up. And I ask myself, "Who am I?"

Most of the time, I can't remember the details of the dreams. But I remember one with clarity.

In my dream I sit atop an eight-foot-tall anthill and watch over my father's flock. As I perch there, I make toy cows out of clay. Beside me lie my knife, my stick, and my spear. I am chewing a sorghum stem and looking at my clay cows, when all of a sudden I hear something running. The curtain of grass opens, and I see a goat of mine, followed by a lion. The lion chases the goat around and around my anthill, and I think that perhaps the goat has run to me to get my help. I get up, grab my spear, and point it at the lion. The lion bows down, afraid of me, and freezes. I seize the lion by the tail and swing it around in a circle. I am so, so powerful. Holding the lion's tail like the handle of a whip, I beat the animal's body against the anthill. Still the lion refuses to move. I switch to my stick and beat the lion's head, then return to swinging it by the tail and whacking it against the hill.

When I look up from beating the lion, I see a group of boys having fun. I drag the lion to where the boys are playing. The boys ask me, "Why are you killing that lion?" I say, "If I kill this lion, he will not be able to attack my goats again."

We talk like that for a while. In my dream I stand like a Dinka boy on watch, with my right leg straight, my left leg bent at the knee, and the handle of my spear tucked under my shoulder, its point stuck in the ground like a third leg.

"What do you want to do with that lion?" one of the boys asks.

"I want to throw it away," I reply. "I will take it far away and get rid of it so it cannot harm anything in my village again."

I take the lion to a place where I can cast it into a swift-flowing river, where the current will make it disappear. Just as I start to toss it in, though, it comes alive and stands up. In the blink of an eye, it grows strong again. The lion chases me, intent on catching and eating me. I run very fast, until I trip over a bunch of grass and fall. The lion leaps toward me...and I wake up.

I don't know what the dream means. Certainly I am no Sigmund Freud, whom I have read about in one of my classes. I never had to kill a lion, having only chased hyenas from the farm when I was young. But I wonder. My dream is about protecting the things I cherish from a powerful force coming in from the outside. And just when I think the force has been subdued, it rises anew and threatens me. Now, I suppose I could be the lion—my name Bul means "lion." But more likely, I think, the dream would make sense if the lion wore a djellaba.

Some of my friends among the Lost Boys have nightmares. They see their loved ones killed by bullets and shrapnel or seized by the roiling waters or the crocodiles of the Gilo River. How long they must relive the horrors of their childhoods I do not know. They have come halfway around the world, thousands of miles from their African homes, yet they cannot leave Africa behind. Nor should they, I think. They, and I, must learn to be Dinka in America. With God's grace, we must learn to treasure the best of our experiences and apply them to our new lives. We must keep moving forward. When a man finds himself in the middle of a swamp—be it a literal quagmire or a figurative one, like drugs, divorce, or despair—going forward is the only way to get free.

I know my way out of a swamp. I must educate myself. I must provide for my loved ones. And I must make sure that I do all I can to help my people, in Sudan and in America.

Since 2004, I have taken on added responsibilities. They have complicated my life but also brought great gladness.

ALMOST FROM THE DAY I ENTERED KAKUMA IN 1992, I TRIED to find my family. I wrote about 70 letters and gave them to the Red Cross. The agency sent tens of thousands of messages from the Lost Boys in Kenya across the Sudanese border to try to re-unite families. Some of the Lost Boys had success through such methods, and I was willing to give it a try. Nothing came from my letter-writing campaign. Still, I did not give up hope. When I got to America, I learned that it often took years for families scattered by Rwanda's civil war of 1994 to find each other. For that matter, American newspapers and television broadcasts still occasionally carry stories of the reunions of European families scattered by World War II. Surely in America, where I had my own phone and access to the Internet, I could search more ef-fectively for my family than I did in Africa.

Two days after arriving in America, I wrote letters to my friends in Kakuma. I told them how good I found life in America, how the country flowed with milk and beef, and how well Susan Meyer and her church friends had treated me. Susan took the letters and mailed them for me.

One of my Kakuma friends who received one of my letters traveled to Uganda for a while. He told the people he met about the Lost Boys in America, and in particular he mentioned his friend, John Dau in New York. That placed the message on the traditional news medium of the Dinka, the storytelling chain that spreads information from person to person, until it reaches the farthest corners of the county.

A man living in Uganda whose name was Goi heard the news and became intrigued. Goi asked my friend, "Who is this John?"

"It is John Dau, from the Nyarweng clan," my friend said.

My friend did not know Goi was my brother. By the longest of odds, at a camp hundreds of miles from any place I had ever called home, two people I loved came together to pass along the most improbable of messages.

Goi went home and told our mother, "I found a man who talked about a Nyarweng named John Dau today. He said John is alive."

"No," my mother told Goi. "John is dead."

Goi decided to get more information. He went back to my friend and started peppering him with questions. What did this John look like? Where did he come from? What was his father's name? When did he go to America? What did he say about his life before he became a Lost Boy? Goi also volunteered information about the shelling of Duk Payuel in 1987, and how the family got separated that night.

John, in a dark suit, stands with his brothers Goi, right, and Aleer,
and Angok Ayiik, the wife of his half brother, in Uganda in January 2006.

They compared answers and thought there were too many co-incidences. Goi invited my friend to his home to meet Abraham Aleer Deng, our eldest brother. Aleer heard the evidence and de-cided to write to the return address on my letter.

When I got home from classes at Onandaga Community College on October 18, 2002, the sight of the big letter in the apartment mailbox sparked my curiosity immediately. Ugandan stamps covered the back of the envelope, and the words above the handwritten address said, "Dhieu Deng Leek," a name I had not used in a long time. I took the envelope inside my apart-ment and opened it with trembling hands. Out spilled a letter and photographs of an old man and woman. They looked like my mother and father, only grayer and more wrinkled.

"John," Aleer wrote, "if you are my brother, please, can you write to us? And if you are not my brother, please throw this letter away."

It sounds like a cliché, but I literally jumped for joy. Two sentences into reading the letter, I held it up as if it had been a thousand-dollar bill. I bounded around the tiny living room like a jackrabbit.

"We are still alive—mother, father, and all of your brothers and sisters, plus a sister born after you left, named Akuot. Unfortunately, our three uncles were killed in the shelling, along with their families." The letter went on with news of how the family had settled in a camp along the Sudan-Uganda border. It ended with a Ugandan phone number.

I called Susan Meyer. I called Brandy Blackman. I called Jack Howard. I called the InterReligious Council of Central New York, the agency that had sponsored my resettlement in America and set up my contacts with First Presbyterian Church in Skaneateles. I couldn't call enough, fast enough, to tell everyone. At church on Sunday, I announced that my loved ones lived, and I had been given a great blessing.

"Be happy with me," I said. "I have found my family."

I wrote a letter to my parents and mailed it. Then, after waiting enough time to make sure the letter had arrived, I followed up with a call. Ron Dean, one of the members of Living Word Church in Syracuse, gave me a plastic telephone card charged with $30, good for several hundred domestic minutes. At the exchange rate of 11 minutes of American calls for each minute of connection to Uganda, it gave me only a little while to talk. I had precious little time to reestablish the ties to my family after an absence of 15 years.

The phone rang in Africa. I heard the receiver click as someone picked it up.

"This is Goi."

"Hello. This is John."

Goi handed the phone to Aleer. We spoke just a few words, enough to learn that Mother was in the kitchen, when the connection got cut off. I tried calling again but got nothing. The call simply would not go through. I looked at the clock: one in the morning my time. I decided to wait until morning and try again. At dawn in Syracuse, as the sun sank in Uganda, the phone finally rang again at my mother's house.

I spoke to my brothers first. I filled them in as quickly as I could on my journey of survival with Abraham and my many years in the Ethiopian and Kenyan refugee camps. I told them how I had come to America, gotten a job, and started college.

Goi and Aleer started crying. I cried too. But when they tried to hand the phone to my mother, she refused to speak to me. She accused Goi and Aleer of lying to her, to try to make her feel better.

"Mother, mother, weep no more. It is I, John." I wanted so much to tell her those words. She would not listen. She would not even allow herself to hear.

I spoke to Goi and Aleer over a crackling transatlantic telephone connection. They relayed my words to our mother, who stood nearby. It must be a trick, she said. John died in 1987. Of that she was certain. She wouldn't take the receiver from my brothers, who urged her to speak into the mouthpiece.

"Tell Mother, it is me, John," I said.

I heard a muffled exchange as Goi and Aleer spoke to my mother. Then, Aleer's voice came back on the line.

"She said, 'You guys are lying to me. That is not my son.'"

That was the start of 48 hours of agony. I could not get my mother to talk to me, and I could not be sure when the minutes on my card would run out. With a heavy heart, I said good-bye to my brothers and hung up.

Two days later, with a fresh phone card, I tried again.

This time, my mother reluctantly accepted the phone from Aleer and Goi. I pressed my case.

"Mother, this is John. I am the one."

"No," she said. "You are not my son."

She must have had begun to have a change of heart, though, because she decided to test me. Among the Dinka, mothers give their children a variety of nicknames. Few outside the family know what they are.

"If you are my son, tell me the other names I used to call you," she said.

"Did you call me Makat?" I replied. "Did you call me Runrach? Did you call me Dhieu?"

Makat means "born when people are running away," *Runrach* means "bad year," and *Dhieu* means "cry." My nicknames referred to my being born during the year when a raid by the Murle tribe killed two of my father's brothers. For a split second, silence filled the space between us. In certain critical moments in my life, I have found that time expands until it consumes the universe. I lived a lifetime waiting for the silence to end.

Then, my mother's voice.

"It is you! But your voice seems different."

"I'm not the 13-year-old you used to know," I said. "I'm now a grown man. Today, I'm tall."

We spoke awhile longer, but I felt my mother still had doubts. I decided to settle them once and for all. I sent her money from my job to help pay the medical bills of my oldest sister, Agot. First Presbyterian Church of Skaneateles sent money, too—$300 from the congregation and $700 from Penny and Bill Allyn. No one would be so generous without a reason. My mother realized the news had to be true. I called her two or three times a week from then on.

My family had fled west and south from Duk Payuel on the night of the attack. They lived as internal refugees for a while in southern Sudan before returning to the village. A second djellaba attack drove them south again. When I called, my mother, sisters Agot and Akuot, brothers Goi and Aleer, two stepbrothers, and three stepsisters lived at the Ugandan border. My father had returned to Duk County, as soon as it was safe, with the youngest of his wives. He had added another wife since we last saw each other, and, as is the custom among the Dinka, made his home with the latest of his brides.

I began a phone and mail campaign to try to bring everyone in my family to Syracuse. It culminated with my filing family reunification papers with the Immigration and Naturalization Service early in 2002. The INS considered the case over the next few months and settled it with a compromise by helping some but not others. The immigration lawyers denied entry to my brothers and sisters, because they were self-supporting adults. However, the INS allowed my 14-year-old sister, Akuot, into the U.S. as a minor. My mother, Anon Duot, then won permission to resettle in order to take care of Akuot. Unfortunately, the line got drawn when I tried to bring my father to accompany my mother. He refused to enter the country without his new wife, which the INS told him would have violated American laws against polygamy. The bureaucracy that decided who got in and who stayed behind reminded me of the Dinka story of the hyena and the goats. The hyena desperately wanted to enter the goats' hut so he could kill and eat. He bargained with God, saying, "Just let me inside. That's the hard part. Going out will be easy." For an immigrant, it's harder to get into America than to leave the country after gaining entry.

Two years later, in February 2004—immigration red tape takes forever to clear up—my mother and sister landed at Syracuse Hancock International Airport. Syracuse's newspaper and television stations had learned about the reunion and joined me at the end of a secure corridor to await the arrival. Christopher Quinn's documentary cameras captured the reunion for his film. As my mother walked along the corridor, she looked at me and my roommates waiting to greet her. I could tell she struggled to pick me out, so I stepped forward. She threw her hands in the air and embraced me. We collapsed on the floor, rocking back and forth, as my mother chanted in Dinka.

"*Yecue doc ben, yecue doc ben,*" she sobbed. I translated for the reporters: My mother said her thanks to God.

That embrace lasted a full five minutes. I could have held her for hours.

She carried with her a cross and two Sudanese *gupo* baskets to give to First Presbyterian Church of Skaneateles as a way to thank its members for supporting me since my arrival. The gupos blazed in colorful designs of red, green, black, and white yard; Dinka use them to store valuables, collect the offering at

Akuot, the sister John never knew, flies into his arms at the Syracuse airport in 2004, while their mother, just out of the picture, cries in jubilation.

church, or carry dry food such as groundnuts. The round baskets of my mother's gupos were separate, but she conjoined the lids to symbolize the unity of the Sudanese and the American people. Those gupos now hang in the Skaneateles church.

I also had gifts. I carried two bouquets: roses for my mother, lollipops for my sister Akuot.

Akuot Deng Leek: *When I got off the plane with my mother and walked through the airport at Syracuse, I strained to look for John. Several Dinka waited for us at the end of a walkway in the terminal. Which one was my brother? I figured it out when a man stepped ahead of the others and advanced toward us. He was very tall—the tallest in our family—and he was crying. He kind of crouched as he hugged us. I screamed and I cried in joy, and so did my mother. I think I might have said, "Is that you?" As I looked at him, though, I could see the family resemblance.*

Reporters asked me how I felt. What a silly question. I felt everything. Great love for my family. Great relief at their safe arrival. Great concern for those they left behind. I knew many challenges lay ahead. My mother spoke no English. She would have to adjust to life in a city where only a few dozen people could communicate with her. My sister, whose English skills at least let her carry on simple conversations, would need to go to school, learn the customs of a new country, and make new friends. Both got a taste of culture shock when they stepped out of the heated terminal into a frosty winter day unlike anything they had seen in Africa, and then walked to a car that I told them I owned and drove. At least they would have my experience to guide them through the confusion, I thought. I had arranged for them to take an apartment in the same complex where I lived, so I could be nearby when they needed me.

I did not say so at the time, but I felt one more thing above all others. It was a private thing, so I did not share it. But I felt, very strongly, the grace of God. I can take no credit for it; grace is not something anyone can earn. Rather, grace opened before me like the door, and I walked through it. I knew I had been blessed. How else could anyone explain the impossible odds I had overcome—the dangers, the miles, the despair. God had not forgotten me after all.

MORE DOORS OPENED, AND MORE BLESSINGS CAME. I GOT INTO Syracuse University, and I found the woman I wanted to marry. It was as if God had chosen to make up for my years of torment by granting me many good things in a short span of time.

Martha Arual Akech and I lived in Pinyudu at the same time, but I don't think we ever met. Martha had lost her parents when

John embraces his American family—Akuot, Martha, and Anon, John and
Akuot's mother—at the home of friends Bill and Sabra Reichardt.

the djellabas attacked her village in the same year they shelled
Duk Payuel. She made her way to Ethiopia with her three-year-
old sister, Tabitha. Their survival placed them among the rare
and lucky Lost Girls.

The first time I recall noticing Martha was in Kakuma. She
made quite an impression on me. Some Lost Boys teased her and
acted mean. She kept her composure and ignored them. It was a
courageous performance. Not long after that, I saw her again at
a Sunday night dance in her group area.

I approached her later, at her home in the Dinka manner, which
is to say politely and slowly. I asked if I could talk to her, because I
liked her. She was smart, practical, and strong in her Christian faith.

She turned me down. But in a good way. Something in the
way she told me to leave made me think she acted out of Dinka

custom, which forbade her to encourage a suitor in any way. She never gave me a specific reason she disliked me, so I thought I had a chance with her. I kept coming back to ask if I could be her boyfriend. She kept saying no, but she always let me come back the next day. This went on until finally she said yes, she would allow me to visit, and we could be boyfriend and girlfriend. That lasted a few months, until she left Kakuma in December 2000 to fly to Seattle with her sister.

I feared I would never see her again.

When I got to Syracuse, I asked around and got in touch with Martha, who was living in Seattle. We began talking and exchanging e-mails. In December 2002, after I learned my family had survived, I saw Martha again. We met at a reunion of Lost Boys held in Grand Rapids, Michigan, because so many had settled there. I flew from Syracuse on a ticket donated by the Skaneateles church. She stayed with one of her girlfriends in Michigan, while I stayed with my friends. We drove to a restaurant that first night, then spent as much time as we could just talking. In the mornings and afternoons, I met with the other Lost Boys in a big Lutheran church. We wanted to organize to speak politically with one voice on behalf of southern Sudan and to establish organizations to provide college scholarships for Lost Boys in the U.S. In the evenings, I met Martha in the home where she was staying. She had her friends and extended family with her, as did I. It was all very proper, according to Dinka tradition.

It was hard to think nothing but politics in the mornings and then try to ignore all debate and discussion to focus on Martha in the evenings, but I think I pulled it off. I tried to give my full attention to everything in its proper time.

About a thousand Lost Boys attended the gathering. It was fun to see people I had not seen since I lived in Kakuma, and to eat real Sudanese *ayod,* a maize-wheat porridge that the Lost Girls griddled to make flat, golden-brown cakes like Ethiopian bread. In three days of talks, we formed the Duk County Association in the U.S. as a continuation of a group we had created in Kakuma. We pledged to help Duk County rebuild from the devastation of civil war, making it attractive and worthy "not only for ourselves and those who follow us," we said, "but also to honor all our beloved sisters, brothers, parents, relatives, and friends who we lost to the war." The Lost Boys of Duk, together again after their dispersal, vowed to place health care and education at the top of their list of desired improvements.

We said we would work in harmony and integrity toward our goals. Little did we know how quickly political divisions would arise to challenge us. We should have guessed. We Dinka are headstrong and proud.

That was not my only disappointment at Grand Rapids. So many of the Lost Boys had adopted the clothing and hairstyles of American youths. They wore jeans that hung far too low, baseball caps, funny jewelry, and weird hairstyles. That just killed me. What would the elders have said if they had seen those boys? It is good for people to embrace their new country but not to such a degree that they forget their heritage. At least, it is not the Dinka way. It seemed ironic that so many Lost Boys could pledge their love of Duk County yet forget to honor their Duk ancestry through their clothes and manners. That was not respectful.

Martha stayed true to her roots, however. She worked hard as a nurse's assistant at a Seattle nursing home and supported herself and her sister with her salary. She lived practically and dressed modestly. After our meeting in Grand Rapids, we began seeing each other regularly, each of us flying to the other's city. To save money, we talked of living in the same town. The decision taxed us terribly. Which one of us should move? Martha had her sister Tabitha to think of, and by 2004 I had my mother, who spoke no English and knew nobody in Seattle. I convinced Martha that the move would be difficult for my mother, who could neither go with me to the West Coast nor live alone if I left her behind. Martha agreed to move East.

"You know what?" I told myself. "This is the girl. The one."

I had promised the elders at Kakuma I would not go with an American girl. That was easy; I did not want one. Martha was a Dinka, she spoke the Dinka language, she knew the Dinka ways. And she was very pretty.

My parents helped with the marriage negotiations. My mother got my brothers to send for my father, and we talked on the phone.

"This is the girl I want to marry," I told my father.

"Okay," he said. "Let's find out whether we are related and whether she comes from a good family." He made inquiries in Africa. Her family came from the village of Abek, a few miles from Duk Payuel, so it was relatively easy to find people who knew Martha's relatives. My father learned that her parents lived good lives. Nobody saw them die, so we hope to find them alive someday. Martha's grandparents and brothers and sisters and cousins and aunts and uncles all passed muster. I waited for a year for my father's investigations to be complete. At last, he said he could find nothing but good things about Martha, and he gave me his blessing.

Martha Arual Akech: *I went to school in Kakuma. That's where I learned a little bit of English. Not as much as the boys, though, because Sudanese women* are so busy. They do a lot of chores—fetching water, fetching firewood, cooking, and so on. So we girls didn't take the lessons as seriously as the boys. We learned some things, but we didn't have a lot of time to practice them. I had almost no chance to read when I got home from school. Still, I learned enough English to help me later.

I finished primary school, passed the test for my certificate, and had begun the first year of high school when I was selected to come to America. I met John that year in Kakuma. Our schools were next to each other. When I left my house to go to school, I passed by his school. I had seen him around before that time, on the way to school or in the school kitchen where we both ate lunch. I remember him as one of the tall Sudanese guys. But there was no attraction then either way, from him or from me.

People passed by my house a lot on the way to school. They saw me in my compound as they walked to and fro. According to John, the first time he really paid close attention to me was when I was going to school and he walked behind me. He saw two boys being mean to me, but I was polite and did not talk back to them. He told me, later, that he watched me keep my cool, and he said to himself, "I like her."

Boys often came and stood by the compound gates and waited for the girls to walk by. John came one morning, riding a bike, to my compound. One of the little neighbor girls came and told me, "There's a man standing by the door." I was inside the house, braiding a friend's hair at the time. I looked through the window to see who it was. If it had been one of the guys I didn't want to talk to, I would have sent the little girl back to tell him I wasn't home. But I spoke to him, and he answered, "I just want to know when you will be free, as I want to talk to you." I didn't really have any idea if he was coming for me, or for somebody else. Some guys ask a girl about her sister or her friend before they approach that girl, and John may have wanted to talk about someone I knew. I told him to come back later.

When he came back, he told me he liked me and wanted to be my boyfriend. I told him, "I don't like you," but I did not give a specific reason. That meant

I liked him. See, a Dinka girl would never say anything to a boy the first time they talked to indicate she liked him. What the girl wants to find out is if the guy really likes her. And if he does like the girl, he will come back the next day if she tells him to go away. The girl keeps sending him away, and he keeps coming back and coming back. That's how she knows.

So I said, "No, I don't like you. No, no way."

So he said, "Why?"

I answered, "I do not know you very well."

And he said, "That's why I came, so you can get to know me."

He probably knew I liked him. He kept coming back. Each time I told him to go away, he asked me to let him have one more day to talk to me. I don't know how many times he came back like that, asking each time for one more day, before I said yes.

John and I were together for about six months before I had to leave. We did not go out on dates. There was nowhere in the camp to go, nowhere for a girl to date. And it was not accepted for a girl to be seen with a man outside her home, except at the dances on Sunday nights. Most of the young people went to the dances, where they might or might not see a boyfriend and girlfriend. If the boy or girl were there, they could dance together. That was the extent of our relationship, other than walking and talking together.

One of the things that attracted me to him was the way he thinks. I had guys come to me before in Kakuma, but when I saw John, I compared him to those other guys and said, "This is a man." If he has something to say, he says it. He gets his back up when he feels strongly about things. I liked that.

I also liked it that he always took responsibility, and he was very caring. A lot of boys had problems, and he would sit them down and help them solve their issues. I could see him doing good work from far away. And I never heard anything bad about him at Kakuma. Camp is big, but if you did something wrong, it always got around. I knew who the bad guys and the good guys were at camp. John was one of the good guys.

I didn't know if he was going to be accepted into America too. He came to say good-bye to me before I left, and he said, "Don't forget me."

I told him, "I can't promise you I will wait for you. I don't know what will happen here, or what will happen there. If things work out for you, that would be great." John was kind of disappointed about that. He said he would think about me and wait to be with me, no matter how many years it would take.

I wanted a traditional Dinka marriage. That meant I had to give a dowry of cows to Martha's family. We made the arrangements and agreed on the contract in October 2005. Martha's uncles in Twic County, Sudan, and my father in the camp on the Uganda border concurred. At that moment, in the eyes of my people, we were married. If I had a mallet and a peg, I would have smacked the peg into the dirt outside my apartment to announce—*whack!*—that everyone endorsed the arrangements.

Like my father when he married, I lacked the wealth to seal the deal. I owned no cows, and my pay stayed only a few dollars an hour above minimum wage. I started saving money to send to Sudan, so that our proxies could buy and exchange cows in the Dinka manner. If I did not pay the dowry, I could not claim and name our children.

Martha, my wife, moved into my apartment. It was empty by the end of 2005, my roommates having moved on to independent lives. The adjustment to living with a woman confounded me at first. I had lived with men for nearly two decades. Out of sheer necessity I had learned to cook and to clean in Pinyudu and Kakuma, which married Dinka men never do in Sudan. I wanted to revert to our roles as man and woman, but sometimes my plans just didn't work out. Martha came home one night from the hospital after a long shift and felt too tired to cook. So I cooked for myself as a married man. Hard to imagine for a Dinka, but I did it because I love her. I've done it again and again, as the need arises, and tell myself it is a compromise I must make as an American. I am not in Sudan, after all.

Our division of labor took on added importance when Martha became pregnant in 2006. She had taken a job as a phlebotomist, drawing blood for analysis and transfusion at St. Joseph's Hospital, where I worked in security. We celebrated when our hospital co-workers tested Martha and announced she was expecting. The sonogram came back with a clear picture: We would have a daughter before the end of the year.

I arranged to build a house in Syracuse with the help of a city program that encourages low-income first-time homeowners to take out mortgages for homes within the city limits. At first, the program administrators wanted to deny my application, saying I earned too much money to qualify. They changed their minds when I showed that my income exceeded their limits only because I worked so much overtime at the hospital.

The whole family will live there—Martha, me, our daughter, my mother, and my sister. My mother and sister can help with the baby. I will leave the car with my family during the day and ride a bicycle to work. I had five bikes stolen at the apartment complex, where thieves cut the chains and rode away in the middle of the night. At my new house, I will lock the bike in a secure place.

As a Dinka, I must have a son to continue my name. That does not mean I love my daughter any less. Women have more of a sense of humanity than men. They are big-hearted, and they bring happiness wherever they go.

The prayer I say for my daughter, for my children, no doubt is the same as the prayer of many, many Americans. I want her to have a better life than I did. I pray for my daughter to be my "make up girl." Through her, I will make up all that I lost. My parents took good care of me, but I left them and had to raise myself. I will not let my daughter grow up without my help. I will set up a bank account for her, with money going into it every week, so she will have the finest education and learn more than I know. I will make sure she learns to appreciate her family. I will see to it that she never suffers from want.

I know I will be strict with her, as my father was with me. That is the best way to raise a child. Teach the child at a young age to have discipline, to respect elders and family, and the rest of life's lessons will take care of themselves. This will give my daughter the best of two worlds: The gifts of Dinka culture, in a land where those gifts will take her as far as she wants to go.

The duty of naming the baby belongs to my mother, as representative of the women on the husband's side of the new family. By tradition, the name Agot has been set aside for my daughter. It is always the name of the oldest girl in my family; I have eight aunts named Agot. My second daughter will be Akur, also because of family custom. The first son born to Martha and me will be Leek and the second Aleer. That's the system. My contribution to my daughter's christening will be what Americans call the "middle name," which is actually another family name among the Dinka. I want her to be Agot Dhieu-Deng Leek. That way, my father's name will live on in America.

To take some of the financial pressure off my growing family, I secured a Pell Grant, a federal financial award for undergraduate education that does not need to be repaid. I've also secured additional aid to attend Syracuse University through a

New York State program that helps pay the tuition of first-time, low-income students. I thought about a major and settled on public relations. An advisor interviewed me about appropriate classes for my first semester and quickly determined that I had chosen wrongly. Instead of public relations, I wanted a public policy major in the public affairs program. The advisor, Joey Tse, told me public affairs deals with government policies, while public relations focuses on communicating ideas. Every government policy that affects people naturally has to be communicated, so in reality the two are not completely separate. But the advisor essentially was right. I want to make a basic difference in the lives of refugees and immigrants. I want to make changes in policy that will make lives better.

Joey Tse told me to take a class from Bill Coplin, a professor in the Maxwell School who teaches public policy. On the first day of class, Professor Coplin demonstrated the importance of such policy on a basic level by cutting up a student's fake ID card. He asked for comments, and I raised my hand. Almost alone among the students in class that day, I told him that if we don't like the law, we may work to change it, but until then we must obey it. He took an interest in me and spoke to me after class. From then on, he worked with me not only to master the basics of my various classes but also to assemble the skills I would need as an American university student. He told me I had to learn to type, then set up a series of typing lessons. He showed me how to use a computer to set up spreadsheets and plan PowerPoint presentations. And he arranged for tutors to help me with my speaking and writing. It was more than any student should have a right to expect from a professor, yet it was exactly what I needed to have the confidence to express myself.

I know these skills will help me influence people on behalf of international refugees.

My dream is to get a job with the United Nations and work in Africa or America. If I have the time and money, I would like to study immigration law. Refugees in Africa would best be served by someone who knows the ins and outs of international law, yet who understands the depths of their troubles firsthand. Oppressors hurt people because of their religion or their politics or their ethnic or racial background. Too many victims lack someone to speak for them on the world stage. The peoples of southern Sudan, for example, are still scattered in Uganda, Ethiopia, Chad, Congo, the Central African Republic, Kenya, and other countries. Ending the diaspora requires people with a variety of skills and the motivation to use them. One thing Professor Coplin's class taught me was to look for the people in power and watch how they exercise it. On the ground in faraway refugee camps, the people with power are immigration agents and lawyers. I need to change the laws so they will let more refugees out of their misery. That is my mission.

I DECIDED TO DO WHAT I COULD TO CHANGE LIVES IN A CONCRETE way. When I arrived in Syracuse, the Lost Boys hadn't organized themselves. We needed a forum, I thought, a foundation, to channel our energy. With the help of others interested in such an organization, I set up the Sudanese Lost Boys Foundation of New York. Our members include about 150 Lost Boys in Syracuse, about 45 in Rochester, and a few more in Utica and other towns. We set up the foundation to accept and disburse charitable donations. My intent was to create a funnel for money to help the Lost Boys pay for college tuition, books, computers, and other things they needed to succeed in America. The foundation office also served as a place for Lost Boys to relax and discuss issues affecting them. We raised $35,000 in the first year.

The most amazing donation came from the philanthropic Rosamond Gifford Foundation of Syracuse. When I talked to other foundations, they said no, no, no to my requests for donations. The breakthrough occurred when I approached Kathy Goldfarb-Findling at the Gifford. I found her office on the Internet when I Googled the words "foundation" and "Syracuse." I called her and said, "My name is John Dau, of the Sudanese Lost Boys Foundation of New York." She said, "Okay, what do you need?" I told her the foundation I represented did good work helping Lost Boys go to school in the U.S. but that we needed money. She told me to visit her in her office downtown the next day. As I made a note of that, I asked her again what her name was. "Kathy with a 'K,'" she said. I remembered that and have called her that ever since.

The next day, I put on my dark suit—it is so hard to find clothes to fit a skinny man who stands six feet eight—and went to her office with some of my friends. Kathy-with-a-K took us to another room and made us feel welcome. She invited me to say why I had come. I don't remember what I said, but I didn't say much before Kathy excused herself, got up, and left the meeting. When she returned, she held out a check. We were stunned. She gave us $5,000 on the spot.

Kathy Goldfarb-Findling: *There were two things that struck me immediately about John. The first was that he was so clearly trying to create structure and organization within the community of Lost Boys, and he was working very hard at finding a focus for them. That was the first thing I found to be a bit extraordinary. Then, he was in a leadership role, he was comfortable in that role, and he was trying to accomplish something that to me, appeared to be really difficult to do: To organize these young men around the idea of creating a scholarship fund to further their education. Given that they were all in relatively low-paying jobs and sending a good deal of money back to the refugee camps where they had come from, and where a good deal of their families still resided, it seemed to me that he had taken on a difficult task.*

That gave us the momentum we needed. She recruited others to support our foundation and even organized a fund-raiser during the showing of a PBS documentary about the Lost Boys on Syracuse television. Kathy's foundation paid for four brand-new computers in our office and even picked up the expenses when eight other Lost Boys and I traveled to a national reunion in Phoenix, Arizona. Many Sudanese, including some still in Africa, have benefited from Kathy's generosity. I cannot thank her enough. In America, nobody seemed willing to take the Lost Boys Foundation seriously until the Gifford Foundation stepped up and made its support very public.

After a year as president of the foundation, I stepped down to give others a chance to serve. That was at the end of 2004. By that time, I had plans to raise money for other projects. One involved creating the Sudanese Association of Central New York, an umbrella organization that includes women, families, children, and others who can't technically be called Lost Boys. Another involved bringing American-style medical care to Sudan. I didn't want to announce the health care project while raising money for scholarships, because I thought they would detract from one another. However, after I left my office as foundation president, I felt free to act.

I spoke to "Grandfather" Jack Howard and told him I wanted to build a medical clinic in Duk County. Grandfather Jack didn't bat an eye, although he later told me the idea moved him profoundly. He said it would take a lot of work, but it could be done. I chatted with relatives in Sudan and Uganda too, and they said the villagers of Duk County supported the idea wholeheartedly.

Penny Allyn, who had helped me when I moved into my apartment and went with me on my first trip to the grocery store, was married to Bill Allyn, whose family co-owned Welch Allyn, a huge company that makes medical diagnostic equipment. With Grandfather's help, I wrote and polished a proposal to create a foundation to build a clinic in my homeland. Although the Welch Allyn company could not make a corporate donation because of rules limiting its charity to local causes, members of the family gave as individuals. In just a few weeks, Grandfather and I got pledges from the Allyn family totaling about $40,000. We figured that represented about a third of what we needed.

After that, Grandfather and I launched the project publicly. With the endorsement of other Lost Boys from around the United States, we created a nongovernmental organization to operate efficiently overseas. We obtained the proper Internal Revenue Service status, so donors could claim contributions as deductions on their income taxes. We called our project the American Care for Sudan Foundation. Our minister at First Presbyterian Church of Skaneateles announced it to the congregation, and the members promptly gave us an additional quarter of what we needed. Volunteers came forward to help push the project. We established a board for the clinic and staffed it with a lawyer, a doctor, a contractor, a Welch Allyn company officer, and others whose practical experience would help the clinic become a reality.

Boys play a traditional Dinka game in the dirt of Duk Payuel,
John's Sudanese village, where he plans to build a clinic.

Our best advice came from a nonprofit, missionary group out of Arkansas that had done work in Africa. The group, Tech Serve International, told us to buy everything we needed in the United States and ship it to Sudan. That way, we would get the best deals on materials, yet still pay local laborers to assemble the clinic building. Most assembly would have to take place after dark, we learned, as the slightest touch against the bare metal framing would cause severe burns under the blazing sun and 120°F midday temperatures.

The plan calls for first clearing the ground with teams of oxen and compacting the dirt with logs to prepare it for construction. Local laborers will do that work for $1.25 an hour—a pittance by American standards but a good wage in southern

Sudan. A thatched fence about the size and shape of the outer edge of a football field will surround the compound. Inside, workers will erect a simple, steel-frame building, 92 feet by 38 feet. More than a dozen rooms will include proper spaces for childbirth and recovery, which are crucial in a region noted for high infant mortality. There will also be four examination rooms and a sterile room for sewing wounds and setting broken bones. Supplies to keep the clinic running will initially be funneled through the foundation, but the people of southern Sudan likely will press the government to pick up any slack. Already, high-ranking officials of the new Sudanese government, including the head of intelligence, have endorsed the clinic. A Sudanese doctor in Canada has volunteered to staff the building when it opens, and Dinka nurses are ready to go to work, too. Services will be free to the patients.

Our initial budget totaled $115,000. That's a lot of expensive equipment to place on the ground to await assembly. Grandfather asked me if I had any fears that the Dinka would steal anything left unsecured. I told him that if they did, they would be dead men; the natives would defend their clinic with their lives. Besides, I hope they do not have long to wait. I expect construction to begin when the ground dries in 2007. Perhaps by June it will be ready for its first patient. I hope so. For 50 years now the Khartoum government has pledged advanced medical care to the dark-skinned tribes of southern Sudan without delivering on the promise. For five years, an international relief organization has been trying to open a healthcare building in the southern Sudanese town of Poktap, all the while promising swift completion to the village elders. When my pastor at First Presbyterian, Rev. Craig Lindsey, went to Sudan to look for possible clinic sites, one of the elders told the organizers of the project, "If you fulfill this promise, you shall have a full and blessed life. If you lie to us and do not fulfill your promises, as others have done, may you and all whom you care about die a painful and long death!" And he meant it, I'm sure.

"Grandfather" Jack Howard: *I have a great relationship with John. I have been a mentor to him for several years. He calls me nearly every day, to ask for advice about taking classes, or moving in with Martha. It makes me feel good that I can be an important part of his life. The amazing thing about him is that he is so intuitive. It came out of the blue sky that he wanted to build a clinic, and he did it. The credit for the clinic goes to John and the Lost Boys. It just never would have happened without John Dau.*

I expect the clinic to have an immediate impact. More than 19,000 residents of Duk County who fled to other parts of Su-dan during the civil war will probably return once the nation has a secure peace. The county's elders fear that the influx of returnees will place a heavy burden on the food producers, and the sudden introduction of so many people likely will spread chicken pox and other communicable diseases. But sufferers of many other diseases—including malaria, guinea worm, and kalazar, a deadly disease also known as black fever that spreads through contact with the sand fly—will find relief for the first time in memory at our clinic.

The Dinka deserve the wonders of modern medicine. When I lived in Duk County, young children suffered from a disease called *taach*. It's a kind of chronic fever, and the symptoms last for two months. The victim's father typically applied a homemade Dinka remedy. He put a piece of metal in fire until it glowed red-hot. Then he placed it against the victim's skin on the neck, back, or knee. The skin smoked and melted, and the burn left a nasty red welt. Some said it made the pain of taach go away. I always suspected it merely took the patient's mind off the existing pain and substituted another that felt even worse. If I can open this clinic, maybe the babies born in Duk County will never be burned again.

As southern Sudan has moved toward a new era of freedom, Duk County hasn't had a single medical dispensary to meet the challenge; residents of my hometown still have to walk 75 miles to another village if they wish to receive modern health care. Thanks to the many Lost Boys who talked with the foundation directors and helped plan the clinic, the building has been designed to meet the needs of the Dinka and to be built as efficiently as possible. The best way for Americans to help Africans, I believe, is to get Africans in the United States to oversee any philanthropic redevelopment. African immigrants had to fend for themselves to succeed in America, so they know how to get things done and how to get the most from a dollar. But having also lived in their home countries, they know who has to be bribed and who can be ignored, as well as how to appeal to the values of the indigenous people. I call this concept "Africans for Africa." The same thing would work in other regions—Southeast Asians for Southeast Asia, Indians for India, etc. It certainly works better than throwing money at an inept and corrupt government and hoping some of it spills into the right pockets.

Fund-raising efforts for the clinic coincided with the completion of *God Grew Tired of Us*, Christopher Quinn's documentary. After he put the finishing touches on the film, I got a lot of financial help in unexpected places. Liz Marks and her twin daughters, Lily and Isabel, teenage students at the Dalton School in New York City, saw Christopher's documentary. They asked me to speak at the school, and I did. Lily and Isabel asked people to donate to the Duk County clinic, and they raised about $14,000. I was very impressed with the determination and smarts of these two girls. Liz also raised money to help pay my way to Sudan at the beginning of 2006, so I could inspect the ground for the clinic and reestablish family ties. Christopher's girlfriend, Victoria Cuthert, also gave me a sizable donation toward my trip.

I had spoken to my father before the trip, and he suggested we build the clinic on a piece of land that his family had farmed since God made the world. He had a specific place in mind. It had good water, even in drought years, but we had not grown maize or sorghum on it for a while.

I wanted to walk all over the spot and talk to the elders to make sure there would be no problems. And, to be frank, I wanted to see my boyhood home again.

I had only 20 days off from the hospital to see my family and homeland before returning to Syracuse. Given that I had not seen my brothers, sisters, and father in 19 years, it did not seem long enough.

I booked a plane from Syracuse to Kampala, Uganda. My brothers met me at the airport. I recognized them from the pictures they sent me; they looked quite different from the way I remembered them. I am sure I looked different, too. My brothers slaughtered three goats to welcome me back. They invited relatives and neighbors to a big outdoor feast.

After five days with my brothers, we rented two cars and drove to Juba, where I chartered a small, propeller-driven plane to take us home. The flight lasted an hour. It might seem extravagant to hire a plane for such a short journey. I had no choice. Land mines dotted the roads heading north out of Uganda.

When the plane landed in Poktap, we picked up another rental car and drove to the village where my father had resettled. As we approached, I saw things I had not seen since I was a boy. Long-horned, long-eared cows, white and tan. Boys carrying milk in gourds. Boys in cattle camp. Faces with Dinka scars on the foreheads. As we drove through the village, we heard voices saying, "The children of Deng Ayuel are here!" They trilled a joyful Dinka chant, *Yeyeyeyea-ah!* One of them ran very fast to tell my father.

He had gone to the landing strip, expecting us to arrive there. Instead, we had driven over the dusty, red-dirt roads to his home. I met his youngest wife before I saw him. My brothers and I were all very thirsty, as our car had broken down three times on the road, and we had nothing to drink while we waited out the repairs. I asked for water, but my father's new wife said that out of respect, we could not drink anything until he returned. We waited 25 minutes, scanning the horizon, before we saw him coming on foot with his neighbors and the village elders.

He was still a respected judge, still a big man in the village. Figuratively, I mean. I could not believe how short he looked. Of course, I was looking down on him at the time, instead of up at him as I had as a child. I noticed that the scars on his forehead that distinguished him as a Dinka had faded with time.

We cried together, and he put his arms around me. He still had the wrestler's strength in his arms. He gripped me and my brothers in a big circle and gave a prayer, right there in front of his house.

All smiles, John hugs his father, Deng Leek, at their reunion at
Poktap, Sudan, in 2006.

"He was lost to me, oh, Lord," my father said, "but now he is alive. And I thank you for that, Lord." It reminded me of the welcome given by the father of the prodigal son in the Gospel of Luke.

I stayed with him for five days. He slaughtered five goats and one cow for the village to celebrate. I opened a case of wine I bought in Uganda, so the celebrators could drink. It was the only time I ever bought wine.

My father kept touching me during the length of my visit, as if to reassure himself he had not imagined my existence. He seemed proud.

"This is the first child who brought America to our country," he said. "This is he first child who really told of our problems to

Dinka children and their families in Duk County wonder what to make of
the well-dressed American. John's car, its hood open, broke down often.

the American people. And now he brings us a hospital." There
is no Dinka word for "clinic," so I did not try to correct him. I
showed him some pictures of First Presbyterian Church of Skaneateles, and I took pictures of southern Sudan to share when
I returned.

We drove the 18 miles from my father's village to Duk Payuel
to inspect the site my father had selected. I got out of the car and
sat on the ground at the edge of a stand of grass that stood eight
feet tall. This feels like my country, I thought, even though I have
not seen it for so long. I visited the huts where my family slept on
the night of the attack, walking around and reliving the events
in memory as if watching them on a movie screen. I bent over

and scooped up the dirt, running the grains of dust through my fingers. I visited the place where my mother buried my placenta after I was born. The Dinka never throw the placenta away. Instead, they hang it in a gourd outside the door where a baby has been born. Later, the family buries it to make a spiritual connection between the child and the place of birth. I stood where my placenta had been placed in the ground and felt my spirit reaching down, like roots of a thirsty tree seeking water.

I tossed stones into branches to dislodge the palm fruits I had eaten while tending cattle. I found the ancient beehive, still active, where I gathered honey as a boy. Best of all, I found my tree, a tall *kuel,* with one long, curved branch that brushed the ground. As a child, I used to cut its bark, collect the sap that ran out, and chew the congealed gum. I also rocked on the long, low branch with my friends. In 2006 I sat again on the same limb and said, to nobody in particular, "Swing me!"

It was so good to be home. Too bad it could not last. My time grew short, and I had to return to the United States. Unfortunately, I had booked no return to Uganda. No planes had arrived at the Poktap landing strip on which we could make a return flight. My uncle, the governor of Jonglei state, said he would have liked to help my brothers and me, but he had no planes to put at our disposal.

"Lord," my father prayed aloud, "find a way to send my sons back home."

Very soon, within an hour, a plane landed. I negotiated with the pilot, and he agreed to fly us to Lokichokio, on the Kenya border, for a thousand dollars. It was our only option for transportation, so I willingly paid it. We hugged my father and boarded the plane. Sudan dissolved beneath me as the plane headed into the sky.

From left, John Dau, Panther Bior, Daniel Pach, and filmmaker Christopher Quinn pose for a portrait at the 2006 Sundance Film Festival.

After an uneventful flight, we rented a car at Lokichokio and drove to Uganda. Along the way, we drove through Kakuma town. My friends still in the refugee camp heard I would be passing, so they tried to meet our car. We did not know of the planned reunion, and in our haste to catch a plane we did not stop. I later heard they slaughtered two goats, which they ate without me.

I SAID MY GOOD-BYES TO MY BROTHERS AND FLEW TO SYRACUSE on January 18. Four days later, I was on a plane again, this time for the world premiere of *God Grew Tired of Us* at the Sundance Film Festival in Park City, Utah. I had never heard of Sundance, but Christopher said it was an important event, and he really wanted me to attend. I got off work again and flew to central Utah in the middle of winter.

As I stepped off the plane, I looked east toward a towering chain of snow-covered mountains. Although I had not been in icy mountains before, they were not the strangest part of the journey. Almost as soon as I emerged from the secure corridors of the airport into the public reception area next to the baggage claim, I stepped into the most topsy-turvy world I had ever seen.

Hollywood.

CNN wanted to interview me. So did NBC's *Access Hollywood*. A buzz had been building in Salt Lake City, the biggest population center near Park City, about Christopher's movie. People thrust cameras at my face and turned on bright lights. Then they fired questions at me. I answered them as politely as I could, but I felt like an animal in a cage. Fortunately, there were many Lost Boys at Sundance to take some of the interviews. About 140 of the boys who were living in Utah watched a special screening. Afterward, one of the them, a University of Utah honors student named James Alic Garang, told the *Salt Lake Tribune*, "A film like this will get the word out to the American people, who might not know about the Lost Boys—or even where Sudan is. The world has been turning a deaf ear to Sudan for a long time." I agreed. While being the subject of attention might seem fun, it meant nothing compared with the good the publicity had done for Sudan.

After the initial screenings, the pace of the interviews and the requests for introductions increased. I met many people Christopher said were celebrities. A nice man, very sincere, shook my hand, and spoke to me. He said his name was Brad

Pitt. I had not heard of him, so I asked him what he did. He said he worked as the executive producer of Christopher's documentary. Sometime later, somebody told me Brad also acted in movies.

I attended all of the showings of *God Grew Tired of Us*. As the lights came up at the end of the film, Christopher introduced me and the other two Lost Boys featured in the movie, Panther Bior and Daniel Pach, and asked us to take questions.

"How is it in Africa now, John?" somebody asked me from the audience.

"Oh, I just got back four days ago from Sudan," I said. "I am building a clinic in my homeland. It is going very well."

A woman came up to me after the talk and said, "John, I want to help your clinic. Whom should I write a check to?" I gave her the name of the American Care for Sudan Foundation, and she filled out the check on the spot. Then, she tore it from the checkbook, handed it to me, and disappeared into the crowd. I glanced at the check. Twenty-five dollars. Nice. Then I looked more closely.

I had missed the zeroes. It was $25,000.

I showed the check to Christopher. "Oh, my," he said.

I wanted to thank the woman who gave me the money, but she apparently wanted to remain anonymous. I did not see her again at Sundance. I later learned her name and that she came from Texas.

The foundation got another check, for $5,000, from another Texan, and I got to take a half day off. A viewer who liked the movie paid to have Daniel, Panther, and me go tubing down the mountains at Park City. We sprawled in inner tubes and skimmed across the snow on a very cold day. Needless to say, I had never done anything like that in Sudan.

At the end of the festival, the film won the Grand Jury Prize and the Audience Award, the fourth documentary in Sundance's 25-year history to take the top awards from both critics and public. The attention can do nothing but good for southern Sudan. Americans will realize how badly my homeland has been hurt by the war, and how the skilled people necessary for its redevelopment have been scattered to the winds. With America's help, sparked in part by Christopher's film, the Dinka will replant, rebuild, and reestablish democracy. Because of the film, I have already seen doors open to me that never would have opened otherwise. I spoke to UN Secretary General Kofi Annan's personal secretary about my Africans for Africa concept in early 2006.

I am sorry that John Garang will not help lead southern Sudan into a new age, because I appreciate what he did in his 22-year fight against the Khartoum government. In July 2005, three days after he took the oath as vice president in Sudan's transitional government, he died in a helicopter when he was returning from talks with the Ugandan president. Some southerners suspected foul play, but the Comprehensive Peace Agreement, which he helped negotiate and which led to the Government of National Unity, gives southern Sudan the best prospects for lasting peace in more than a century. The agreement will bring half of the nation's oil revenue to the south, and that money will strengthen the towns and tribes, as well as the SPLA units that surround and support them. I frankly do not know how Garang managed to get the Khartoum government to agree to share revenue. Even more astonishingly, he won autonomy for the southern regions, to be followed in 2011 by a referendum on independence. Ten states in the south, including Duk County's state of Jonglei, will vote on whether to stay with Khartoum or break away. Southerners favor independence by huge margins in every straw poll, so I expect the ten states to become a new country. Maybe they will call it Kush, to cement the nation's identity to its biblical foundations.

I hope to return to Sudan in 2010 and 2011 to campaign for independence and to be there when the people of Kush achieve it. This is my generation's duty. We have to see independence through to its realization. Previous generations failed, and that is why southern Sudan suffered for so many years.

Much could still go wrong. The Khartoum government has proved itself adept at playing one dark-skinned tribe against another, primarily Nuer against Dinka, to destabilize the south. It is quite possible that the djellabas will renege on their president's promise to let the south go free and take its oil reserves with it. We must not let that happen. The front lines in America's current war run through many countries where religious ideologies clash. Keeping southern Sudan strong will pay dividends in the war on terrorism and create an American ally in a strategically contested part of the world.

It will be tough getting all of the Lost Boys to agree on a political course of action. We tried to do that at the Phoenix convention and found our attempts to elect a leader and set an agenda regretfully splitting along tribal lines—Dinka against Nuer, Bor against Bahr el-Ghazal, and so on. I am confident, though, that the people of southern Sudan will focus on their common desires and dreams as they shape the future of my ancestral homeland. If we keep our eyes on the prize of independence, we will ignore the distractions and temptations certain to be placed in our way by the Khartoum government.

Finding unity in a shared vision is my prayer for my new homeland.

Celina Martinez, graduate student at Syracuse and John's writing tutor: *I told John once, "Language is power." He was silent for a second, and said, "Language is the reason we have fighting among the tribes in Africa." He says these amazing things. Another time I told him that, considering his life story, he was really lucky. He said, "I don't feel lucky."*

America has many tribes. Irish, German, Mexican, Greek, Chinese, Italian, and on and on through scores of other ethnicities, religions, and languages. Jews and Christians and Muslims. Great-grandchildren of slaves and great-grandchildren of slaveholders. Those who crossed the ocean in first-class cabins on luxury liners and those who traveled in steerage. Red-state citizens and blue-state citizens. Unlike the Dinka, whom God placed along the Nile long, long ago, Americans live in a young and restless country. Everyone is an immigrant in this nation of immigrants; even the so-called "Native" Americans once traveled to this continent from Asia. As an outsider to the U.S., who knew next to nothing about America before arriving on these shores in 2001, I have observed many things that others have stared at but failed to see. Too many Americans have put on blinders. They see only what they choose to, not taking the time or effort to try to understand the big picture. I believe a macroscopic view of America must take account of all things that make this country great, as well as the things that stand in the way of its achieving even more greatness.

When I talk to my American friends about this country, the conversation reminds me in some ways of the parable of the blind men and the elephant. In the story, a group of men who have been blind all their lives encounter an elephant on the road. They have never come across one before, so they place their hands on the beast to try to understand it. One man places his hands on the animal's great, gray flank and announces, "It is just like a wall." Another feels the elephant's long ivory tusk and declares, "It is just like a spear." A third grabs the trunk and says, "It is just like a snake." And so it goes, with each man exploring a different part and none able to articulate the true nature of the beast. Everything in America presented itself as new to me; I have seen with fresh eyes the head and heart and belly of the beast.

I believe a young woman in my class at Syracuse University mainly saw the elephant's blundering feet and not its great heart. I had given a talk about perseverance in Professor Coplin's class, and I told stories of my life in Africa and America. Lisa rushed up to talk to me afterward. She wanted to know whether Africans felt America had done enough to help them. Lisa accused the United States of neglecting some big problems, and she said some very critical things about my new country. I told her to sit down. I explained to her how so many people, some of whom I had never met, gave me warm clothes, bought me groceries, set me up in my apartment, and helped me go to school. I told of how my new country encouraged me to succeed by giving me access to grants and loans to further my education.

Is this enough? I told Lisa it was enough for me and for anyone else helped by such generosity. The Lost Boys had never known such gifts, and they could never have expected them in the closed societies of Africa. In America, many treasures get taken for granted, because people see them every day. As an African who grew up with so very little, I told Lisa I thought America had done right by me, and I blessed my new country. I looked in her eyes and saw that she was thinking, maybe about things she hadn't considered before. After that, she asked me to meet some of her friends and speak at their meetings. Now we enjoy talking often, and she has made plans to put on a concert to raise money for the clinic.

Without even pausing to think, I can tell you America's greatest strength is its enormous spirit, manifest in its generosity. Americans deserve huge credit for giving to those in need. They open their checkbooks and make donations to people in Africa, in Asia, in Latin America, and in devastated New Orleans, and they seldom know personally who benefits from their altruism. Nowhere else in the world do people give so much, so freely, with no expectations in return. Look what happened when I got my first job and needed someone to give me a ride. I called a friend, Jim Hockenbery from Living Word Church, in the middle of the night and asked him to help. Now that I understand how my requests violated American customs, I feel embarrassed for my actions all those years ago. Yet at the same time, I feel a great love for all who sacrificed sleep or time with family to help me out, no questions asked. You tell an American you need assistance, and chances are you will find in his or her response the spirit that made this country grow and prosper.

I look at Jack Howard, my new grandfather, and I see a man determined to do all he can to help others succeed. An elder by any standard, in his 80s, he has the energy of a teenager and refuses to give up on any task. When the Lost Boys came to central New York, he treated them like his grandchildren. Jack has done so many things for me, from showing me the value of each American coin, to introducing me to candy bars and asking me if I liked them, to pushing the Duk County clinic toward its grand and glorious opening day. All the while, he has encouraged me to do what I could on my own. This is so good, to urge others to succeed, while being there to help when needed. He has a clean heart. I want God to give Jack Howard years more to live, so he may continue to go good things.

Then there is Professor Bill Coplin at Syracuse University. He taught me many things that had nothing to do with public policy, because he knows education extends far beyond the walls of a classroom. He helped me to prosper and to remember to take care of myself as I try to take care of the Lost Boys and the people of Duk County. "Before you can feed others, you must first feed yourself," Bill told me.

Professor Bill Coplin: *The first time I called on John in class and heard his accent, I thought he might be Nigerian, maybe a highly trained student whose parents worked in the diplomatic corps. He is a mature, thoughtful student, but he likes to argue. He's stubborn, too. That probably helped him survive when he was in Africa. He has a huge capacity for hard work, and he takes a tremendous amount of responsibility. He kicks himself, and that's crucial to success. The fact that he survived impresses me. Even more, I am impressed by his being such a nice person, despite everything that happened to him. Maybe his challenges made him what he is, but I think he was special to begin with.*

America is full of people like Jack and Bill. People like them have made America a welcoming place to immigrants for generations. Nobody can cause me to fail in America; nobody stands in the way, as they do in traditional African societies, where privilege, wealth, and membership in the insiders' group count for more than integrity and hard work. The United States has no group actively working for others to fail; rather, it is populated by many who seek to promote goodness.

In what I've seen of America and Americans, race and social class do not seem to define the individual; even physical handicaps are not relevant. My successes and my failures are my own, and I like living my life that way. True, I had people like Jack Howard and Susan Meyer and Bill Coplin to help me, but I know that millions of Americans like them are waiting to help others who take the trouble to help themselves. There is no other country in the world like that.

America's greatest weakness, I believe, lies in how it has drifted far from the love of family, at least as the Dinka understand that love. Among my people, a child can never know the world on its own, or even through the eyes of just a mother and father. Young parents cannot impart all of the wisdom necessary to raise a child. They are off cultivating crops, building huts, cooking—the hundreds of tasks required to keep food on the table and a roof overhead. Therefore, aunts, uncles, and grandparents help instruct a child about Dinka values. Even nonrelatives of a certain age are treated as family members, assuming the right to correct a wayward child; if strangers saw a Dinka boy or girl misbehaving, they would admonish the child and receive the parents' thanks for doing so.

Special honors and respect go to all who have gray hair, especially grandmothers. They watch the little children all the time, teaching them how to speak, how to act, how to be good Dinka. When my grandmother in Duk Payuel saw me acting up, she would say, "Stop that! You will destroy the family name!" And then she would tell me what to do to bring honor to the family. Like children everywhere, I grumbled from time to time, but like every Dinka, I learned never to say a disrespectful word to her or any other elders. My mother will live with me in my house until she dies. She will teach the Dinka tongue to my baby, making it her first language. Grandmother will help raise my children to be good Dinka, while I will raise them to be good Americans.

Here in Syracuse, among my neighbors, fellow students, and co-workers, grandparents generally do not live in the same home as the children. Young families claim they want to live alone to assert their independence—but at what a cost! They lose the advice and support of grandparents, and they are not there to return the care their grandparents are due. I think with despair about old people getting sick alone or falling and break-ing their bones (I witness their agony at the hospital), and I see how the pain of their bodies gets compounded with the anguish of loneliness.

I think America has lost much of the benefits of the tribe by putting its elderly in rest homes. And by clustering children in day-care centers—so many young calves mooing together in one pen! By separating the generations of a family, the circle of life gets broken.

For 14 years I lived without a family of blood relatives in the refugee camps of Pinyudu and Kakuma. I learned that if you do not have a family, you must *make* a family in order to survive. Without Abraham, who became my family as I walked from Duk Payuel to Ethiopia, I would have died before finding ref-uge. Without the dozen Lost Boys who became my family and shared food rations and cooking duties, I surely would have starved. Without those at synagogue who helped me feel the spirit of the Lord flowing through me like water, my soul would have withered. Without my classmates who progressed with me through grade school, pushing me to master the lessons in the Dinka manner just as I pushed them not to fall behind, none of us would have gotten an education.

The Lost Boys invented families, bound together not by blood but by the culture of tribe. I looked upon the elders of Pinyudu and Kakuma as my parents and grandparents. Similarly, I became like an uncle to the littlest of the Lost Boys in the camps. I doctored them and cooked for them when they fell sick; disciplined them when they acted rudely; and taught them the Dinka traditions through actions and stories. I am still an uncle to those young men, even though we are separated by thousands of miles. I cannot forget them. I must continue to help my hundreds of nephews, nieces, and cousins.

One people, sharing one circle of hope. That is my prayer not only for the scattered children of southern Sudan but also for the extended family I hope to make bloom, the latest in a long line of immigrants, in this magnificent land of second chances.

ACKNOWLEDGMENTS

MANY PEOPLE HAVE HELPED ME NOT JUST IN WRITING THIS BOOK but also in my life. As the book is about my years in Sudan and America, it is hard to separate the influences that shaped these pages from those that molded who I am today. I do not have room to thank everyone, so I will name a few and beg the rest to take heart. You know who you are; your good deeds have not been forgotten.

I must first thank Mike Sweeney for his time and patience. Mike is soft of speech, quick to understand, and kind. And next, Bill Coplin, the professor at Syracuse University who has done much to help me. It is unusual for an American professor to go the extra mile, as he has done for me.

I don't know what to say about Abraham Deng Niop. Without him, this book would not exist, because I would not have been here to write it. Bless you, Abraham, for being like a father to me.

My family has been amazing. When I awoke in the middle of the night and talked about the book, my wife, Martha Akech, listened and understood. She helped me come up with good words. I love you, Honey. My mother, Anon Manyok Duot Lual, struggles with English and will not know how I praise her here. Still, I must acknowledge her wisdom and her contribution. She helped me remember things from long ago, which have found their way into these pages. Thanks also to my sister Akuot Deng Leek. She took time from her high school studies to contribute to the book.

At my church in Skaneateles, Grandfather Jack Howard and his wife, Ruth, helped get many things started in my life. Jack never said, "No, John." The Rev. Craig Lindsey, a good shepherd, inspired me with his sermons and his ready offers of help. He enriched my life by returning from Sudan with news that my father had changed my name, according to custom, to Dhieu Deng Leek. Now that name will live on in America—a great gift. Susan Meyer and her family were so caring for such a long time. It is no small gift to introduce someone to new things, such as a first ride on a roller coaster. And without the support of Penny and Bill Allyn, there likely would be no clinic in Duk County. Their generous donations made people believe.

Palath Thonchar, my longtime friend, is like my blood brother. We supported each other in Kakuma. We were, and still are, family. I thank him for his contribution to the book. Santino Atak also has been good, making things easier for others in America through his wisdom. God bless.

I must thank Joe Scicchitano at St. Joseph's Hospital for hiring me. He saw how much I wanted to work. His leadership helps make the hospital great.

When other organizations said "no, no, no" to me, Kathy Goldfarb-Findling of the Gifford Foundation said yes. After she produced a $5,000 check, I knew anything was possible.

Thanks also to Bill and Sabra Reichardt, who have helped Abraham and my half-brother Aleer with payments toward their college tuition in Africa. Education will be mother and father to loved ones far away.

To Christopher Quinn, thanks for bringing the problems of southern Sudan to the attention of the world.

And finally, I must say thank you to a tiny girl whom I will get to know very well in the coming years. Agot, my lovely daughter, you are my future. So many times, I feared I would never live to see my first child. God, who has blessed me so many times, has outdone Himself.

RELIEF ORGANIZATIONS
INVOLVED IN SUDAN

JOHN DAU SUDAN
FOUNDATION
518 James Street, Suite 200

Syracuse, NY 13220
info@johndaufoundation.org
www.johndaufoundation.org

ACT INTERNATIONAL
ECUMENICAL CENTRE
ROUTE DE FERNEY
150 P.O. Box 2100 CH-1211
Geneva 2, Switzerland
http://act-intl.org

ACTION AGAINST HUNGER
247 West 37th
Suite #1201
New York, NY 10018
www.actionagainsthunger.org

CATHOLIC RELIEF SERVICES
P.O. Box 17090
Baltimore, Maryland 21203
www.crs.org

CHURCH WORLD SERVICE
28606 Phillips Street
P. O. Box 968
Elkhart, IN 46515
churchworldservice.org

DIRECT CHANGE
919 18th St. NW
Suite 950
Washington, DC 20006
www.directchange.org

INTERNATIONAL
RESCUE COMMITTEE
P.O. Box 98152
Washington, DC 20090
www.theIRC.org

LUTHERAN WORLD RELIEF
PO Box 17061
Baltimore, MD 21298-9832
www.lwr.org

REFUGEES INTERNATIONAL
1705 N Street NW
Washington, DC 20036
www.refugeesinternational.org

UNITED STATES CONFERENCE
OF CATHOLIC BISHOPS
Migration and Refugee Services
3211 Fourth Street NE
Washington, DC 20017
www.usccb.org
Through USCCB, you can volunteer
to help Lost Boys in your area make the
adjustment to life in the U.S.

FURTHER READING

Bixler, Mark. *The Lost Boys Of Sudan: An American Story Of The Refugee Experience*. Athens: University of Georgia Press, 2005.

Deng, Alephonsion, Benson Deng, and Benjamin Atak. *They Poured Fire on Us From the Sky: The True Story of Three Lost Boys From Sudan*. New York: Public Affairs, 2005.

Eggers, David. *What Is the What: The Autobiography of Valentino Achak Deng*. New York: McSweeney's, 2006.

Khalid, Mansour. *War and Peace in Sudan*. London: Kegan Paul, 2003.

O'Ballance, Edgar. *Sudan, Civil War and Terrorism, 1956-99*. Houndmills, England: Macmillan, 2000.

ONLINE SOURCES

A personal home page where you can learn more about John Bul Dau
http://sites.maxwell.syr.edu/johndau/

The home page of the Duk County Association in the United States. John is acting president of the association, which brings together people from Duk County in the U.S. and Sudan.
www.dukcounty.com

The home page of Abek Community Development Program, associated with the Sudanese community of John's wife, Martha
http://abekcommunityusa.com

The Website for people from the Sudanese district of Bor, which includes Duk County
www.borsouthcommunity.org